LIFE

★★★ OF THE ★★★

PARTY

KENNETH F. SIMPSON
and the
SURVIVAL OF THE REPUBLICANS
IN 1930s NEW YORK

BY KENNETH D. DURR

MP

Montrose
Press

Durr, Kenneth D.

The Life of the Party: Kenneth F. Simpson and the Survival of the
Republicans in 1930s New York

Library of Congress Control Number 2009920882

ISBN 9780972887472

Printed and bound in the United States of America

TABLE OF CONTENTS

FOREWORD

Kenneth Simpson was a flame behind glass in 1930s New York, a bright thing on display: a curious character, a minor celebrity, a political chieftain. The flame was fed by a rich mixture—filial duty and a strong sense of justice, a thirst for recognition, and a yearning to be a player in the big game. Born into a world of possibility, Simpson enjoyed enough privilege to believe in the perfectibility of the world, but not enough to lose touch with the travails of less fortunate early twentieth-century New Yorkers.

As a young man, he could hardly have helped but marvel at his own capabilities, outshining even the best and the brightest in his prep school and college years. But in his early life, Simpson was, even more than boyhood hero Theodore Roosevelt, "pure act." He was eager to apply himself, but unsure of what to apply himself *to*. He was early attracted to the Republican Roosevelt's vigorous "Bull Moose" progressivism, but politics was then an ungentlemanly pursuit. So rather than renounce a genteel upper middle-class existence, Simpson became a different kind of political boss: a Republican of liberal leanings, a machine politician of culture, at once a clubroom swell and a street fighter.

Simpson immersed himself in the day-to-day struggles of urban politics and, in the critical decade of the 1930s, loomed large in a compelling corner of political history—the struggle of the Republican Party to find its way out of the political wilderness in Franklin Roosevelt's America. As his tactics succeeded, his influence spread even beyond New York City. Simpson's was a call to action rather than an appeal to ideas or grand strategy. He started from the optimistic assumption that the Republican Party's path back to power was as simple as figuring out what it took to win the next election. Nor would his essential optimism allow him to nurse grudges when positive action was more appropriate. He evinced no highly principled resentment over the "best people" losing power during the New Deal, only insisting that the best people had gotten it wrong and that the first step toward getting it right would be to get the common man on their side.

That Simpson was a brilliant tactician was borne out in his masterful handling of the 1937 municipal election in which he simultaneously ensured the everlasting defeat of Tammany Hall and brought Republicans to power in Depression-era New York. But in the end, Simpson's scope failed him, and opponents like Thomas Dewey, who were less tactically brilliant but more strategically shrewd, prevailed.

Understanding what made Simpson's light burn so brightly is difficult, but seeing into his soul is impossible. What we can see is the glass that refracted the light—the structure of a life, formed out of countless decisions and compromises that kept the draft from the flame. Simpson was a good son from a genteel, though not aristocratic, family. An expert—if not brilliant—student and a dashing young officer and gentleman, he went to the right schools, formed the right associations, and ingratiated himself to the most influential people. Gathering these accoutrements of success may have seemed easy to outsiders, but something in the pursuit cost Simpson greatly. For if he displayed an uncanny ability to succeed early on, he also betrayed a definite lack of imagination later as he became ever more hedged in by choices made and not made, and by the consequences of his own contradictions. He "married well" but found closer companionship in another woman, although it was a relationship that he could never entirely accept. Chance started Simpson into a lucrative life of corporate law, but he rejected it for a shot at courtroom stardom that he could not sustain.

But whatever his disappointments, there was always politics—that he loved more than the law. In the one-on-one transaction, whether in barrooms or clubrooms, Albany or Washington, Simpson found the stage most appropriate for his performance. But it is tragic, somehow, that there always had to be a stage. For Simpson, like so many outwardly strong men, was deeply vulnerable. He sought mastery, but whether as colonel of the Knickerbocker Greys or as a political boss, he was most comfortable achieving it through others, as if a direct relationship with the masses—such as that upon which contemporaries Wendell Willkie and Fiorello La Guardia thrived—would have left him too exposed. The youth whose acting career ended almost as soon as it began spent the rest of his life making sure that a proscenium intervened between himself and his public. That was the glass refracting the flame, making it dance and twinkle and delighting political journalists in the late 1930s. But it was also the bell jar within which nothing could live for long.

And so it was for Kenneth Simpson, who did not so much burn as blaze. As he did so, he illuminated the strengths and failings of a party that had lost its way and helped it find a path forward, first in New York City and then in the U.S. Congress, where the flame finally burned itself out.

Influential as Simpson was in the late 1930s, however, the nature of his achievement is evident in his very obscurity. For Simpson's political struggle for the life of the Republican Party in the 1930s was betrayed by the progressive ideals that were rapidly becoming obsolete: he wanted less to make a new world than to make a better place out of the old one. And although Simpson had many colleagues, he was no prophet and so he left no disciples. Perhaps one of the greatest tragedies of his life was that Simpson remained spiritually cut off from his fellows even as he yearned for—and flourished in—their companionship. The protector of Republicanism in the 1930s was indeed the life of the party.

A biographer could hardly hope for a more colorful subject than the life of Kenneth Simpson. While it was this story that made the project most enjoyable, the hard work of research and writing was made easier by the assistance of many people. Chief among them is Kelly Simpson, who opened his files without reservation and with constant encouragement along the way. Darwin Stapleton at the Rockefeller Archive Center brought me together with this story in search of an author and provided invaluable guidance at the outset of the project. I am indebted to those who held the keys to the archives, particularly Barbara Heck at Yale University, Louis Jeffries at The Hill School, David Menegon at the Knickerbocker Greys, and Jennifer Lee at Columbia University. Genealogist Barbara Doxey also shared information on the Simpson family.

As always, History Associates Incorporated in Rockville, Maryland, has been a great place to research and to write. I am indebted to historians Caitlin Verboon, Mary Bays, James Rife, Randall Lewis, and Laura Moore, all of whom helped with research tasks. Gene Fielden created the bibliography, and Jennifer Randazzo and Gail Mathews meticulously proofed the manuscript. I am also indebted to Kurt Hanson, an independent historian and even more independent thinker, who applied a keen understanding of politics and history to every page of the manuscript. He helped fix what was fixable and was generous about what was not. Some shortcomings, no doubt, remain, but I hope the reader is compensated by the compelling story of a remarkable man.

CHAPTER ONE
A YOUTH IN THREE ACTS

On an April afternoon in 1905, a resolute, red-haired eight-year-old strapped on his marching snare as the last few carriages and motor cars pulled up to Park Avenue curbs. The men came north from well-appointed offices downtown; the women east from Fifth Avenue, hurrying along little girls in white crinolines and pink and blue bows. Under the red brick vault of the Seventh Regiment Armory, officers in brilliant dress uniforms towered over scores of little boys in grey, white gloved and sporting French-style kepis that led one observer to exclaim, "Look at all the little bell hops. What's going on?"[1] Then Kenneth Simpson and his comrades began rapping out "First Call" to open the 23rd Annual Reception of the Knickerbocker Greys. "The Greys," founded by a society matron to instill discipline among The Four Hundred's fractious heirs, was then in its heyday. It was, of course, exclusive. Most of its 150 members were enrolled at birth, among them Van Rensselaers, Vanderbilts, and Harrimans.[2]

Kenneth Simpson thrived in this company. He had joined as a private the previous fall, had made every one of the twice-weekly drills, and was one of seven drummers second class. Although Kenneth's father was a well-known physician, he was a relative newcomer to New York society. Accordingly, Kenneth had yet to achieve distinction in the Greys. Less prominent boys were usually assigned to the drum corps—there were no Vanderbilts in its ranks—and Kenneth's perfect attendance was, in a sense, ignominious: more affluent boys frequented Europe and Palm Beach during the winter. Kenneth was not even much of a percussionist; he had won no drumming medal nor would he ever. But he excelled at sizing up a complex situation and understanding its fundamentals. As the Greys paraded before doting parents and admiring little girls, he was no doubt aware that New York's best were marching to his beat. It must have felt good.[3]

Center, Kenneth Simpson, drummer boy in the Knickerbocker Greys. *(Courtesy of Dave Menegon of the Knickerbocker Greys)*

HUDSON TO MANHATTAN

Kenneth's parents had raised him to consider what you did to be more important than "who you were," unusual in New York society, where family trees were carefully tracked and sometimes judiciously pruned. But then, they were newcomers. Kenneth's paternal ancestors were of Scotch Irish descent. Sometime before the Revolution, they made their way into Virginia's Piedmont and intermarried with Old Dominion families like the Langhornes and Flournoys, picking up some Huguenot blood along the way. George Nicholas Simpson was born a Virginian in 1814, but by the time he reached adulthood he had decided to try his luck farther north in the still-young nation.[4]

While the Scotch-Irish were exploring the James River, the Dutch were settling the Hudson River, four hundred miles to the north. By the mid-nineteenth century, their vast landed estates and vowel-rich names were already fading to pentimento on a canvas painted over with the vigorous strokes of Yankee enterprise. In the 1790s, as European wars threatened their New England ports, merchants from Nantucket and Martha's Vineyard had established an inland port on a high landing about thirty miles south of Albany. Hudson, New York, became the state's third largest city, its Quaker and Episcopalian blue bloods sensibly tolerant of the grog shops and bawdy houses frequented by the sailors and teamsters who kept the port humming.[5]

By the 1840s, railroads were beginning to challenge navigation as a carrier of commerce in the Hudson valley. Sometime during that decade, George Simpson found work on one of the rapidly lengthening lines. By the time he was thirty-six years old, George Simpson had worked his way up to the prestigious and well-paid position of conductor, married Irish-born Caroline Benedict McCann, and settled down in Hudson. One of the town's notables, George even served a term on the Hudson City Council. In 1852, George took a position with the Hudson River Railroad—the first to link Albany and New York on the east side of the river—and soon gained a reputation as one of the line's "most careful men."[6] In 1855, eighth child William Kelly Simpson was born into this secure and settled family.

Then things fell apart. In early January 1860, George was conductor on the Albany Express. One morning, a steam pipe on the southbound locomotive began malfunctioning; the train stopped repeatedly for repairs that day. In the afternoon, just north of Tarrytown, the engineer was forced to stop again—on the blind side of a curve. George sent a brakeman around the curve with a flag, but the brakeman took too long. A rear end collision killed one passenger immediately; others died during the next few days. The railroad had a rule in those days: the train conductor, like the captain of a ship, was always culpable and, in the case of a fatal accident, was always dismissed. George Simpson's career was over. At about the same time, Caroline Simpson died at age forty-three, most likely of tuberculosis. George moved five-year-old son William and the rest of his family to Hudson's 4th ward, eked out a living as an innkeeper, and began to put his life back together.[7]

It did not take long, for George met Sarah Hull Jenkins, and they were married in 1863. Sarah belonged to one of Hudson's founding families and was a cultivated woman. A devout Episcopalian, before her marriage relatively late in life she had traveled widely. Sarah brought her parents to live in the Simpson household, helped George land a position at the Hudson customs house, and saw to it that young William got a good education.[8]

William Kelly Simpson grew up to be a remarkably good-natured young man, so much so that he preferred the informal "Kelly" to the more decorous "William" even as he ascended the social scale. His rise began at Cornell in the early 1870s. Although there was likely some help from the Jenkins estate, Kelly worked his way through college, a necessity that did not seem to affect his academic achievements. Upon graduation in 1876, he was admitted to New York's College of Physicians and Surgeons, which was associated with Columbia College. He graduated from medical school in 1880 and was married the next day.[9]

Kelly Simpson and Anna Farrand had much in common, including a Huguenot and Irish background, the early loss of their mothers, the Episcopal Church, and Hudson. Anna was the fifth child of Joseph Steevens Farrand and Elizabeth Carroll. Joseph Farrand was born in England, a man of means sufficient to emigrate to New York City and set up as a grain broker. He married Irish-born Elizabeth in 1844 and began raising a family in Manhattan. Anna was born in 1856, but just four years later, Elizabeth Farrand died. Just as George Simpson had done, Joseph Farrand

Dr. William Kelly Simpson. *(Courtesy of Dr. Kelly Simpson)*

started anew. In 1864 he married Helen Peake. More children followed, and Farrand raised them not as an urban businessman but as a landed gentleman. Anna Farrand spent her teen years on the family's 140-acre farm in Greenport, New York, just outside of Hudson.[10]

Kelly and Anna were married at Hudson's Christ Church Episcopal and then moved down the river for good, although a sentimental attachment would always remain. In New York City, Kelly developed a specialty in laryngology at the New York Foundling Hospital. There, he assisted physician Joseph O'Dwyer in perfecting a method of keeping respiratory patients' swollen airways open with a tube. It was Kelly, in fact, who first applied this technique of "intubation" on an adult patient. Later, Kelly renewed his association with the College of Physicians and Surgeons. He became assistant professor of laryngology in 1892 and began working toward a full professorship, helped along by the "strong personal magnetism and essential friendliness," as one colleague put it, that made him popular among students and faculty alike.[11]

The Simpsons appear to have settled easily into the cultural life of late nineteenth-century New York. Kelly, in particular, had a deep appreciation of the arts. He belonged to a private choral group directed by Frank and Walter Damrosch, even serving as its president for a time, and belonged to the Lotos Club, where he communed with Mark Twain and other illustrious literati. Anna Farrand Simpson, like her longer-established society sisters, dutifully patronized each season's charity events.[12]

The Simpsons began a family in 1887 with the birth of daughter Sarah Hull Jenkins Simpson, later nicknamed "Sallie." A son, Louis Flournoy Simpson, was born in late 1891 but died less than two months later. In February 1892, in the midst of a long, cold, winter, Louis was buried in the Hudson City Cemetery near his grandfather, who had died in 1885. It was springtime, however, when the Simpsons, now reaching middle age, expected their third child. On May 4, 1895, Dr. Simpson delivered son Kenneth Farrand Simpson, at home at 952 Lexington Avenue.[13]

ROOTS OF A REFORMER

Kenneth Simpson was born in a city that had risen to greatness only recently and had not completely adjusted. In the early nineteenth century, the old Dutch trading town vied with other eastern cities for dominance in the new nation. It gained the advantage after the Erie Canal opened a water route from the commercial East to the agricultural West in 1825. By the end of the Civil War, New York City was the nation's center of transportation and banking, and two-thirds of America's imported goods landed on its wharves. But it was the gathering in of people, not merchandise, that truly transformed the city. In the 1840s came the first big influx of Europeans, mostly Irish and Germans. In the 1870s came another, and every successive wave seemed more impoverished and more troublesome than the last. Manhattan's horrified old-stock merchants and bankers either fled to the suburbs or moved north up Fifth Avenue.

The immigrant influx fueled a political transformation. New York's venerable political machine, the Society of Saint Tammany, emerged just after the Revolution when Aaron Burr turned a patriotic social club into a powerful political organization. As New York's elite closed ranks against the newcomers, Tammany Hall, allied firmly with the Democratic Party, drew them into their web of obligations and benefits. Tammany politicians trudged the neighborhoods, kissed babies, doled out jobs, bailed out miscreants, and asked for little more than a vote in return. They bought the people of New York cheaply, as it turned out, for Tammany blithely ignored mounting social and economic problems while rewarding its own with what one turn-of-the-century politician called "honest graft."[14] By the late nineteenth century, Tammany was ruled by Richard Croker, who had worked his way up from street fighter to ward captain, alderman to "boss." Meanwhile, mud and filth collected in the streets, whole neighborhoods took sick from polluted wells, and corruption added a premium to every penny paid by a New Yorker. Two cities—one wealthy and privileged, the other poor and dirty, 1.5 million people in all—simmered in one pot.

The vessel bubbled up at times, particularly after the spectacular lootings of the Tammany "Tweed Ring" were exposed in the 1870s, but it never boiled over, and few seemed inclined to look under the lid. One who did was a Danish immigrant who had lived on the streets for a time before landing a job as a newspaperman. Jacob Riis acquired one of George Eastman's new Kodak cameras, bought a magnesium flash device, and took to the slums to capture for astonished Americans, in a book published in 1890, *How the Other Half Lives*. Riis's revelations helped touch off a tide of reform that lifted William L. Strong into the mayor's office. Strong was the first of what were dubbed "fusion" candidates: Republicans who worked in coalition with other—usually left-wing—splinter parties against Tammany. Since the city's corruption problem was rooted in a tangled alliance between Tammany and municipal officeholders, particularly the police, Strong needed someone to clean up the force. He chose an unusual elite New Yorker with a high-pitched voice, prominent teeth, endless reserves of energy, and an exceptional ability to get things done.

Kenneth Simpson was two days old when Theodore Roosevelt became New York City Police Commissioner. His infant ears no doubt heard the news because Jacob Riis, who had signed on as Roosevelt's assistant, was a friend of Kelly Simpson's. Roosevelt's solution to the police corruption problem was simple: since it stemmed from selective enforcement of the laws, he would uphold them all—all including the sabbatarian laws that kept otherwise law-abiding citizens from drinking on Sundays. Roosevelt disinfected the force, but at the price of angering New York voters, who were delighted to see his tumultuous career continue in Washington as Assistant Secretary of the Navy.[15]

By then, Kelly Simpson had achieved something like equipoise, and geography had much to do with it. The mid-century tectonic collision of wealth and poverty had heaved up a range of chateau-style mansions all along Fifth Avenue, but to the east was an immigrant wilderness. By the 1890s the construction of the Seventh Regiment Armory had encouraged a few middle-class citizens to venture toward Park Avenue, but from Third Avenue to the East River lay dense neighborhoods of German and Irish immigrants. It was between this wealth and poverty that Kelly Simpson settled down. At the turn of the century, he was still making payments on a brownstone at 952 Lexington Avenue near the corner of 69th Street.[16]

The tumult to the east was no doubt echoed in the turn-of-the-century Simpson household. Kelly's stepmother had come to live after George died. She kept the family involved in the affairs of St. James's Episcopal Church, just a few blocks away on Madison Avenue, until the day she died in 1897. Anna Farrand Simpson's siblings, older sister Jemimah and widowed younger sister Ada Saxton, lived in the household as well, and one of Kelly's fellow physicians even boarded with the family for a time.[17]

Despite this crowded household and many professional obligations, Kelly Simpson appears to have spent a good deal of time with the son that he called

Anna Farrand Simpson and son. *(Courtesy of Dr. Kelly Simpson)*

"Kent." Kelly and Anna Farrand Simpson had established very different relationships with their son. A heart condition had made Anna something of an invalid and unapproachable. Kelly delighted in activity and was gregarious. Anna was somewhat autocratic, but Kelly became a partner in a few of Kenneth's boyhood pursuits. The two conspired regularly to escape Mrs. Simpson's supervision and take in a baseball game.[18]

Kenneth's baseball companion was beginning to attain eminence in New York medical circles, where he was known for his wit and in demand as an after-dinner speaker. By 1904, Kelly Simpson was full professor of laryngology at the College of Physicians and Surgeons and consulting at four other hospitals. He was, by all accounts, a fine surgeon with what a colleague described as "delicacy of hand and surety of touch." But it was with less glamorous, if more practical, forms of treatment that he was associated, particularly intubation and the treating of head colds and infections with douches. Now New York's top laryngologist, Kelly Simpson looked down his share of eminent throats, but he continued to consider himself more a general practitioner than a specialist. More of the patients at his Lexington Avenue practice came from the poor neighborhoods by the river than from the wealthy enclaves near the park, and he treated them for nominal fees, which he sometimes could not collect.[19]

Close proximity to urban poverty likely made Kelly Simpson more attuned than most to the stirrings of reform. But due to the creation of Greater New York, Roosevelt's overzealousness, and mostly because that was how it always went, the rest of New York tired of reform and in 1898 voted Tammany back in. Then, three years later "Boss" Croker left town as spectacular hearings detailed Tammany's latest transgressions and ushered in to office yet another "fusion" mayor, Columbia College president Seth Low, who introduced civil service to New York, boosted education, and lowered taxes before falling victim to another bout of reform fatigue.

Kelly Simpson sympathized with Seth Low. But he venerated Theodore Roosevelt, now nationally famous as the nominal leader of an improbable assembly of elite easterners and grizzled westerners called the "Rough Riders," the heroes of the Spanish-American War. Elected governor of New York State in 1898, Roosevelt continued to garner headlines; an 1899 speech put "the strenuous life" in the American phrasebook. By then, Roosevelt had learned from his misstep as police commissioner—he understood that politics is the art of the possible. As a "regular Republican" governor willing to work with Republican boss Thomas Collier Platt, and as vice president to the conservative William McKinley, Roosevelt disappointed some reformers, but not Kelly Simpson. One day Kelly talked a local merchant out of a cardboard display piece for Moxie, America's first mass-marketed soft drink. He brought home the statuette of Roosevelt bearing the inscription "Lead the strenuous life—Drink Moxie" and installed it in his son's bedroom.[20] The cardboard Roosevelt was likely in Kenneth's bedroom when an assassin's bullet made the real one, then only forty-two years old, President of the United States, an office that he called a "bully pulpit" from which to advocate strenuous living and reform.

Kenneth Simpson spent his formative years listening with reverence to the abundant words from the bully pulpit. While reform played itself out most visibly in politics, there was also a more personal approach, known as the "social gospel," adopted by a few crusading individuals. Middle-class reformers usually began with a paternalistic attitude: they expected right thinking and clean living to remedy all social ills. Advocates of the social gospel had reached a more nuanced understanding. They realized that new social and economic millstones were grinding the urban poor into the cultural bedrock of American individualism. They believed that the government had to protect the powerless many from being harmed by a powerful, self-interested few.

That understanding usually came from working and living among the urban poor, something that Kelly Simpson had done. Probably for the same reason that he dragged the cardboard Roosevelt home, Kelly Simpson sent his son for schooling with a social gospel acolyte, Robert Howard Syms. Syms was preoccupied with the complications of the urbanizing, industrializing city. He opened the Syms School in the fall of 1899 in order to develop a new generation of boys more attuned to this new life. He supplemented academics with physical and manual training and took pride that in his classroom "the birch is absent."[21] Kelly Simpson enrolled Kenneth at the Syms School, although only for a time. There is no record of what Kenneth learned about social justice, but he had seen a true believer. In 1907 Syms, who had been struggling with a book on the city's "sociological problem," became deranged. He ended up insane in Bellevue Hospital.[22]

Kelly Simpson found it easier to expose his son to the fine arts. In 1904, the music-loving physician noticed that the box office manager at Carnegie Hall seemed to have a stubborn cough. He successfully treated the man, who reciprocated with regular free concert tickets. Sometimes Kelly took his children along, but as he grew older, Kenneth began to take in the symphony alone or with sister Sallie—he was, from a young age, comfortable in a world of orchestras and evening clothes.[23]

Kenneth was still as much grade school boy as cosmopolite, and like his contemporaries he explored a fantasy life of story on his own and the concrete urban surroundings with friends. He eventually learned to appreciate literature, but Kenneth had an early weakness for a good tale. One of his favorites was *Trail of the Lonesome Pine*. He may well have recognized something of his father's situation in a plot that revolved around a cultivated outsider becoming involved in the affairs and intrigues of a close-knit "uncivilized" people. The landmarks of his young life, now long gone, to him seemed permanent: Presbyterian Hospital, Lenox Library, and Union Theological Seminary. The gothic windows and "cathedral-like edifice" of Hunter College made a deep impression on a worldly yet wide-eyed youth.[24] Among these unchanging edifices there was much going on. The cable cars, still running along Lexington Avenue, were slated to be scrapped. Steam trains ran below Park Avenue and belched smoke from apertures in the pavement. Over on Fifth Avenue, an automobile occasionally shot by, and delighted local children shouted "get a horse"—which, of course, still meant something.[25]

Indeed, the modern city emerged during Kenneth's youth. Regular trash collection began the year he was born. The Flatiron Building went up in 1902, and the Fifth Avenue horse cars gave way to the subway in 1907. In 1910, construction began on the Woolworth Building—briefly to be the tallest building in the world—designed by the father of Kenneth's friend, Cass Gilbert Jr. There were, of course, summer camps in the Adirondacks and vacations in Maine, but Kenneth was always most at home in New York City. For the rest of his life, it was the canvas upon which he would paint his dreams. This was no platitude, for Kenneth Simpson had already realized one dream.[26]

Kenneth took the Knickerbocker Greys quite seriously from the start. Faced with a complex yet clearly-defined institution, he plotted a route to success and achieved it. He played a boy's role, perhaps, but he did it masterfully. A song written by drillmaster Charles Hoyt defined the discipline and ideals of the group. "We are in earnest in our work, for they command best who best obey," the chorus went. "We are proud to wear the uniform so neat, for it means a self-control that is complete."[27] Kenneth Simpson was the kind of boy who took sentiment like this seriously, and he regularly won the medal for neatness, displaying a sartorial bent that remained throughout his life.[28]

Kenneth obeyed as required and commanded when he could. His rise in the Greys was steady: from private to lance corporal to sergeant to lieu-tenant—one grade per year. In 1907, he quit the drum corps to become com-mandant of Company D and won the coveted officers medal. The next year Kenneth was major, First Battalion, and won the officers medal again. Finally, in November 1909 when the Knickerbocker Greys assembled for the season, Kenneth Simpson, at age fourteen, was colonel—in charge of 150 of New York's most privileged and promising boys. The next spring's program, indi-cating that he had arrived, printed his full name for the first time—Kenneth Farrand Simpson.[29]

WORKING "THE HILL"

It was hardly swimming holes and fishing poles, but New York and the Knickerbocker Greys were childhood for Kenneth Simpson. In the fall of 1910 it was time to prepare for college. The door to prep school may have been opened by one of Kelly Simpson's wealthier patients, George Walbridge Perkins. Perkins had built the New York Life Insurance Company into the world's largest and in so doing reinvented the entire industry. That achieve-ment made Perkins a million-dollar-a-year partner in the Wall Street invest-ment banking firm of J. P. Morgan, where he assembled the International Harvester Trust. Kelly Simpson shared with Perkins an admiration of Theodore Roosevelt and a concern for social justice. Kenneth Simpson shared with Perkins's son, George W. Perkins Jr., the aspirations common to teenage boys. And both were going to "The Hill."[30]

In early October 1910, Kenneth Simpson stepped off a train into the grey Pennsylvania steel city of Pottstown, about thirty-five miles northwest of Philadelphia. It must have been disquieting—more than a few of the privi-leged youth who prepped there lay awake at night with the clanging of metal ringing in their ears and the glare of the blast furnaces flashing across their dormitory windows. But those were mere apparitions, for The Hill School, perched high above Pottstown like some Victorian junior Olympus, was a world away from the mills. "The Hill" was established in 1851. A half-century later, professor John Meigs had brought the school to prominence by pro-moting "mental discipline and exact scholarship" and a curriculum heavily

weighted toward the Greek and Latin classics. The Hill provided an alternative to rigidly pietistic New England boarding schools and was equally effective—no student ever failed to get into college.[31]

Kenneth was entering in his "fourth form" year—the equivalent of tenth
grade in prep school parlance. Joining him in residence at the brand new
"Upper School" building were familiar faces like Cass Gilbert Jr. and George
Perkins Jr. There were also familiar names in his class, including scions of
the du Pont and Weyerhauser families. As the boys settled nervously into
their quarters, Kenneth might have provided welcomed assurance. By then
Kenneth had in abundance the kind of confidence that colonelcy in the Greys
bestowed. His heritage and education had made him sharp. He could think
fast and, in what one student called his "witty, fast-talking Irish line," talk
faster.[32] This raft of verbiage, coupled with a buoyant personality, enabled
Kenneth, observed George Perkins Jr., to "make things nice and cheerful" for
others even under tough circumstances.[33]

The fresh new dormitory must have been welcomed relief in a school that
was overlaid in a stifling veneer of Victorian propriety. The aging master's
wife, known as "Mrs. John," kept it burnished, enforcing proper dress and eti-
quette and ushering the students, one by one, into her rooms to enquire about
their souls. Days were spent mostly in the "Old Schoolroom," its molasses-
colored oak and pine varnished as thick as the layer of cultivation that the
school was expected to impart on its charges. But tradition did not beget
lethargy, for the educators on the hill were as efficient as the steelmakers in
the valley. "Every moment was disposed of; our whole life was regulated by
bells; and—till we reached the sixth form, at any rate—we had hardly an hour
of leisure," recalled Kenneth's classmate Edmund Wilson.[34]

That fall began the process—in between the bells—of finding "a place" at
The Hill. A few, like Wilson, were destined to spend the long library hours
of the literati. Kenneth held his own with them. He was on the board of
the Hill School yearbook, *The Dial*, all through school, and his closest friend,
Alfred Bellinger, earned a literary reputation that exceeded even Wilson's at
the time. Kenneth's biggest aspiration, though, was to become an actor. He
made drama club his first year, playing a minor role in the Victorian farce
"The Private Secretary." Perhaps he could not abide bit parts, for although
Kenneth remained in the club, he never acted again.[35]

For most boys, sports offered the surest route to success. Classmate John

Overton, for example, developed athletic prowess at The Hill that carried him to stardom at Yale. Kenneth, however, played only tennis, and that "indifferently," although in 1912 he participated in Thanksgiving Day festivities that included a sack race, a tug of war, and backward running—in which he came in fourth. Prep schools allowed minimal scope for superabundant teenage hormones, making social activities rare but monumental. In that realm Kenneth had no troubles. Many classmates—Perkins included—were obliged to take their sisters to the big sixth form dance in May 1913. Kenneth brought older sister Sallie—but as chaperone. He chose a date for the ball from among at least two young ladies. But Kenneth was hardly preoccupied with girls. His passion was far more specialized and he developed it early, for in the school newspaper Kenneth had found a new way to lay down a beat for his contemporaries to follow.[36]

The *Hill School News* was then only nine years old, but it had already assumed a position of high status on The Hill. The Hill traditionally sent its best graduates to Yale, and its paper was unabashedly modeled on that institution's legendary *Yale Daily News*. Like its collegiate counterpart, the *News* provided a powerful voice for the students. Power attracts ambition, and since this was abundant at The Hill, the *News* chose its staff through competition. As at Yale, aspiring newspapermen were known as "heelers," a term borrowed from urban machine politics. Almost from his first day, Kenneth had decided to "heel the *News*," cornering his fellow students with subscription blanks, soliciting advertisements from local merchants, and ferreting out and typing up stories. Kenneth's way with words, his fast-blossoming salesmanship, and an ability to turn out copy served him well. He won an associate editor's post during his first term.[37]

Another steady climb ensued. In his fifth form year, Kenneth was one of three editors. In his final, sixth form, year he was elected business manager—second in command at the *News*, although the record suggests that he was second among equals. The *News* reflected Kenneth's ambitions: it grew from four to sixteen pages to become the largest school newspaper in the country. Among profiles of other prep schools and stories about Yale, it printed exhortations to self-discipline and civic engagement. At times the exhortations were less than compelling. Hemingway and Fitzgerald had yet to dismantle overly ornate Victorian American prose, and faculty advisor Howard Bement, described by one historian as a "skilled rhetoritician in both the good and bad sense of the word," would not have allowed it anyway.[38] Bement taught Kenneth how to write, but the student always retained a bit of the teacher's pretentious tone and workmanlike construction.

DEBATING PROGRESSIVISM

By sixth form year the *News* had become something of a "bully pulpit" for Kenneth. But even it proved inadequate, for Kelly Simpson's encouragement had taken effect—Kenneth Simpson was preoccupied with politics. And by then, the politics of reform, sprung from the efforts of authors and activists, nurtured by local and state politicians, and watered by the words of Theodore Roosevelt, had a name: Progressivism.

Party politicians of the late nineteenth century had shut their eyes to the changes that transformed the nation and undermined old sources of stability and security. The Republicans who dominated the era catered to the aspirations of business rather than to the needs of people; they stoked the furnace of industrialization but paid no attention to the many who were burned. "Populist" protest from farmers and workers was dismissed as the grumbling of losers. By the turn of the century, though, "respectable," old-stock Americans had begun to awaken to the nation's problems and Progressivism, described by one journalist as Populism that had "shaved its whiskers washed its shirt . . . and moved up into the middle class," was born.[39]

By his second year in office, President Theodore Roosevelt began to harken to the concerns of Progressives. In 1902 he struck back against monopoly in the Northern Securities Case and intervened in a nationwide coal strike, not on the side of the owners but as a neutral. He signed the Newlands Act that directed national resources to be used for the public good rather than for private gain. He appointed to the Supreme Court the brilliant jurist Oliver Wendell Holmes, more inclined to decide cases on a pragmatic assessment of the consequences rather than on ideology and business interest.[40]

Roosevelt worked on a national canvas woven by governors like New York's Charles Evans Hughes and California's Hiram Johnson and hundreds of mayors, councilmen, and activists. All sought, through a host of initiatives, to come to grips with the problems created by industrialization, immigration, and urbanization. Their goals included furthering democracy through electoral reform, curbing the power of corporations through antitrust measures, and creating greater efficiency in the economy by harmonizing business interests. This latter goal ensured that there was a marked pro-business vein in Progressivism, and mining these ores most energetically was George W. Perkins Sr. Despite his enduring reputation, Roosevelt was seldom heedless. He had learned not to favor one constituency enough to alienate another. His successor had missed the lesson, however.

In 1909 Roosevelt left office in grand style. He entrusted his Progressive mantle to Vice President William Howard Taft and went hunting in Africa. Though a formidable legal mind, Taft was not an adept politician, and he had never been a Progressive at heart. Taft alienated Progressives by favoring wealthy constituents and backing venal Secretary of the Interior Richard Ballinger over crusading Forestry Chief Gifford Pinchot in a battle over the public lands. When Roosevelt returned, he began planning to take back Progressivism for the Republicans.

In the midst of this conflict, over the 1911 Christmas break, sixteen-year-old Kenneth Simpson issued his first public political statement. Commenting on state politics in a letter to the editor of the *New York Times*, he argued that the election of a Republican legislature indicated "disgust at the result of one year of Tammany rule at Albany" and urged the party to select a reformer for the speakership.[41] The statement demonstrated a budding political astuteness. Kenneth was paying the kind of close attention to state and local matters that characterizes an effective politician. He was clearly a committed Republican, but he was also a Roosevelt man. Roosevelt's tiff with Taft, however, was fast rendering these two allegiances incompatible. The break came in the summer of 1912 when the Republican Party renominated Taft. Roosevelt abandoned the Republicans and, bankrolled by the fortunes of George W. Perkins and publisher Frank Munsey, created the Progressive Party. When the Progressive Convention opened in Chicago in 1912, Kenneth was there, a guest of George Perkins Jr. The Progressives went down to defeat in the fall, but what Kenneth saw that summer must have either fascinated or appalled him, because he spent most of the next year talking about it.[42]

Debate was a cornerstone of Hill School life. There were two clubs, "Q.E.D." and "Wranglers," and two camps within each of thirty-five to forty boys that met every Saturday night. Debating suited Kenneth as much or more than journalism. In it he found the outlet for his performer's instincts that he had not found in acting. In fourth form, Kenneth won second prize in debating honors. In fifth form he won one of three gold medals for "excellence in elocution."[43]

In the fall of 1912, as the sixth form year began, Kenneth's debating skills were first rate and the issues of the day close to his heart. The year's first intra-camp debate weighed whether it would be in the nation's best interest for the Progressives to win the election. Kenneth and classmate Oliver B. Cunningham argued for the affirmative. The January inter-camp event debated whether the President should serve a six-year term or not. Kenneth, arguing for the affirmative, received first prize: his virtuosic performance got mixed reviews in the *News*. "He sought, by rapidity of utterance, by clarity of argument, and by forcibleness of manner to nullify the effect of his opponents' points," the reviewer wrote with some admiration, while warning of "the danger of excess in his peculiar method."[44]

Excess does not appear to be something that Kenneth worried unduly about: his classmates regularly poked fun at his overly enthusiastic, hard-sell approach. But he got results. Early in the sixth form year he convinced his professors to schedule a debate with the rival Hotchkiss School at the end of the year. Then, for the rest of the year, he breathlessly promoted this first interscholastic prep school debate in the pages of the *News*. Kenneth may have influenced the subject matter as well. The terms of the debate were, "resolved, that the Progressive Party should have no permanent place in American Politics." As the April 26 match with Hotchkiss approached, Kenneth applied most of his substantial energy to preparing his team, which included Alfred Bellinger and Perkins as alternate, to argue in the affirmative. He even persuaded Perkins to ask his father for some arguments against the continued existence of the party that he was even then trying to hold together. Perkins Sr. does not appear to have willingly undermined his position, even for a prep school debate. Kenneth, however, showed no such compunction. He won the debate, and he and Bellinger shared gold medals for excellence.[45] The Hill offered yet another outlet for public speaking—the mandatory sixth form oration. At the height of the 1912 campaign season, Kenneth chose as his topic "the progressive movement in politics."[46] By the time he delivered his lecture in early 1913, he had ensured that he was not the only one lecturing about politics on The Hill.

Kenneth believed that his classmates did not receive ample instruction in politics and government. High schools taught civics, he reasoned, and Yale—ever the cynosure for Simpson—even had a Civic Club. In early October 1912, just two weeks after school opened, Kenneth convened a meeting of his peers and tried out his arguments. "After we heard that it was not one of his money-making schemes, and that he wanted to start a new Civic Club," wrote the sixth form historian, "we were all back of him."[47] Kenneth drafted Howard Bement as faculty advisor to the Civic Club.

The Civic Club hosted distinguished guests like the Comptroller of New York City, the president of Columbia University, and, of course, George W. Perkins. Kenneth wanted even more notable speakers, but they charged sizeable fees. Within ten days he had solved that problem. Classmate Curtis Bok had a very wealthy and influential father, Edward Bok, who published the *Ladies Home Journal*, then the most popular magazine in the world. When the elder Bok visited one day, Kenneth appealed to him to fund a series of lectures by distinguished political men. Bok agreed, and it was decided to name the lectures in honor of schoolmaster John Meigs, who had died the previous year.[48]

The first Meigs lecturer was a former governor of Pennsylvania. Seth Low was the second, in March 1913. The lineup kept improving. Particularly

The Hill School Civic Club, 1913. Simpson is front row center; George W. Perkins Jr. is front row left. *(Courtesy of the John P. Ryan Library, The Hill School)*

popular was Democratic Missouri Congressman and Speaker of the House Champ Clark, who recounted his role in deposing the despotic former speaker "Uncle Joe" Cannon. Some of the boys thought no one could top Clark, but Kenneth knew one speaker who would. The seventeen-year-old president of the Civic Club traveled to Oyster Bay to invite Theodore Roosevelt to The Hill. Roosevelt agreed.[49]

Kenneth's persuasive powers likely owed something to his ability to frame a successful argument, but they probably owed more to his inexhaustible supply of verbiage. The fifth form yearbook, written in parody of an airship's log, called him "our regular gas machine."[50] The sixth form yearbook called him "Marc Antony Simpson," one of The Hill's prodigies.[51] His confidence, precocity, and persistence could, on occasion, make him something of a know-it-all. A parody issue of the *News* noted that Kenneth would "readily supply advice on getting out an extra issue of the news" and concluded, "P.S.—Information on any other subject cheerfully furnished."[52] Kenneth had enough of a sense of humor to run the barb. Even the eminent George Perkins Sr. was both put off and impressed. After Kenneth invited him to talk to the Civic Club, Perkins wrote his son that "I received a letter from your master man—he of about 4 foot 6 or so—asking me to come down and speak on the 31st."[53]

On Monday, June 9, 1913, Theodore Roosevelt came to Pottstown. When George W. Perkins's special train pulled into the station, the Rough Rider waved his hat, jumped down from his coach, and was whizzed to The Hill in a special car. Extended proximity to the great man may have been too much even for Kenneth. That afternoon, when he stood before the crowd to make the introduction, words—for the first time, apparently—failed Kenneth, so he borrowed a few from the 1912 Progressive convention to introduce "a man who needs no introduction."[54]

For an hour, Roosevelt offered instructions to a youth preparing for a lifetime in politics. One of his firmest rules was one he himself had broken in 1912: accomplish what is possible rather than attempt what is not. He castigated "those who have excellent purposes and no power to achieve them." "I preach to you," said Roosevelt, "the doctrine of realizable idealism."[55] Having dispensed the philosophy, Roosevelt then touched on execution, telling the students that "the man who doesn't play as though he has a spare neck in his pocket isn't of much use. If you go into political life, and can't hold your own in a rough-and-tumble, you will be of no use."[56]

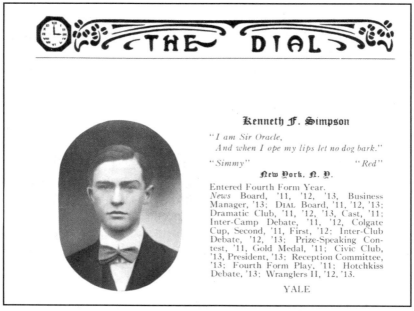

Simpson's page in the Hill School Yearbook in 1913, his sixth form year. *(Courtesy of the John P. Ryan Library, The Hill School)*

This was the capstone of Kenneth's prep school career. The next day came the awarding of prizes, the annual address, and graduation. The class had voted Kenneth "most energetic," "biggest bluffer," and "most successful in business." [57] He was prominently featured—and lightly ribbed—in the class speaker's presentation. It must have been a bittersweet event, however, because although Anna Farrand Simpson and her sister Ada Saxton attended, Kelly Simpson did not. He was ill and would spend most of the next year in sanitariums. [58]

Kelly Simpson had wanted his son to go to Yale. He himself had hoped to study at Yale's Sheffield Scientific School but had been, as he put it, "side-tracked." [59] Perhaps for that reason he had sent his son to The Hill, which provided reliable entry to Yale. Kenneth was going to need even more of the energy and initiative that he had displayed at The Hill, for Yale, with its secret societies and superachievers, had a reputation as the most unforgiving of alma maters. Kenneth well knew this. Just a few months earlier, he had republished in the *News* an article from the *Yale Daily News* by recent graduate William C. Bullitt, who would go on to be the first United States Ambassador to the U.S.S.R.

The standards of excellence at Yale were so high, Bullitt wrote, that "95 percent are graduated perfectly moral, perfectly conventional nonentities." "The rest," he concluded, "are men of tremendous efficiency, but old before their time."[60] Kenneth had no intention of being a nonentity but had little time to worry about the alternative: the Yale entrance exams were in a week.[61]

YOUNG MAN ON THE MAKE

Kenneth's performance on the week's worth of examinations in subjects ranging from algebra to Xenophon—classmate John Overton called them "mental torture"—gained him admittance to Yale without condition.[62] And so he passed from his second expertly played role to a third. It would be the toughest yet, but Kenneth was now a tougher player. At age eighteen he was no longer the slight, four-foot-six "master man" that George Perkins remembered: his height was topping five feet nine. He would never make five-ten—never be tall—and there was always that hair that at The Hill had earned him the unoriginal nickname of "Red." But Kenneth had a slim and consistently well-groomed and attired figure that was none the less impressive. Most striking, however, was his countenance. His blue eyes were deep, penetrating, and hinted at defiance, giving him an adult look of confidence just a bit earlier than his counterparts.[63]

With most of the rest of the freshman class of almost four hundred, Kenneth moved into Wright Hall, a brand new gothic building in the center of the New Haven campus. As he settled in, Kenneth received a letter from his father counseling him as to next steps. "Be careful about acquaintances," Kelly Simpson wrote. "Let the procession pass for awhile and then you can get your proper footing."[64] His first toeholds that fall included being elected vice president of the debating club and winning entry into the highly selective Zeta Psi fraternity.[65]

By late November, when Kenneth wrote to commiserate about the Yale football team's loss to Harvard, his father had moved from Battle Creek to Clifton Springs Sanitarium: he claimed to be "trying out health resorts."[66] In early February 1914, Kelly Simpson died at home of a cerebral hemorrhage—he was only fifty-eight years old. He was buried with his father, mother, and Sarah Hull Jenkins in the hilltop cemetery at Hudson. Kelly's death left Kenneth to his own devices. Much of the $60,000 estate was tied up in obligations that Kelly had assumed for other family members. Anna Simpson considered curtailing some of these, but Kenneth insisted upon honoring them all. Kenneth would put himself through school, piecing together funds from two scholarships, two years of teaching Sunday school at New Haven's St. Paul's Church, and whatever other work he could find.[67]

Kenneth excelled academically but he was no "grind," and he professed later in life to have been "profoundly bored" by the Yale curriculum.[68] The only subject he truly enjoyed was history—French history in particular—and he won the Andrew D. White prize for best historical essay one year. In history, presumably, he found highly practical instruction about how to get things done. He saw no point in study for its own sake and disdained philosophy, which, he later wrote, "doesn't do anybody any good."[69] It probably helped that Kenneth roomed with the studious Alfred Bellinger during his sophomore year. In the next he made Phi Beta Kappa. But in his outlook on academics, Kenneth was squarely within, rather than without, the Yale mainstream. The popular 1911 novel *Stover at Yale* put things in perspective. "You've got to do a certain amount of studying here," an upperclassman told Stover. "Better do it in the first year and get in with the faculty."[70]

By the turn of the century, the competitive pulse of industrial America had penetrated Ivy League institutions—Yale most of all—to create a new kind of student, one to whom "getting in with the faculty" and gaining other forms of leverage were far more important than learning for its own sake. Yale had become a launching pad rather than a refuge for reflection. These "young men on the make," as journalist Henry F. Pringle called them, considered college to be mostly about taking "the first vital steps toward material success after graduation." They did not get diverted by coursework, split their time between school in New Haven and society in New York, and chose either football or the *Daily News* as a way of "doing something for Yale." The best measure of their success was getting tapped for one of Yale's senior societies.[71]

For a young man on the make, Kenneth handled academics perfectly. He did not make the weekend trek to the city as often as his counterparts, however, partly because of his Sunday school obligations and partly because— as was understandable for a young man who had heretofore reached every goal he had set—Kenneth was not hedging his bets. He staked everything on rising to the top right there in New Haven, on the *Yale Daily News*.[72]

Kenneth began heeling in his freshman year when he was one of three in a field of thirty to be the first in the class of 1917 to make it. During an eighteen-week trial, every heeler covered the same beat—everything and anything. They were expected to sell large volumes of advertising and to write between 800 and 2,000 words per night. It may have seemed counterproductive to have so many young men chasing the same stories, but it worked well for the *News*—desperate heelers so annoyed professors, administrators, and students that most sent every conceivable piece of "news" that they had straight to the editorial office to avoid the bother. Kenneth had done all of this before, of course, but the *Hill School News* had been a weekly, and the stakes had not been so high. Heeling the *Yale Daily News* was notoriously rigorous—one heeler in a later year so exhausted himself as to take sick and die shortly after making the staff.[73]

Kenneth's boundless energy enabled him to bear the drudgery and exhaustion, although not without earning from his classmates the nickname "wretched."[74] Upward mobility was not the only reward, however. The *News* was Yale's window to the rest of the world. The big stories came to the members of the *News* board first, and they served them up to the campus in the morning paper or—when the stories were really big—on bulletin boards to the crowds that assembled in the old Berkeley Oval.[75]

It was in the spring of Kenneth's freshman year that one such big story indicated that international events might impinge upon cloistered campus life. Mexico had been ruled for decades by a strong man whose overthrow had spurred a struggle for succession that threatened to draw in the United States. In April 1914, overzealous Mexican officials arrested a few American sailors in Tampico. The sailors were hastily released, but when the Mexicans refused to salute the American flag an international incident resulted. One Sunday night Kenneth was at the news desk when word of the event came in. Kenneth and his colleagues posted the news in the Oval, and the students rallied and marched around campus demanding speeches from teachers and administrators. Kenneth was exhilarated but somewhat surprised that the Yale students had turned an international incident into a "typical spring party." "The college absolutely refuses to take anything seriously," he wrote his mother.[76]

Kenneth took the *News* seriously, however, and his efforts paid off. In early 1916, having faced stiff competition from the other associate editors, Kenneth Simpson took over as chairman of the 1917 board of the *Yale Daily News*. In the statement of principles that he ran in the February 11 edition,

Kenneth offered his own rendition of Yale's achievement-oriented mission, stating that "the goal of education is service, the highest goal of all, the public service."[77]

PERSPECTIVES

For Yale, much would depend upon what Kenneth Simpson's definition of public service was, and that was shaped by a sense of perspective gained during the summers of young adulthood. There were no trips to Europe or balmy days on Long Island estates, but Kenneth's worldview grew broader because of it.

Although George Perkins Jr. had gone to Princeton, Kenneth kept in touch after prep school and the relationship continued to provide opportunities. In 1913, in another of its periodic revolts against Tammany, New York City elected John Purroy Mitchel mayor on a Fusion ticket. In the summer of 1914, the outbreak of the First World War in Europe had spurred a sharp spike in the price of food. The mayor created a "Committee on Food Supply" and appointed as chairman George W. Perkins. Although Perkins did not offer much beyond platitudes and self-publicity, he continued to look into food distribution, first for the mayor and then for the governor. Somewhere along the way, he got his son's former "master man" appointed to the mayor's commission. In the late summer of 1915, Kenneth stayed with the Perkinses for six weeks, presumably exploring food issues some of the time. Those weeks turned out to be most eventful, however, for the unexpected aftermath of an evening's exploration of Times Square.[78]

On the night of September 24, 1915, patrolman Rogan of traffic squad C came across a "wordy wrangle" unfolding at 44th and Broadway. The words were punctuated by the sounds of the slaps that two young women were taking at a young man's face. The young man was Kenneth Simpson, the women were ushers from the Vitagraph Theater. They insisted that Kenneth had made repeated inappropriate advances: he insisted that he had just parted from two friends when one of the girls had inexplicably hit him with a newspaper. Rogan chose not to sort things out—he marched them all down to the station. Kenneth was arrested and then released on his own recognizance until the next day.[79]

There must have been a few strings pulled the night of the 24th. Kenneth made his court appearance in Yorkville on the Upper East Side rather than in Times Square. He also brought along a phalanx of character witnesses, including an eminent lawyer, the bishop of St. James's Episcopal Church, and aunt Ada Saxton. Kenneth was acquitted. The outcome was not terribly surprising—the judge said he would have let Kenneth off even if he had been found guilty. There may have been something to the charge, for Simpson did indeed have a predilection for flirting. But on the other hand, the two young ladies, who had promised to produce witnesses, never did. Kenneth may have shrugged the whole thing off as bad luck, but slipping so suddenly into the legal system must have given him a better sense of the fragility of social status than he had had before. [80]

If the scrape in Times Square allowed Kenneth to see society from the bottom up, events the next summer gave him a look at politics from the top down. Again, George W. Perkins was involved. In 1916 he was desperately trying to hold together his troubled Progressive Party, whose moderate members had been returning to the Republican fold. Theodore Roosevelt was determined to have the Presidency back, and although the party was being kept alive largely due to the ideological fervor of western radicals and the ready checkbook of the eastern Perkins, Roosevelt knew that it had no better chance of winning in 1916 than it had in 1912.

Roosevelt wanted to run as a Republican, but there were two problems. First, the Party machinery was under the capable control of Charles D. Hilles, chairman of the Republican National Committee and a Taft man. Second, in the eyes of party regulars, Roosevelt, in running once as a Progressive, had committed a cardinal sin. Roosevelt believed that his only chance of winning was to use the Progressive Party one last time as a lever to pry the nomination out of the Republicans. The ever-faithful Perkins agreed to give it a try. The Republican Party Convention was scheduled for June 1916 in Chicago at the Coliseum. Perkins saw to it that the Progressives met in the same city at the same time in the Auditorium. Perhaps the Republicans, seeing the tide of support for the Rough Rider that was sure to arise from the Auditorium, would be unable to resist a sure victory and nominate Roosevelt. Perhaps.

When Perkins arrived at Chicago's Blackstone Hotel on the first of June he ran into Charles Hilles in the lobby. The two exchanged pleasantries, and Hilles told reporters that he thought the two parties would "get together."[81] So far, so good. In 1916 it was still not proper for a presidential candidate to show up at his own nominating convention—he had to feign the disinterest that the founding fathers had believed to be most appropriate. But Perkins knew that he and Roosevelt would have to make some quick decisions, so he had a private telephone wire established between his suite at the Blackstone and Oyster Bay. Perkins got his son a floor pass to the Progressive Convention. He would relay messages quickly to and from the floor. Perkins also wanted someone to stay by the telephone just in case—who better than George's friend Kenneth?[82]

The Progressives were all for Roosevelt, but the Republicans were not. They believed that they had found a Republican who was both "regular" enough to placate the conservatives and Progressive enough to win the general election: former New York governor, now Supreme Court Justice, Charles Evans Hughes. Perkins now had to keep the Progressives from committing suicide by nominating Roosevelt, a nomination that Perkins knew that Roosevelt would reject. While the Republicans moved inexorably toward Hughes and Perkins tried mightily to keep the Progressives from balloting, the private wire buzzed. Kenneth manned the telephone in Perkins's bedroom while a succession of eminent politicians trudged in and out. Usually he did little more than pass off the receiver, but on one occasion Roosevelt mistook Kenneth for his old running mate, Hiram Johnson, and began one of his typically one-sided conversations until Kenneth interrupted to straighten things out.[83]

By then, all that would save the Progressives from disaster would be for them to nominate Hughes also. But Roosevelt would have none of it. Although Hughes had once established a record as a reformer, he had been "above politics" on the Supreme Court and was now refusing to take a stand on anything. Most Progressives considered him "too straight-laced to inspire enthusiasm" anyway.[84] On Saturday, June 10, Kenneth's phone duties ended. Shortly after noon, the Republicans nominated Hughes. At almost exactly the same time, the Progressives nominated Roosevelt. Perkins then read a telegram from Oyster Bay declining the nomination.[85]

The Progressive Party, decapitated in what diehards considered a betrayal, was dead. It was not yet clear how the Republican Party would fare. In a remarkable confluence of luck and good connections, Kenneth Simpson had seen history being made. The stuff of his schoolboy orations, debates, and newspaper editorials had become real life. But if he had learned that he could make his dreams reality, he had also learned some important political lessons. Watching Roosevelt try to extricate himself from his predicament underscored the price paid by those who did not respect "party regularity." Seeing the Republicans choose a second-stringer over a clear winner merely out of principle taught him that that pride did not win elections. And as the Progressives nominated themselves into obscurity, he learned a bitter lesson about the practical problems caused by too much democracy and too little leadership. By that time, Simpson had already been initiated into a very different and exclusive world of leadership and power.

BONES AND BATTERY

The mainsprings of Yale's intricate machinery for creating new generations of influential American business and political leaders were its secret societies. Skull and Bones, founded in 1832, was the most prestigious. It built the first of the mysterious, tomb-like buildings that the uninitiated understood to house unimaginably important proceedings. To ensure that outsiders would have nothing but their imaginations to go on, legend had it that the architect himself was inducted so that he could never describe the interior of the Skull and Bones tomb. Every member pledged to uphold the secrecy and sanctity of the institution, even to the point of being obligated to get up and leave the room when an outsider uttered the name "Bones." Scroll and Key, founded in 1842, was both less pretentious and less influential. Wolf's Head, the newcomer founded in 1883, barely registered on the scale in 1916.[86]

There were counterparts elsewhere, but the dining clubs at Princeton and the social clubs at Harvard were far less selective than the Yale societies. They never managed to get their own members, let alone the rest of the campus, to take them as seriously as Yale took its secret societies. For those "young men on the make" who were intent on stepping from Yale into the highest rungs of society possible—for those who had risen above their peers, made connections, and "done something for Yale"—election to "Bones" and "Keys" marked a turning point of sorts. Legend was—and undergraduates believed it—that the millionaires behind Bones and Keys would henceforth smooth the way for their fellows and be there to catch them if they fell.[87]

May 18, 1916, the day that members of the Class of 1917 were inducted into the secret societies, was therefore a time of great excitement at Yale, so much so that the administration had tried unsuccessfully to exclude all but juniors and seniors from the quadrangle between five and six in the evening.

About eighty men stood an outside chance of being "tapped." Everyone knew who they were. But each society would induct only fifteen, so as the crowds assembled in the quadrangle much of the speculation was over the details—who would make the ultra-prestigious Bones? And who would get the highest honor of all, that of being "last man tapped?"[88]

As the chapel clock struck five, the seventy-five-year-old ritual began again. Every few minutes a solemn-faced senior emerged from one of the tombs, plunged into the crowd, tapped the elect on the shoulder, and gave the command "go to your room." The first man tapped for Bones that day was Prescott Bush, destined to be father and grandfather to two U.S. presidents. Then came track star and Hill veteran John Overton. Kenneth's freshman year roommate and second in command at the *News* Henry P. Isham was next. Alfred Bellinger was ninth man tapped. Sometime around six o'clock, senior and son of a wealthy insurance executive Lawrence G. Tighe waded into the crowd and found Kenneth Simpson's shoulder. He was the "last man tapped." It was, said a *News* correspondent, "one of the most popular elections of the afternoon."[89]

Although the conspiracy-minded delight in overestimating its influence in national and world affairs, there can be no overestimating the personal impact Skull and Bones had upon its members. By his senior year, Kenneth's closest compatriots were all Bonesmen: Bush, Bellinger, Isham, and football player Sam Duryee. They all lived around the Berkeley Oval, but their lives revolved around evenings at the tomb. There was no liquor there, and the clocks were set five minutes fast to remind them that they were a step ahead of the rest of the world. And in the inner sanctum, inexplicably named "322," they sat into the night revealing their innermost secrets—tearing each other down so as to, presumably, build each other up again stronger.[90]

Skull and Bones helped transform a casual acquaintance between Kenneth and Chicagoan Oliver B. Cunningham into a deep friendship. The two had been through The Hill and the first three years of Yale together. They had even competed against one another for chairmanship of the *News*. In Bones, Kenneth grew ever more impressed by "the strength of his personality" and Cunningham's ability to combine scholarly excellence and a worldly outlook. During what spare time there was in senior year, usually Saturday afternoons, Kenneth and "O.B." walked the streets and parks around New Haven, talking incessantly. They usually sojourned at the Elizabethan Club—described in one account as "Yale's gracious literary bastion of watercress sandwiches and afternoon tea"—and then retired to Bones, as Kenneth wrote later, for dinner and "a long wonderful evening."[91]

Membership in another group brought less inspiring but equally memorable results. Kenneth and the *News* had been instrumental in getting Yale to sponsor a student military detachment. The idea had germinated sometime around that night in 1914 when the students joyously marched and war with Mexico seemed imminent. Although some Harvard alumni had come up with the "Plattsburg idea" of training Ivy League men as officers, in the 1910s the field artillery was the glamour branch of the service and Yale's young men insisted on forming their own regiment. With government and faculty support they formed the "Yale Battery" as a detachment of the Connecticut Militia.[92]

Kenneth had planned on going to Plattsburg in the summer of 1916. The Progressive Convention intervened and, by the time it was over, Mexico was again in the news thanks to Pancho Villa and his band of border raiders. President Wilson called out the National Guard and Connecticut mobilized the militia. Within two weeks of Kenneth's return from Chicago, the Yale Battery was mustered in with a flurry of activity on the old tree-lined campus. Crowds cheered the Yale men, but the loudest cheers were from the recruits themselves after learning that they would not miss commencement and the baseball game.[93]

In July, Kenneth and nearly all of his Skull and Bones companions were among the Yale men who arrived at the new artillery training camp near Tobyhanna, Pennsylvania, described by one of them as "a flat, treeless plateau on top of nothing, characterized by dust and rocks."[94] In six weeks of seventeen-hour days, the men learned to handle 3-inch guns, find ranges, and fire accurately. When, during closing maneuvers, they found their target after only three tries, the commissioned officers pronounced them the "best artillery regiment in the National Guard."[95] Still, the Yale men adapted to Army life as all soldiers do—everyone learned to swear at Tobyhanna, one of them recalled. In this first experience in the military, Kenneth again attained prominence—not as the dashing young man at a cannon lanyard, but as an expert pusher of paper. In the middle of September, as the Battery mustered out just in time for the start of school, Kenneth was doing adjutant work, albeit with a sense of humor. When word from Washington threw a wrench into the process, he was heard to exclaim from his desk, "War Department one up!"[96]

THE UNCROWNED KING OF YALE

This first military venture ushered Kenneth into a triumphal senior year at Yale. He arrived on stage bedecked with affiliations and honors, including: the Yale Red Cross Relief Committee, Vice President of the Cosmopolitan Club, Vice President of the International Polity Club, President of The Hill School Club, Class Orator, and Chairman of the College Student Council. He contributed to the *Alumni Weekly* and the student publication the *Eli Book*. Playing even a small part in this many activities would have exhausted most people, but Kenneth somehow stayed fresh for his moments in the spotlight, which, in his senior year, were most of the time.[97]

The *Yale Daily News* harnessed the efforts of dozens of ambitious heelers and a smaller number of contenders for the top slots—during Kenneth's chairmanship, these included underclassmen Henry Luce and Britton Hadden who went on to found *Time* magazine. Although half a dozen editors took responsibility for various issues, most were too worn out by the arduous heeling process to work very hard at it, leaving the paper in almost full control of the chairman, who received tremendous latitude and deference. Wrote Henry Pringle, "Professors are slightly shocked on the rare occasions when he comes to class. They read his editorials with . . . solemnity. . . . They treat him with great respect and rarely question his views."[98] Kenneth summed up his own views in an editorial, writing that "the usefulness of a man's whole education is largely measured by the success and the intelligence with which he meets the obligations of citizenship."[99] It was a civic, rather than an academic, drumbeat that Yale heard from Kenneth Simpson's *News*.

One of the paper's first crusades was spurred by recent experience. The *News* started off the year criticizing the Yale Battery and the militia system as "hopelessly inadequate."[100] It advocated taking the battery out of the state's purview and folding it into the Reserve Officers Training Corps (ROTC) program. Kenneth was, by this time, very good at leading opinion, all the while ensuring that he did not get too far ahead. The process had been long under way and in November it played out—the battery was disbanded and its veterans got credit toward an ROTC commission.[101]

Kenneth's next crusade was equally successful, if less of a sure thing. In the fall of 1916 there was an election under way between incumbent Woodrow Wilson and Republican standard-bearer Charles Evans Hughes. Kenneth was determined to get Yale involved. On October 6, the *News* printed a petition

calling for the organization of a Yale Republican Club. Signers included confi-
dantes like Bush, Bellinger, Isham, Duryee, and an enterprising junior named
Robert Lovett.[102] This was a popular appeal at a school where Republicans
outnumbered Democrats by three to one: five hundred turned out at the
Lampson Lyceum. The club was entirely the product of Kenneth's political
calculus, but he had already learned the politico's trick of putting eminent
faces to the fore and calling the shots from the rear. As president, the group
chose Jeremiah M. Evarts, the grandson of Rutherford B. Hayes's secretary of
state. Charles Phelps Taft, the son of the former president, became vice president. Kenneth agreed to act as club secretary. Then he unveiled his plan.[103]

"I hope to be able to vote in Connecticut this fall," he told his assembled
classmates.[104] They could too, he insisted. Of course, New Haven's board of
selectmen would have the final say over voter eligibility, and they were mostly
Democrats, but Kenneth figured he could deal with that. His logic was good.
In admitting Yale students to the State Militia, he posited, Connecticut had
recognized their citizenship. Having done that, he concluded, the state had
to allow students to vote. The New Haven Democratic establishment did not
see it that way. Students, they had always insisted, were transients still tied
to their parents' households. They recognized Kenneth's new plan for an old
political trick—that of planting "floaters" in an election district to sway the
outcome.[105]

New Haven politicians were not the only skeptics. Having hatched the
idea, Kenneth tried it out on William Howard Taft, who was then teaching
law at Yale. Taft pronounced the idea "hopeless"—but Kenneth expected that
from someone who had lost the friendship of Theodore Roosevelt. With the
News stiffening their backbones, the students began to register. But as word
got out, local Democrats began demanding proof of residence. The *Hartford
Courant* voiced their frustration: "It is a well known fact that the applicants for
the right to vote have nearly all been members of the Yale Hughes Club."[106]

The students were well led and well connected: they even obtained
counsel from a senior partner at the New Haven law firm of Watrous & Day
who argued that Kenneth was right—service in the Yale Battery did estab-
lish citizenship. The politicians made the students work for their achievement. As one recalled, "After superhuman efforts, perjury, and a number
of bad cigars, some few individuals safely reached the polls."[107] In the end,
however, the politicians had been too late. Student votes won New Haven's

first ward for the Republicans for the first time in memory. It was the first election Kenneth Simpson ever carried—it was also the first one in which he was old enough to vote.[108]

The young maestro behind the *Yale Daily News* was just as eager to herald the national vote as he was to contest the local one. A little too eager, as it turned out. As the general election approached, Kenneth looked for ways to give his paper an advantage in covering the biggest story of the fall. His thoughts turned to a private telephone wire, and the result was a direct line from Republican National Committee headquarters in New York to the office of the *News*. What better way, Kenneth thought, to scoop the numerous and conflicting wire services than to get the results directly from those closest to the vote? On the night of November 7, 1916, students gathered in the Berkeley Oval where the *News* board projected the returns—literally—on the walls of the surrounding buildings and employed a megaphone to reach the near-sighted. There was likely plenty of excitement as Hughes took an early lead in the East and Midwest. But then returns from the South and West narrowed the gap, and it all came down to California.[109]

Hughes, as predicted, had been a lackluster campaigner. He had also made a few big mistakes, such as inadvertently snubbing California Progressive Hiram Johnson—the man Theodore Roosevelt had mistaken Kenneth Simpson for. It was not the perfect party. Yale tired and went to bed before the results from California came in. Kenneth, used to staying up while Yale slept, waited on the word. Some newspapers began predicting that Hughes would win, and very early in the morning word came from the Republican National Committee. The California count was not in, but Hughes was a sure thing. Kenneth gleefully pulled the trigger on the special election edition with a two-column photo and the banner headline: "Charles E. Hughes Elected President."[110] Few noticed the subheading "California looks like Hughes" as they perused the daily on their way to chapel.

California did not go for Hughes, confusing more people besides Kenneth Simpson. By one account, when a reporter called the Hughes household that morning, he was informed that "the President" was sleeping. "When he wakes up," the reporter countered, "tell him he isn't the President anymore." Although a competing sheet suggested renaming Yale's august daily *The Yale Daily Hughes*, most on campus seem to have been forgiving. The *News* printed one critical letter to the editor but was otherwise unapologetic.[111]

Not even New Haven could contain Kenneth in his next effort to further "the obligations of citizenship." Events in Mexico and the war raging in Europe had made Americans skittish. Most feared that the United States would stumble into the trenches of France. They had re-elected Wilson who, after all, had "kept us out of war." An influential few, however, were convinced that America was unlikely to remain aloof for long and were raising the call for universal military training.

Kenneth was determined to associate Yale with the influential few. He gathered his Republican partisans, began a new drumbeat in the pages of the *News*, and organized a straw poll. The results being as expected, Kenneth obtained—by what means is not known—an audience with the Senate Committee on Military Affairs. This time, Kenneth arranged to have friend Samuel Sloan Duryee act as nominal leader. But when the Yale delegates testified on the afternoon of January 24, 1917, Kenneth did most of the talking, assuring legislators that "the majority of students at Yale University are heartily in accord with the movement for Universal Military Training."[112] Unwilling to waste an opportunity, he also threw in some criticisms of the militia system.[113]

In early March, Kenneth spoke to a less exalted but possibly more influential crowd—the Yale alumni of 1891. They found his talk on "The Undergraduate of 1917" impressive and were reassured that standards had not slipped since the "good old days."[114] Later in the month came the senior class elections. To Kenneth Simpson went two first place awards: "hardest worker" and "most likely to succeed." He won third in the "done most for Yale" and "most brilliant" categories and also ranked in "most versatile," "most scholarly," and "most admired." Kenneth won far more recognitions than any of his counterparts. It was a remarkable performance by any standard.[115]

Although he had chosen Princeton over Yale, Edmund Wilson, Kenneth's classmate from The Hill School, found occasion to visit his old friends in New Haven. He was there one day when Kenneth's mother visited the campus and happened upon English professor William Lyon Phelps, noted for his incandescent wit. "Ah, Mrs. Simpson," began Phelps. "I suppose you know that your son is the uncrowned king of the campus?" Anna Farrand Simpson fixed Phelps in her gaze and asked, "Why uncrowned, Professor Phelps?" Phelps was speechless.[116]

THE NEXT BIG THING

It was still easy, in early 1917, for Americans to jest about kings. Europeans were sick of them. As their empires decayed, they had refused the reforms that a rising populace demanded. Instead, they had formed alliances and promulgated secret agreements to prop one another up—alliances and agreements that had led to this most terrible of all wars. European youth were dying in French fields while American youth, as Kenneth had written, "refused to take anything seriously." But Wilson could no longer keep America out of war after the Germans, long bottled up by the British Navy, made the desperate decision to wage unlimited submarine warfare. On February 3, the United States severed ties with Germany. Nevertheless, Kenneth later wrote, "the prom, for the moment, dwarfed wars and rumors thereof in the interest of the campus."[117]

The deadline to join ROTC approached a few days later. The *News* urged students to sign up, and 201 did. Among the 37 seniors was Kenneth Farrand Simpson, Sergeant Major, Field Artillery. A few days later the 1917 *News* board issued its last edition. Others beat the drum as Kenneth and his classmates concluded their college careers and began their military ones. The first Yale contingent actually called up was the Yale Naval Aviation Unit, a group of self-trained fliers that included former Hill School student and future Secretary of Defense Robert Lovett. It was still something of a spring party, however. Again, students marched around campus, cheering and soliciting speeches from faculty.[118]

It took the actual declaration of war, on April 2, to prompt Yale to begin mobilizing in earnest. By the middle of the month there were more than a thousand men "doing calisthenics before chapel and filling every available corner of both Sheff and the College Campus for drill during the afternoon," Kenneth wrote. Being Yale men, of course, some were still intent on jockeying for position. Those concerned that the war would soon be over scrambled to get in as soon as possible. Others waited to see if they could get a commission from Washington. The Marines recruited a few, but most Yale men insisted that "the artillery's the only thing."[119]

The "young men on the make" of 1917 were going to have to wait to find out where their efforts landed them on the ladder of success—first they would see what the war would bring. Kenneth had given that some thought, and it naturally revolved around politics. On April 24, he competed for the

Yale Graduates, 1917. From left: Knight Woolley, Simpson, Alfred Bellinger. *(Courtesy of Dr. Kelly Simpson)*

prestigious DeForest Speaking Prize, speaking in Lampson Lyceum on the future of political leadership. Kenneth painted with a broad historical brush and ventured that, in this war, "the government will have to perform a far larger task than it has borne in the history of our institutions." He argued that as government becomes larger, the party system upon which it rests would have to become stronger. Most importantly, he said, it would have to draw upon better men. Alluding to the Tammany of his youth, Kenneth stated that, "We must find in the young men of this generation the new type of politician which shall supplant the representatives of that class, peculiar in America, who, making politics a profession for personal profit has long since lost sight of the higher significance of the term."[120] Kenneth shared the DeForest prize with another classmate who also spoke on the war and within days left for training camp.

In New York City, at The Hill School, and at Yale, Simpson had attempted what few would have dared and achieved more than most would have dreamed. His disadvantages—second-tier standing in "society" and the need to work his way through college—had toughened him. His natural gifts—a keen intellect, a quick tongue, and seemingly inexhaustible reserves of energy—had proven easy to summon. Kenneth had made these first, second, and third acts in his young life seem almost too easy. He could learn every line and command any stage—as long as he knew the script. The youth had mastered some familiar roles, but the adult who would become "the new type of politician" would have to invent a new one entirely. For Kenneth, as for others of his generation, World War I would mark a divide between a youth filled with clarity and promise and an adulthood of ambiguity and disenchantment. In *This Side of Paradise*, Amory Blaine, Princeton, Class of 1917, faced the same future. "I know myself," he exclaimed, "but that is all."[121] For F. Scott Fitzgerald's hero, this was enough. Did Kenneth Simpson know himself? He had barely had time.

CHAPTER TWO
THE LONG APPRENTICESHIP

The land south of Ayer, Massachusetts, lay fallow in the summer of 1917. There was nothing promising about it: mostly scrub oaks and old tree stumps left behind long ago. But in Washington, D.C., plans for an overnight transformation were being laid. Armed with blueprints and timetables, the War Department raised upon the Massachusetts countryside a city for 10,000 soldiers in only a few months. In 1917, transformation was not a concern for Kenneth Simpson. His life had been one of steady unfolding rather than substantive change, a series of youthful successes that seemed sure to lead to adult achievement. Big plans were beside the point. But fifteen years later Simpson was still preparing, still waiting for achievement worthy of his beginnings. It was a long apprenticeship—too long, perhaps.

SOLDIER AND SCHOLAR

The Central Powers had wagered that they could defeat the Allies before the Americans had time to raise an army. It was to ensure that the Germans lost that bet that the United States Army built, along with dozens of other posts, Camp Devens, near Ayer, Massachusetts. In a mere eighteen months, the Army fielded 2 million American soldiers. Captain Kenneth Simpson was among them, arriving in Europe just in time to help topple the Central Powers.

A few of the Yale men had joined the Regular Army, but most, like Simpson, remained in the Reserve Officers Training Corps. In the summer of 1917, Congress created the National Army, filled its ranks with conscripts and volunteers, and drew its officers from the reserves, and on August 15, 1917, Simpson entered active service as a captain of the field artillery in the 76th Division, assigned to Camp Devens.[1]

For a while, Devens remained more construction site than Army camp. Under relentless hammering and sawing, the scrub oaks and stumps gave way to

Simpson entered active service as a captain, field artillery, in 1917. *(Courtesy of Dr. Kelly Simpson)*

barracks and buildings. As workmen built up the camp, Simpson helped build up the ranks. On September 4, he became Adjutant of the 302nd Field Artillery Regiment. It was up to him to put the processes in place that turned 1,000 raw recruits into soldiers and to create an administration to keep the regiment running. As recruits from across New England drifted into Camp Devens, they soon encountered Captain Simpson. One reluctant draftee hoped a tantrum would absolve him from service, but ensconced behind his desk, Simpson met the outburst with equanimity—he assigned the man to a battery and summoned the next.[2]

By October, the ranks were filled. Training began as the New England autumn turned into one of the coldest winters on record. There was still, apparently, some question about how best to utilize Captain Simpson, for in February 1918 he was sent to the Army School of Fire at Fort Sill, Oklahoma. Simpson took readily to this training. He was particularly engrossed by the meticulous mathematics involved in projectile fire. When he returned to Camp Devens, however, Simpson discovered that this penchant for complexity could be something of a liability.[3]

Upon Simpson's departure, Captain Coolidge, formerly in command of one of the regiment's six batteries, had filled in as Regimental Adjutant. When Simpson returned, he was reassigned as Adjutant of 1st Battalion, which included two batteries. There was no denying that this was a demotion, the first such setback for the ambitious Kenneth Simpson. One explanation may be that Captain Thomas Jefferson Coolidge III, of Boston Brahmin stock, a descendant of a past President and a relative of a future one, was well connected. But the regimental historian offered another explanation. While Simpson "established a standard of the highest efficiency," he wrote, "Captain Coolidge's methods on the whole followed simpler lines."[4]

In the summer of 1918, the captain went overseas ahead of his regiment to attend reconnaissance and orientation school in England. By mid-August, when Simpson rejoined his regiment en route to Camp de Souge near Bordeaux, the United States had joined in the final campaign of the war, the Second Battle of the Marne. The Americans were preparing to go into action alone for the first time. Their mission: to push back a bulge in the German line at St. Mihel, near Verdun.[5]

It had been more than a year since a close-knit group of Bonesmen had left New Haven. Sam Duryee was commanding a battery in Simpson's own

302nd Regiment. Prescott Bush was also an artillery officer. A few had scattered farther and taken a quicker route to the front. John Overton had joined the Marines and was killed by a shell fragment while leading his unit. "O.B." Cunningham had joined the Regular Army, convinced that he would be of more use working his way through the ranks than idling in officers training camp. On September 17, the first day of the American offensive at St. Mihel, Cunningham was killed when an enemy shell destroyed his forward observation post. Simpson learned the news while at Camp de Souge. Alone in his quarters, Simpson swatted flies, gazed out at the pine barrens, and penned a plaintive letter to his mother, writing that Cunningham "was the nearest thing to a brother that I've ever had."[6]

Simpson had taken a longer route to the front, but his chance was coming soon enough. The great climax of the war, the Meuse-Argonne offensive, was already in the works, and the 302nd Artillery was assigned to pin down the eastern end of the line near the Heights of the Meuse. Simpson's unit shipped out by rail to a point near Verdun, a bleak terrain littered with ruins, pocked by shell holes, and strewn with barbed wire. After a day's march, the First Batallion arrived at Rupt-en-Woevre, and on November 5th it went into position to provide artillery support for the second French colonial corps. Things were changing fast. By the 10th, although some were still fighting in the Heights of the Meuse, the Germans were in retreat all along the front.[7]

Overnight, rumors of an armistice ran through the ranks. The First Battalion, however, which had yet to fire a shot, was busy moving into an exposed position. As the sun rose on the 11th, it was protected by little more than the morning fog. At 6:55, word came down that the armistice would take effect at 11:00 A.M. But as the sun rose higher, the mist burned off and the Germans began ranging shells—mustard gas—toward the First Battalion. The officers pleaded for permission to return fire, but hearing nothing they waited expectantly for eleven o'clock, when finally the shelling stopped. The First Battalion had been a year preparing for a day in battle, but that was enough. That night both Germans and Americans along the Heights of the Meuse sent up red, green, and white rockets in sad celebration.[8]

The end of the war left the United States Army with a big problem: what to do with 2 million soldiers laboriously shipped overseas? They could not all go back at once. Officers took the opportunity for travel—Simpson spent Christmas day in Paris, attending services at Notre Dame Cathedral. Enlisted men could hardly be set loose; instead, it was decided to send them to college. The Army began building its own makeshift campus and also began arranging for doughboys to enroll in European schools.[9]

Simpson was enthusiastic about the idea. He envisioned himself ensconced in the hallowed halls of Oxford, and he lobbied hard for a spot there. But Simpson spoke very good French, so the Army nipped his Anglophilia in the bud and instead made him a Francophile for life. On January 7, 1919, Simpson left the 302nd to take command of the American School Attachments at the Universities of Aix and Marseilles, twenty-five miles apart in the South of France. A week later he was in Marseilles, and with a staff of 23 making arrangements for 86 students to study law and letters at Aix and 178 to study science, medicine, and engineering at Marseilles. A visiting officer found "an extremely capable young officer, of pleasing personality," and pronounced Captain Simpson "In every way fully capable of conducting the University activities."[10] Simpson's charges remained quite content during the next three months, in no small part due to extracurricular activities arranged by the enterprising commandant.[11]

Among the new acquaintances Simpson made in the South of France was the French commander of the port of Toulon. One day Simpson sprung an idea on the admiral: why not take some torpedo cruisers, which were just sitting in port, out with a detachment of soldiers for a tour? Simpson had Corsica in mind. The admiral liked the idea, but the American commanders quashed the idea—that is, until Simpson invited them to come along. In April, Simpson took 150 officers and men on a week-long vacation in Corsica. In Ajaccio, the birthplace of Napoleon, the soldiers-turned-students staged a baseball game for the amused locals. After a few days there, they finished out the week in Bastian. All along the way, the contingent was greeted with keys to cities and cannon salutes befitting heads of state. It was a triumphal conclusion to Simpson's brief career as university administrator, for by then the student population was dwindling. In recognition, the French minister of Public Instruction and Fine Arts decorated Simpson as Officier d'Academie.[12]

Simpson took his time returning from overseas. He arrived in Paris in the early summer of 1919 just as Wilsonian Progressivism drew its last breaths. America had entered "the war to end all wars" during the final flurry of reform in which it had approved the women's right to vote and prohibition.

Now a conservative backlash had set in. Woodrow Wilson did not notice; he was intent upon remaking the western world in accordance with progressive ideals at the Paris peace conference. Simpson basked in Wilson's reflected glory during some earnest late-night conversations at the Hotel Crillon with Yale historian and fellow Bonesman Charles Seymour, whom Wilson had assigned to create modern nations out of the ruins of Austria-Hungary. Late in June, Simpson visited England. He stopped for a few days in Oxford but spent most of his time in London, where he made the best of some remarkable, if inexplicably formed, connections. Twice he had tea with renowned writer Hillaire Belloc. Simpson dined at the House of Commons with a member of parliament, and he attended a ball at the estate of Mrs. Waldorf Astor.[13]

In the fall of 1919, out of active service, Simpson resumed his interrupted education. Harvard had been home to the nation's top law school since the 1870s when Christopher Columbus Langdell implemented the "case-book method" of studying law. It was not hard to get in, but it was difficult to stay in, because Harvard Law School had a demanding and unforgiving program. First-year students took the "five great common law classes," which included civil procedure, contracts, criminal law, principles of liability, and torts and property. Teaching the latter was legendary professor Edward "Bull" Warren. On the first day of each class, Warren delighted in announcing: "Gentlemen, look at the man on your right and the man on your left. Next year one of you three will be gone."[14]

Simpson was in no danger. He kept up a "B" average, very good for Harvard Law when grades of "C" and below were quite common, and he achieved an A-plus in his first year contracts class. The class of 1922 was the largest yet, with almost half of the law school's total enrollment, and they stuck together—during his first and second years, Simpson roomed in the red-brick Walter Hastings Hall with a Yale classmate. But Simpson also became close with second year student John Jay McCloy, destined to become one of the most influential men in twentieth-century American politics and diplomacy. Both men just missed making the law review and found the curriculum more challenging than anything they had previously encountered. "I had to run as fast as I could to keep up," recalled McCloy.[15] Simpson also kept running fast. He took Felix Frankfurter's public utilities class in his second year but did best on evidence. In his third year, Simpson's strongest subject was corporations. Throughout, he never let his grade point average slip.

For Simpson, law school was not as memorable as his colorful undergraduate career—he almost never spoke of it later in life. But there were some pleasant diversions. Simpson attended an occasional social event, mostly with old Yale friends, and he was selected for the Signet Club and the Lincoln Inn Society, Harvard Law's dining club in an old house on Brattle Street where "Albert the Steward" waited on law students taking a break from memorizing cases.[16] Simpson still had to work to supplement his income. Again, he tutored during the winter and in summers he returned to journalism, working as a reporter for the *New York Sun* covering Boston society and ultra-posh polo matches at Narragansett Pier, Rhode Island.[17]

Simpson's society features contrasted sharply with the headlines of the late teens and early twenties with their dire warnings of class warfare. The Russian Revolution and widespread labor troubles after the war had set off a "Red Scare" in the United States that scaled even the walls of Harvard. In 1920, Felix Frankfurter, President Roscoe Pound, and a few other professors formally criticized the government's abrogation of freedom of speech during and after the war. Outraged alumi arranged a "heresy trial" in May 1921, and the controversy split the almost uniformly progressive Harvard Law student body cleanly in two. Some, like Dean Acheson, a Frankfurter favorite, became lifelong Democrats. Others, including Simpson and McCloy, stuck with the Republicans despite the party's conservative turn.[18]

Simpson graduated from Harvard Law School in a class that, true to Bull Warren's prediction, was about two-thirds its original size. In the summer of 1922 he returned to Europe, visiting as far east as Constantinople. That fall, back in New York City for good, Simpson moved into the Yale Club next to Grand Central Terminal and prepared to embark, at long last, on his career. Through prep school, college, war, and law school an old obsession survived—the yearning to perform that had once left Simpson longing to be an actor. For Simpson had decided to become a great courtroom lawyer. His next move, therefore, was puzzling.[19]

FALSE START AND GOOD START

During Simpson's third year, George W. Wickersham spoke at Harvard Law School. Simpson would not have missed an appearance by the former Attorney General of the United States, and perhaps he was swayed by Wickersham's lecture topic, "some practical considerations concerning the practice of law."[20]   Perhaps, like McCloy before him, Simpson was simply attracted by the prestige of Wickersham and his senior partner, brother of former President Taft.   Whatever the reason, in October 1922, Simpson accepted a position at the estimable New York firm of Cadwalader, Wickersham & Taft.[21]

Cadwalader provided its lawyers with far more opportunities to face business barons than juries. Most of its work involved corporate transactions and negotiations, particularly in matters of corporate finance, trusts, and estates. Toiling away in offices and backrooms—seldom courtrooms—were

The young corporate lawyer in 1924. *(Courtesy of Dr. Kelly Simpson)*

more than a dozen associates and thirty-four staffers, which made Cadwalader one of New York's first big corporate law firms.[22]

Simpson was likely disappointed to be detailed to some of the firm's least notable cases. In his first year he handled some receiverships and represented a building contractor seeking the recovery of costs. Early in 1924, Simpson represented an ice cream machine company in a dispute involving $75. There was work for some larger clients as well, but smoothing out details for corporations, however large or small, never appealed to Simpson. For despite his schoolboy entrepreneurship and the administrative bent shown in the Army, Simpson did not have an instinct for business—he never really considered accumulating capital a concrete accomplishment.[23]

In the early 1920s, for example, one of the former "heelers" for Simpson's *Yale Daily News* came up with an idea for a weekly news magazine with topical stories told in punchy, compelling prose. Henry Luce thought that he would call his magazine *Time.* He also thought that it would be easy to raise the starting capital from among his Yale colleagues, particularly his highly successful fellow Bonesmen. When Luce made his pitch to his former boss, Simpson claimed to have no savings to invest. "I suppose I could raise some money to put into such an idea," Simpson continued, "but even if I had it, *Time* is such a lousy name that I wouldn't risk a penny on it."[24] Luce raised the money elsewhere, and the fortune that would have accrued to Simpson went to men with better business instincts.

Simpson did make it to trial on occasion. He recalled one of his most high-powered appearances to be "representing the Farmers Loan & Trust Company as executors of the estate of Willie Waldorf Astor against Mary Sweeny for five dollars in arrears."[25] It was during one such ignominious visit to the courthouse that Simpson poured out his plight to court official Peter Gaffney. Simpson, it appears, had not entirely forgotten about politics, and Gaffney suggested that he get involved in his local political club.[26]

New York politics in the 1920s was complex to say the least. There was an administration for each borough and another for each county in Greater New York. The city, of course, had its own mayor, a powerful board of estimates, and a toothless board of aldermen. The whole was divided into sixty-two assembly districts—twenty-three of them in Manhattan, which professionals called "New York County." Each assembly district had its political clubs: Democratic, Republican, and an odd Socialist club for good measure.

Reformers painted the clubs as havens for opportunists seeking special favors and influence, and Tammany's unsavory institutions lent some credibility to this claim. But New York's political clubs were critical because they linked the entire Byzantine construction of metropolitan politics to the people and provided a structure within which grassroots activists could work. As Theodore Roosevelt put it, "absolutely no good work can be done in politics without an organization."[27] Democratic or Republican, the business of most of the clubs had long been done in bars. The 19th Amendment did away with that, so the 1920s became the heyday of the clubhouse. Few of these were any better than the brawling bars that they had replaced. Most were "insider" bastions where neither women nor newcomers were welcomed. But not all.

One evening in early 1924, Kenneth Simpson approached, perhaps a bit apprehensively, an unassuming brownstone on Madison Avenue. This was the home of New York's 15th Assembly District (abbreviated "15th A.D.") Republican Club. The 15th A.D., which wrapped around the east side of Central Park from 52nd Street to 104th Street and extended over to Third Avenue, spanned most of Manhattan's wealthy neighborhoods. The star in the 15th A.D. Republican Club's firmament of notable alumni was Theodore Roosevelt, who had lived there when the district had been designated the 29th. Upon crossing the threshold, Simpson encountered not crass politicos shooting dice and uttering monosyllables but a surprisingly genteel crowd. One observer wrote that "the casual visitor of the Fifteenth A.D. Republican club is likely to find the lounge thronged with men in tuxedos and women in evening clothes, engaged in sprightly, animated conversation."[28] The 15th A.D. Republican Club was also different because it took political education seriously—voting one's conscience, after all, was easier for the affluent upper east siders than for most New Yorkers.[29]

The most important people in any assembly district were the president of the club and the district leader—and these were never the same person. The president was an organizer—he kept in touch with the rank and file and kept the clubhouse running. The district leader was the local political boss: he established the positions that the club would take, and he made the deals and decisions that the club members lived by. He also presided over the activities of forty or fifty precinct captains (called "ward heelers" in another day), each of whom was responsible for keeping tabs on the populace and getting out the vote on election day. If one had the right temperament, "ringing doorbells" could be great fun. Every good precinct captain wielded at least a little patronage power, even if it was just a bit of extra pull for aspiring public employees having trouble on civil service exams. These precinct captains were usually elected to the county committee, where they became foot soldiers for county leaders.[30]

The New York County Republican Committee had been led for years by a diminutive, bespectacled, and politically astute Hungarian-born Jew named Sam Koenig. A resident of the immigrant lower east side, Koenig had started out in city politics in 1888 and had backed reformer Seth Low at the turn of the century. Unlike the "silk-stocking" Republicans (so designated after women who wore then-extravagantly expensive hosiery), Koenig was not overly burdened by ideology: for him, politics was about cutting the best deal possible. This made him good at papering over differences and so, not surprisingly, he rose to prominence by keeping the Progressive split from destroying the local Republican Party.[31]

Most Republicans tolerated Koenig's expedient approach when times were good. In 1920 they were. Voters were disillusioned by the Wilson administration and its war, so Republicans outpolled the Democrats in the urban elections. But then the tide turned for reasons far larger than Sam Koenig, as alien immigrants became hyphenated Americans and voted with Tammany. Local Republicans were also saddled with defending prohibition and tarred by supporting a large transit fare increase called the "ten cent fare." Reform-minded Republicans, however, were eager to lay the blame mostly at Koenig's feet. They resented his willingness to cut deals with Tammany. They were convinced, probably correctly, that Koenig had become far too content with second place: they wanted to win elections, or at least lay the groundwork for future victories. Koenig acknowledged that he had one other liability. "Some of the bluebloods," he maintained, "never could reconcile themselves to being led by an East Side Boy."[32]

One such blueblood was William Chadbourne, a former Bull Moose Republican, corporation lawyer, and resident of the 15th A.D. By January 1924, Chadbourne was thoroughly disgusted with "the weakening of our party in New York County."[33] He warned that even the 15th A.D. could be lost to the Democrats if the organization closed itself off to "public spirited men and women." Chadbourne founded the Lenox Hill Republican Club to fight for the soul of the New York Republican Party. He hoped ultimately to unseat Koenig, but he began by assembling a slate to take on the leadership of the 15th A.D. Republican organization.[34]

The Republican head of the 15th A.D. was Frank Coleman, a former assistant district attorney, municipal court justice, and strong leader. Every organization had a female "co-leader." The title was usually honorific, but Coleman's co-leader was anything but passive. Mrs. Ruth Baker Pratt was the smart, energetic wife of a financier and quickly becoming a political power in her own right. The only thing that the Chadbourne faction had against Coleman and Pratt was that as "regular" Republicans they were defenders of Sam Koenig. Chadbourne hoped former state senator Schuyler Meyer could unseat Coleman and begin to challenge Koenig. Assisting him were a few dozen young, affluent Republicans, recent college graduates who agreed that the party would not get anywhere "so long as it stands for the principle of barter and trade."[35] Kenneth Simpson was not one of them. He already knew too much about politics to take such an uncompromising stance.

Instead, on that evening in early 1924, Simpson appeared before Frank Coleman and offered to go to work for him. Coleman had been acquainted with Kelly Simpson and was happy to offer an opportunity to his son. Being a novice, however, Simpson got a thankless, and apparently hopeless, assignment. He and fellow newcomer Frederick Warburg were assigned to work as precinct captains and run as Coleman delegates to the county committee in two election districts that were loaded with Meyer supporters. Warburg, twenty-six, was the eldest grandson of Jacob Schiff and had practically inherited a position in the Kuhn, Loeb investment banking firm. But his heart was no more in investment banking than Simpson's was in corporate law. Together they set out to do the impossible.[36]

They started out by scrutinizing the lists of registered voters in their districts. Sure enough, they found many a foe and more potential friends than certain ones. They began ringing doorbells. In other New York neighborhoods, party workers were usually welcomed visitors. But residents of the Upper East Side hardly needed favors. Simpson and Warburg found themselves obliged to bribe doormen, put their feet in doors to keep butlers from slamming them, and otherwise behave like traveling salesmen. The work was taxing, even to Simpson who had learned to love rough-and-tumble. But the benefits were great. In addition to Coleman and Pratt, Simpson became familiar with other influentials like Keyes Winter, Charles Hilles, and Colonel

William Hayward. Simpson also forged strong ties with young contemporaries like Newbold Morris and Stanley Isaacs.[37]

On April 1, 1924, election day, hardly a silk stocking could be seen in the 15th A.D. Party workers wore galoshes and stood knee-deep in slush, thanks to an unseasonable snowstorm that hit just before the polls opened. Snow and overconfidence kept Meyer supporters in Simpson's 25th election district at home. Simpson left them in peace but kept tabs on his friends. Thirty minutes before the polls closed he noticed that one had not voted. Simpson tracked him down, put him in a taxi, and took him to the polls. Both Warburg and Simpson won their districts—the latter by two votes—and became Republican committeemen. Meyer had never stood a chance, but Simpson's effort was not forgotten. As he came in time to realize, the reputable young corporate lawyer had crossed a Rubicon of sorts: few affluent New Yorkers considered precinct politics to be a respectable pursuit. One businessman active in the 15th A.D. had even been offered a raise if he would give up politics. Not surprisingly, these men stuck together.[38]

A few months after the election, Coleman enquired of Simpson, "How are you getting along?" Simpson forthrightly admitted that he was bored, that he wanted to try cases rather than slog through documents. Coleman suggested that Simpson visit William Hayward, then U.S. Attorney for the Southern District of New York.[39] Hayward had earned some renown as the commander of the Harlem Hellfighters, the all-black 369th infantry regiment that had spent 191 days at the front during the war, and he had political aspirations. Although Hayward had 190 days of battlefield experience over the young lawyer, he was impressed with Simpson's Republican credentials. In January 1925, Simpson left Cadwalader to become an assistant U.S. Attorney for the Southern District of New York. Some of his trials were hardly sensational, but they were trials nonetheless. Simpson prosecuted a clothing manufacturer who hid assets and went bankrupt and tried a doctor and two pharmacists charged with narcotics violations.[40]

Simpson had barely begun before Hayward resigned. His successor, Emory Buckner, was partner in a prestigious law firm and determined to put the office on a more professional, less political footing. Buckner well knew that the paramount issue of his tenure would be prohibition enforcement, and although he was uninterested in prohibition "except as a legal problem," he was determined not to be burdened by conflict of interest: when he heard that his nomination had been forwarded to Washington, Buckner held a party where chagrined guests poured his expensive bootleg liquor collection down the sink. Confirmed, the crusading U.S. Attorney launched his soon legendary "padlock campaign." Before he was through, Buckner had closed down hundreds of New York establishments charged with violating prohibition.[41]

The padlocking campaign made Buckner's office the butt of more than a few jokes, but everyone acknowledged that he ran a tight ship. And although the pay was low, the morale was high. "Buckner's administration has been one of the best in the Federal courts," claimed the *Daily News Record*.[42] Convinced that Hayward had hired too many assistants for political reasons, Buckner began edging the unqualified out. Simpson was not one of them. To the contrary, within just a few months Simpson was happy to note that Buckner was getting "more agreeable and commendatory."[43] This approval was not easy to earn. Buckner gave his assistants a heavy load, and he expected them to stay late and complete it. Buckner imposed one other stricture: he insisted that his subordinates join him in swearing off drink for the duration. This was likely a challenge for Simpson. At some point during the early 1920s, he became a heavy drinker. He knew his way around the city's speakeasies well enough that a colleague suggested that he might be invaluable on padlocking detail. Simpson did not volunteer and Buckner did not draft him, but he did go on the wagon. There was another good reason to give up drinking—Simpson was about to be married.[44]

ALL THE RIGHT PEOPLE

Simpson's leisure time was hardly limited to speakeasies. He was also one of the young socialites frequenting New York's charity and debutante balls during the early 1920s. It is highly likely that it was at one of these events that Simpson met Helen Louise Knickerbacker Porter. Helen's bloodline was impressive. Her grandfather was from an old New England family. Upon coming to New York, he had thrown in with a commission merchant, eventually taken over the business, and made it one of the city's most prosperous. Helen's father, Nathan Todd Porter Jr., had gone to Yale, started out in the family business, and then become president of Montclair Trust Company, in Montclair, New Jersey. It was Helen's second middle name that came in for the most comment. Her mother, Caroline Chester Knickerbacker, was a native of Troy, New York, forty-five miles north of Hudson. She was descended from the first Dutch settler in the Hudson River Valley, Herman Jansen Knickerbacker, whose name, famously corrupted by Washington Irving, became synonymous with New York's oldest European inhabitants.[45]

Helen was born May 24, 1893, and with her older sister Caroline grew up in the family's palatial yet placid home in Montclair. Helen followed the predictable path of privileged young women of the day. She graduated from Bryn Mawr, became involved in the Junior League, and joined New York's exclusive Colony Club. But Helen was more than a complacent society girl. During the World War, she worked as a nurse in an American Red Cross mobile hospital unit that followed the French Army, arriving at the front shortly before the armistice. Helen did not slow down after the war—in 1920 she did canteen work with the French army in the Middle East. Between 1921 and 1924, she traveled widely throughout Europe. Then, in 1925, she was thinking about marriage.[46]

Helen Porter was a contrast to Kenneth Simpson. He was passionate and mercurial; she was subdued and reflective. They shared a caustic wit, although hers was usually kept under wraps. Kenneth's whirlwind of activity stemmed in part from insecurity; Helen's self-confidence and self-control made her somewhat detached. Sister Caroline once accused her of never saying anything to her that she "would not say to a casual acquaintance made on a Pullman car."[47] Finally, although Helen was educated and highly cultivated—she could quote Goethe and mixed easily with writers and artists—she was little interested in politics or history. It is easy to imagine her despair at a love letter that read "tonight at the Republican club Judge Hand gave a splendid talk about the Federal Judiciary which I wished you'd been there to hear."[48] Helen was soon resigned to Simpson's enthusiasms, however, and in April 1925 the two became engaged. For a time they debated whether to marry in the summer or to wait until fall—a more socially advantageous time—but Kenneth pressed for June, refusing to wait "until all the right Vanderbilts and Pratts are here."[49]

Although Helen's family took their social obligations seriously, they were nearly as smitten with the handsome young Assistant U.S. Attorney as Helen was. On the afternoon of June 26th, with Sam Duryee as best man and George Perkins Jr., Henry Isham, and John McCloy serving as ushers, Kenneth Simpson stood before the altar of St. James's Episcopal Church. The superstitious may have been concerned, for just then a terrific lightning storm swept the city, smashing the granite ball on top of the natural history building, shattering the cross on St. Patrick's Cathedral, and dumping torrents of rain on the sidewalks. Undaunted, the "Knickerbocker" girl and the precinct politician exchanged vows between claps of thunder. At 5:30 that evening they stepped arm and arm down the steps of St. James's into a clearing evening. They soon set sail to Paris.[50]

Of the two, Helen was most familiar with France, having spent the better part of six summers there between 1912 and 1921. By 1925, they were both so

Helen Louise Knickerbacker Porter, about the time she met Kenneth Simpson. *(Courtesy of Dr. Kelly Simpson)*

attached to Paris that they took an apartment at 1 Rue Git-Le-Coeur, in the Latin Quarter overlooking the Isle de la Cite. It was the right time and the right place—for Paris in the twenties was at the epicenter of a cultural efflorescence that was even then becoming legendary. Within shouting distance of the Simpsons' apartment, patrons of Latin Quarter cafes were discussing Picasso, Pound, and James Joyce. Americans were particularly numerous, inspired by Hemingway and Gertrude Stein to join the expatriate "lost generation." Few were ever at a loss when it came to criticizing America.[51]

The Progressive fervor had, in the end, been too much to sustain. The notion that unrestrained business was the best basis for society—challenged for a time—returned, its reassuring platitudes welcomed by middle Americans fatigued with crusades, wars, and red scares. Influential intellectuals and cultural mavericks lashed back at anything that smacked of "Puritanism" or that restrained "freedoms" of any kind. Claiming to despair for society, they mostly despaired for themselves alone. George Jean Nathan, with H. L. Mencken, cofounder of *Smart Set* and *The American Mercury*, put it bluntly: "The great problems of the world—social, political, economic and theological—do not concern me in the slightest."[52]

Kenneth Simpson was aware of the shifting cultural currents. He had, for example, read H. G. Wells's *The Undying Fire* in the early 1920s and was generally sympathetic to its debunking of Christianity. He certainly had nothing but disdain for the decade's excess of blind business boosterism and the hypocrisy of prohibition. But for him Paris was hardly a means of escape. It meant involvement with new ideas and new people. Among the good friends that the Simpsons made in Paris in the twenties were Bernard Fay, a newspaperman and historian, Alexander Kerensky, the leader of Russia during the brief days between the overthrow of the Czar and the descent of Communist rule, and Gertrude Stein.[53]

Simpson met Kerensky at a party. They soon discovered that they were both frustrated actors and shared a passion for ballet. Simpson urged Kerensky to visit the United States and in March 1927 he did, ostensibly to study "American principles of liberty." He stayed with the Simpsons. It is not clear which of the Simpsons made the first friendship with Gertrude Stein, then a literary giant and living cultural touchstone. Simpson claimed to have met Stein in the early 1920s and credited her with helping launch him in expatriate society. By the mid-1920s Helen was already very close

Simpson meets Alexander Kerensky (left) as he arrives in New York, March 1927. *(Courtesy of Dr. Kelly Simpson)*

to Stein and her companion, Alice Toklas. She continued to see Stein whenever she visited France, often without Simpson. When the family visited, however, it was the loquacious Kenneth who engaged the domineering writer. "There were almost never pauses in a conversation with Miss Stein," wrote Hemingway, a characterization that equally applied to Simpson.[54] The newlywed Simpsons also visited England and Italy in the summer of 1925. They returned to New York in August to start their life together at Manhattan's newest high-class address.[55]

Not until the 1920s did architects figure out how to insulate structures from the noise and vibration of the New York Central trains running under Park Avenue. When they did, it set off a construction boom that redefined wealthy Manhattan. Park Avenue was soon populated with skyscraper apartments, and the epicenter of the social register shifted from Fifth Avenue to 68th Street and Madison Avenue. North thirteen blocks and over one, the Simpsons rented half of the top two floors of a newly built seventeen-story apartment house at 935 Park Avenue. To keep it all running, they employed a cook and a Japanese butler.[56]

The Simpsons and their many guests soon fell in love with the apartment, particularly the roof garden adjoining the luxurious penthouse. They began collecting art. Over the next few years they accumulated Whistlers, a Modigliani, a Picasso, and a Matisse along with dozens of other pieces. Kenneth Simpson also began to read literature, picking up Dostoevsky and embarking, in mid-1926, on Proust, his mastery of which would became a point of pride. Simpson no doubt loved the sense of history that drenched every page of Proust, but his fascination is somewhat curious given the stark contrast between Proust's seductive, slowly unfolding, and insinuating prose and Simpson's aggressive and blunt-edged speech. But music, far more than art and literature, was Simpson's favorite pastime—the family always maintained a subscription to the Philharmonic. Simpson claimed to be a convert to the moderns, but he was steeped in the classics as a child and did not stray too far, preferring Mussorgsky and Prokofiev to atonalists like Webern.[57]

As befitted New Yorkers of their station, the Simpsons undertook a nearly endless round of social engagements. In 1927, they, along with Kenneth's sister Sally, who had married writer and architectural historian Talbot Hamlin and lived nearby, attended a newsworthy dinner party for publisher Conde Nast. The next year they were among notables at a soiree that included sportswriter Grantland Rice, journalist Claude Bowers, industrialist Walter Teagle, and eminent politician William McAdoo. Simpson, who inevitably measured himself in terms of his relationships with others, delighted in these opportunities for conversation, and he pitted himself against heavyweights. At one affair he talked literature with Vita Sackville-West; at another, art with Cecelia Beaux—in neither case did he claim to be much intimidated by his accomplished conversant. Simpson maintained poise and equanimity when discussing art, music, and literature, and the slight, broad "A" Harvard accent that he had picked up along the way added just the right luster to such elevated discourse. But when politics came up, Simpson's composure slipped and he punctuated his conversation with questions like "Do you follow me?" or "Do you see what I mean?"[58]

Social engagements, regular trips to Europe, and an occasional vacation—sometimes in the Adirondacks, sometimes sailing a borrowed yacht on Long Island Sound—formed family life for the couple during the mid-1920s.

A transatlantic couple on shipboard with their young family: Kelly is at left, baby Helen-Louise at right. *(Courtesy of Dr. Kelly Simpson)*

A few landmarks intervened. Anna Farrand Simpson, who had been completely invalid since the early 1920s, died in 1926 while Kenneth and Helen were overseas. She was buried in Hudson alongside her husband. On a much happier note, son Kelly, named after Kenneth's father, was born in January 1928. Soon the precocious toddler and his Irish nanny enlivened the Park Avenue household. Although hardly doting by today's standards, Simpson delighted in playing hide and seek, and he marveled at the way the world looked to the wide-eyed Kelly Simpson.[59]

THE GOVERNMENT'S REPRESENTATIVE

On February 27, 1926, among the papers neatly arrayed in the lobby of the Hotel Crillon and scattered in Left Bank cafés, was the Paris edition of the *New York Herald* announcing the arrival, on the liner *Aquitania*, of an Assistant U.S. Attorney. His mission: to persuade German industrialist Richard W. Merton, the "copper King of middle Europe," to testify in a sensational federal corruption case. By that time Kenneth and Helen Simpson, along with lawyer Martin Littleton and his family, were rattling across the continent on a train bound for Basle. It was a long way to go in order to clean up the mess left by the Harding administration.[60]

The retreat from reform had been a boon to old-line Republicans. The presidential candidate of 1920 did not need Progressive credentials—he needed few credentials at all, for that matter. Warren Harding did meet two qualifications: he looked like a President and he was someone that business leaders could control. The problem was that Harding could not control his friends. Harding made a few stellar appointments to his cabinet, including Charles Evans Hughes and Herbert Hoover. But he also appointed friends—and, as it turned out, scoundrels—like Albert Fall and Harry Daugherty. To the Veterans Bureau he even appointed Charles Forbes, a casual acquaintance made on vacation.

The scent of corruption soon wafted about the White House. Forbes resigned in early 1923, caught reselling Veterans Bureau supplies for kickbacks. Then Harding began to suspect that attorney general Daugherty was selling favors and confronted Jess Smith, Daugherty's personal fixer. Smith committed suicide. Before leaving for an Alaska trip, Harding lamented that "I can take care of my enemies all right. But my damn friends . . . they're the ones that keep me walking the floor nights." Harding died on the way back from Alaska, and no one minded having "Silent Cal" Coolidge in office: Harding's cronies were doing enough talking for everyone—in congressional hearings and courtrooms. "Teapot Dome" emerged in 1924, a scheme in which Secretary of the Interior Fall had leased Naval Oil Reserves to western oil men in return for substantial "loans." Then another story seemed to lead to the attorney general himself.

During the war, the government had seized German-owned assets in the United States, including half the shares in the American Metal Company of New York. The shares were later sold for $7 million. In 1921, Richard Merton decided to get the $7 million back—never mind that he had acquired these "assets" from their former German owners in 1919, well after they had been seized and disposed of. Merton first consulted a young corporate lawyer named John Foster Dulles, who told him the thing could not be done. Then Merton "freshened up" his documents and tried again. Republican National Committee chairman John T. King introduced him to Jess Smith, and with surprising speed, Daugherty's Justice Department instructed Alien Property Custodian Thomas W. Miller to allow the claim. When word got out, the Justice Department had little choice but to investigate. In October 1925, a special assistant attorney general dutifully gained an indictment against Miller, Merton, and some other foreign businessmen. He did not inconvenience his boss by looking much deeper.[61]

In late 1925, the special assistant resigned and U.S. Attorney Buckner inherited the case, and he asked Simpson to look into the matter. Simpson found what the special assistant had hoped not to. It appeared that Merton had reciprocated the favor, providing King, Miller, and Daugherty with nearly $500,000 in cash and Liberty Bonds. Simpson brought the evidence to his astonished superior. On January 22, 1926, Daugherty appeared before a grand jury, the first sitting attorney general threatened with corruption charges. Simpson asked whether "in obedience to the subpoena" he had brought with him ledger accounts from the institution where, it was suspected, Daugherty's share had ended up—brother Mal Daugherty's bank in Washington Courthouse, Ohio. Daugherty read a remarkable statement suggesting that his testimony would either impugn or implicate the late President. He then took the Fifth Amendment. It was one of those moments when spectators gasped and reporters rushed for the pay phones. A few days later Simpson left for Europe.[62]

The earlier indictment of the foreign nationals had been an empty gesture—they could never be compelled to return to the United States. Nor, Buckner realized, did Merton have any good reason to come to the United States now to testify. Nevertheless, he confided to Felix Frankfurter, "I have hopes of getting something."[63] Those hopes were pinned on Simpson even though he could employ little more than diplomacy and friendly persuasion to gain Merton's cooperation. The trip was a two-fold success. First, Simpson worked closely with Merton's counsel, distinguished Long Island attorney and former U.S. Congressman Martin W. Littleton. Simpson soon acquired what he called a "deep affection" and unabashed admiration for Littleton, calling him an "eastern counterpart of Clarence Darrow."[64] Second, Simpson found Merton completely cooperative, providing access to all of his firm's books and papers and agreeing to testify in court. Upon arriving back in the United States, Simpson reported that "all concerned showed me every courtesy abroad as the government's representative in quest of the facts."[65]

That spring, other Buckner assistants were looking for evidence in the United States, reviewing records from the Ritz Hotel, where the conspirators stayed, and combing the accounts in Mal Daugherty's Midland National Bank in Ohio. Simpson himself took a government accountant to Columbus, Ohio, during April. On May 7, Daugherty, Miller, and King were indicted on the strength of the information that Simpson had turned up in Europe. Like so many of the Harding-era conspirators, King promptly died, succumbing to pneumonia. Miller went to dinner.[66]

Simpson and the former Alien Property custodian, it turned out, shared an alma mater, and on September 7, 1926, the first night of the trial, both men were dining at New York's Yale Club. A telephone call came in for Miller, who failed to respond to the page. Simpson, unable to resist, left his own table and answered the call. What Simpson learned is not known, but Miller reported him and the Yale Club threatened expulsion. Simpson brushed it off. "Getting expelled from the Yale Club," he joked, "is like getting expelled from Grand Central Station."[67] But this was a serious lapse in judgment, and the bad blood spilled over into the courtroom: throughout the trial, observers wondered about the source of the animosity between Miller and Simpson.[68]

This was just one of the elements that made for fine theater and big headlines. Another was constant speculation as to what the U.S. Attorney and his six assistants, soon dubbed "Buckner's Six Young Men" or "Buckner's Boy Scouts,"

Characterized by a cartoonist for the *New York Evening Post* as one of "Buckner's Young Men,"
Simpson is at right.

might do next. They were hard to miss, sitting at a long table below the judge's
bench, "almost buried," an *Evening Post* reporter wrote, "under piles and piles of
documents, mountains of exhibits, and prodigious stacks of ledgers." Simpson,
sitting at Buckner's side, quickly emerged as first among equals. "Constantly
during the trial," the *Evening Post* reported, "Mr. Buckner halts his cross exami-
nation of an important witness to whisper in his assistant's ear."[69] The young
assistant did a good bit of questioning early on, until he brought out information that had been forbidden by a judge's ruling. For a time it looked as if this
mistake might cause a mistrial and put an end to Simpson's budding prosecutorial career, but in the end it did not matter. Because Daugherty had burned
his own bank records, there was no way to connect him with the cash. After
three days of deliberation, the jury deadlocked and an ebullient Mal Daugherty
invited Simpson to visit him in Ohio. "I would like to have you out there in time
to go fishing, or give you a little spring water," he said.[70]

Instead of going to Ohio, Simpson returned to Europe to obtain affidavits
that would strengthen the government's case. Both defendants got new counsel,
and a new trial began in February 1927. The old trouble between Simpson
and Miller soon reappeared when Miller's counsel accused Simpson of guiding
Merton in his testimony. The charge was likely leveled out of desperation: in
the end Miller was easily convicted. Although the case against Daugherty was
strong, a lone juror kept him from being the first cabinet member imprisoned
for maladministration.[71]

At the conclusion of the trial Buckner resigned as U.S. Attorney. He had run an exemplary office, taken on a tough case, and kept Simpson at his side the whole time. Still, the two never became close. It had been mostly chance that made Simpson something of a star in the U.S. Attorney's office. Other Buckner lieutenants, after all, had spent tedious months slogging through bank records, but international intrigue sold far more papers than financial revelations from corn-belt banks. This was especially true in the twenties, the age of "ballyhoo," when newspapers, magazines, and those things in between recently dubbed "tabloids" discovered that good stories were not so much reported as manufactured. At mid-decade came a host of sensations, including the Floyd Collins tragedy, the Hall-Mills murder case, and the trial of Leopold and Loeb. In the summer of 1927, Simpson drew an assignment that gave him a part in a similarly sensational story.

"From the first the voyage was going wrong," wrote Jack London in his 1914 tale, *The Mutiny of the Elsinore*. Thirteen years later the book may have enjoyed a spike in sales when newspaper headlines blurred the lines between fact and fiction. In the autumn of 1926, the schooner *Kingsway* left New York for Africa, seeking lumber and cocoa beans for the African and Eastern Trading Company. It was a ship out of another time, a four-masted sailing vessel without even a radio. Sometime during mid-July, the *Kingsway* signaled a dire message to a passing ship that reached federal authorities in New York: "Prisoner has broken out. Have no irons to hold him. This is a desperate man." As the *Kingsway* approached coastal waters in a heavy fog, Assistant U.S. Attorneys Kenneth Simpson and George Mintzer prepared to meet it. On the dock at Staten Island late on the afternoon of July 20, Simpson, who by now knew what reporters liked to hear, vowed to intercept the schooner "if we have to chase her all the way to England."[72] They did locate the *Kingsway*, and that night, as the old ship creaked at anchor off Barnegat Light, learned a remarkable story that all of New York would soon be reading.[73]

As the *Kingsway* prepared to leave New York, it turned out, the ship's captain had become ill. Veteran first mate Fred Mortimer was eager to take on the assignment. But Mortimer, who had been the inspiration for the angry, deteriorating alcoholic "Mr. Pike" in Jack London's story, was passed over for retired Captain F. E. Lawry, pulled from a Norfolk rooming house for one last voyage. That was where the trouble started. It got worse when the outbound ship reached San Juan and the cook resigned. His replacement, Earl Battice, insisted on bringing his wife along. As the vessel left San Juan, however, a desperate woman pulled up to its side in a launch, pleading to come aboard. That was the "wife" that Battice had hoped to bring along—until his real wife caught wind of the trick and had come along herself. The angry wife and suspicious crew made the trip across the Atlantic a rough one, and as the ship approached Africa, Battice slit his wife's throat. The unfortunate woman lingered for seven days, Mortimer curled up in his bunk and died, and the crew grew hungry—Battice was in chains, but he was the only man aboard who could cook. The ship picked up a replacement in Africa, but he made the sailors sick, so for the rest of the voyage Captain Lawry equivocated between keeping the cook in irons and sending him back to the galley.[74]

With or without new information, reporters penned ever more stories about the "murder ship." One of them featured a photograph of Simpson and Mintzer examining the irons that "could not hold" Battice. A new thrill arose when it was discovered that "murder on the high seas" still carried the penalty of death by hanging and that New Yorkers might enjoy the spectacle of a gallows in the old post office. Although the details were delightful, the trial was less than New York had hoped for. U.S. Attorney Charles Tuttle, assisted by Simpson and Mintzer, sent Battice to prison for ten years.[75]

By then Simpson was eager to move on. Assistant U.S. Attorney was understood to be a stepping-stone—Simpson had always been advised not to stay long. The pay made that unlikely in any case; Simpson never adjusted to a government salary of $250 per month and looked forward to making a better living in private practice. On September 12, 1927, confiding to Tuttle that he had a "great opportunity" elsewhere, Simpson tendered his resignation. The New York Times announced the departure of "one of the best known assistants on the staffs of each of the three United States Attorneys under which he served."[76]

LAWYER IN SEARCH OF A TRIAL

With high hopes, Simpson set up practice at 67 Wall Street, in the heart of the nation's financial capital. He did some work in the securities area, representing an odd-lot cotton dealer charged with defrauding customers and attempting to drum up business from victims of another investment scheme. He also conducted legal research for the eminent counsel of one of the Teapot Dome conspirators. In between, Simpson did run-of-the-mill criminal defense work. Referring to the defendant in a narcotics case, Simpson confided to a friend that "getting a poor devil out of a jam like this gives me as much satisfaction as saving some wealthy corporation a few dollars."[77]

Unfortunately, the monetary rewards of Simpson's solo practice did not equal the psychological ones. In January 1928, Simpson became a junior partner in Barnes, McKenna & Halstead, a firm most notable for employing former silent film star turned lawyer Mary Rehan. Directed with a firm hand by Albert Mac C. Barnes Jr., its practice was modest—mostly representing smaller businesses and assisting larger firms in corporate cases. Barnes clearly led Simpson to believe that his outlook was bright: "I expect to specialize in trial work and litigation," he confided to former Yale classmates.[78] What materialized, however, was mostly the inevitable corporate work, although Simpson did soon appear in court defending the colorful granddaughter of Mexican dictator Porfirio Diaz on prohibition-related charges.[79]

Then Simpson met an even more remarkable woman. It began in January 1928, when police charged a twenty-year-old art student named Carol Bodmer with living with a married man. By the late 1920s, morals cases such as this were rare. Most judges would not consider such a case, but Magistrate Jean Norris was not most judges. She was politically well connected, highly pretentious, and the hanging judge of the New York County women's court. The hapless Bodmer worked at an 11th Street studio frequented by New York's artistic crowd, and for help she turned to an influential friend—Mrs. Dorothy Harvey. Bodmer confessed to the "crime," Dorothy Harvey vouched for her character, and Judge Norris sent her to live with Mrs. Harvey in her spacious apartment on 12th Street, to be "guided by her" until sentencing.[80] The puritanical judge may have reconsidered had she known Dorothy Harvey well.

Born in 1884, Dorothy was one of the four extraordinary daughters of affluent Chicago physician E. C. Dudley. Their unorthodox upbringing made them politically progressive and culturally adventurous. By young adulthood, each Dudley sister was armed with a trust fund and going her own unconventional way. In 1919, sister Katherine smuggled documents out of the Paris Peace Conference. She had obtained them from sister Helen's lover, Bertrand Russell. Sister Caroline outdid them by creating, in 1925, "Le Revue Negre," the daring and legendary all-black show that introduced Josephine Baker to Paris and the world.

Dorothy Dudley's niche was in literature. She was part of a group associated with the influential publication *Poetry: a Magazine of Verse*. In 1915,
she married Henry Blodgett Harvey, an advertising man, and although the
two experimented with the expatriate life, Dorothy remained fascinated by
American literature. She stayed in touch with Carl Sandburg, Edgar Lee
Masters, and Theodore Dreiser, whose biography she was writing. Dorothy
Dudley (she used her maiden name professionally) hardly outshone such
luminous correspondents. Her writings reflected the conventional uncon-
ventionality—especially about sex and other "freedoms"—common among
expatriate Americans of the time. Poet Louise Bogan once described her as
a "spoiled Chicago girl who thinks herself a profound thinker and feeler," but
she could not help liking her any less.[81] Dorothy Dudley was eleven years his
senior (eight Simpson thought), but the young lawyer was instantly attracted
to the artistic authoress. The two began a long romantic involvement.[82]

The affair was perhaps unremarkable for one of Dorothy's bohemian
background, but Henry Harvey did not approve. Falsely assured, at some
point, that the affair was over, Henry Harvey forgave and forgot: Simpson
remained his friend and sometime legal counsel. Helen accepted this devel-
opment with surprising equanimity. She appears to have had some prior
acquaintance with Dorothy Harvey and knew and liked her. Although she
could hardly have welcomed it, Helen tolerated and even, in some instances,
facilitated the relationship.[83]

This "understanding" among the Simpsons is probably best understood
in light of similar arrangements among wealthy Americans—and even more
so the Europeans they emulated—at the time. Some would always assume
that Simpson had married for money, but his letters to Helen—and Helen
kept them all—demonstrate that this is not the case. As their married life
matured and the inevitable difficulties arose, there was no sign that Kenneth
ever loved Helen any less than on the day they were married. And Helen knew,
perhaps even better than did Kenneth himself, that if her husband delighted
in Dorothy's intellectual adventure, he needed her patience, empathy, and
wisdom more. Simpson and Dorothy Harvey trysted from time to time, but
their relationship was mostly one of letters: his, pencilled on yellow legal
pads, and hers, on typed or handwritten cards and letters simply signed "D."

Among the subjects that Simpson shared were his triumphs and disappointments as a lawyer. Many of these had some political aspect, for lawyers

were the lieutenants of New York politics, bidden to find footholds in publicity and levers in the law. Reform politics had always remained close to Simpson's heart. The same instincts that had made him an enthusiastic champion of Theodore Roosevelt and an eager advocate for the "poor devil" in a jam led him to champion diverse causes in the 1920s. In 1928, he joined a board of former U.S. Attorneys who came to the assistance of New York cab drivers being preyed upon by unscrupulous finance companies. In 1929, Simpson made headlines as an opponent of the draconian Jones Law, which made sale of a glass of beer a felony in New York State. When corporate lawyer and former Assistant U.S. Attorney Frederic Coudert Jr. organized a lawyers group against the law, Simpson made a statement that was reprinted in the *New York Times*. "I feel it is high time for all lawyers and other citizens who still cherish the preservation of our civil liberties to take as drastic action as they can without inciting rebellion," Simpson wrote.[84] Coudert may have considered his initiative a stepping-stone to office. That fall he ran, unsuccessfully, for district attorney for New York County. Others in the anti-Jones Law crusade may have harbored political aspirations as well, including a young lawyer named Thomas E. Dewey.[85]

Although Simpson harbored his own political inclinations, his avowed objective through the late 1920s was to triumph in trial work. His best chance came in a prohibition case. On the night of April 14, 1927, Albert Johnson was working as a government custodian at a Staten Island Brewery. When two employees were caught on a nearby highway with beer that they had stolen from the brewery, federal marshals arrested Johnson for good measure, even though he was not implicated by the employees. Johnson was jailed for a week before the charges were dismissed. He hired Simpson as counsel and sued for damages.[86]

The first trial was lackluster and the jury could not reach a verdict. The second Johnson trial, which began in May 1930, was far more dramatic. There was, for example, the day that prosecuting Assistant U.S. Attorney James Wilkinson approached Simpson swinging two beer bungs. There was bad blood between the two—Simpson thought he had cut a deal for a client in an earlier case, only to have Wilkinson renege. "What are you going to do, Mr. Wilkinson," Simpson asked, "hit me with those?" Wilkinson brandished fists, "No, I'm going to hit you with these."[87] In the middle of the trial, the Assistant U.S. Attorney challenged the defending attorney to meet him at the Elks Gymnasium. Simpson accepted, although both men apparently thought better of it later. Simpson expected a similar emotional outburst from Wilkinson during closing arguments and prepared accordingly. When Wilkinson delivered a calm, methodical statement, Simpson was flummoxed until he fell back on his prep school debating skills, delivered a brilliant statement, and won the case.[88]

Offering fewer rewards but more notoriety was the role Simpson played in the investigation—with the possibility of impeachment—into the conduct of federal judge Grover Moscowitz. Moscowitz was a Brooklyn federal judge who, among other things, seemed to be favoring former law partners with receiverships. In early 1929, a United States congressman called for an investigation before the House Subcommittee of the Judiciary. Representing Moscowitz was former presidential candidate John W. Davis. Representing Congress was Howard Carter Dickinson, nephew of Charles Evan Hughes. Investigations like these were a good way for lawyers to win their spurs. John W. Davis had done just that in 1913, and now it was Dickinson's turn. He tapped Simpson as his assistant. Simpson proved to be invaluable to Dickinson, although the luster of the case faded fast after Congress refused to do more than censure Moscowitz.[89]

A better outcome occurred after Simpson's small part in the famous Seabury Investigation. In 1930, eager to uncover Democratic malfeasance and perhaps tarnish then-governor Franklin Roosevelt, the Republican legislature charged a commission led by Judge Samuel Seabury with scrutinizing the systematic corruption in the municipal courts and police department that helped keep Tammany in power. One of the first judges caught in the net was Magistrate Jean Norris. Shortly after Simpson testified in February 1931, she was expelled for falsifying records. This gave the investigation a badly needed boost, and in April the legislature widened it to include the district attorney's office. It ultimately unseated happy-go-lucky mayor Jimmy Walker.[90]

AN AVOCATION

These highly public activities all raised Simpson's profile in city, state, and national politics. They did not shake Simpson's own desire to succeed as a trial lawyer, however, and he still considered politics "more of a hobby or avocation than a business."[91] It was an all-consuming avocation, though. Simpson worked hard for the 15th A.D. Republicans, both in municipal elections and as a delegate to Republican conventions, and although it remained the only district able to regularly elect Republican officeholders, the 15th A.D. could not reverse the decline of the party's fortunes. In that respect, Sam Koenig was right when he complained that the "silk stockings" did more for the party nationally than locally.[92]

That was hard to avoid, of course, with so many Republican grandees living on the Upper East Side. One of the biggest was Charles Hilles, a man that Simpson may have met at the Blackstone Hotel in 1916 who was now a neighbor on Park Avenue. Hilles had started out as a reform school superintendent in Ohio. After moving to Westchester County he met William Howard Taft, who asked him to survey voter sentiment in New York and New England. Hilles did so well that he rose to become Taft's personal secretary and eventually Republican National Committee chairman. When Taft's political career ended, Hilles went into business, but he remained a force in the party under Coolidge. Hilles was at home with the leaders of American business but also pleasantly unassuming. He once showed up at the polls in a dinner jacket and, finding the party workers overwhelmed, put off his dinner plans to round up voters himself. Party loyalty and political acumen transcended the ideological disagreements inevitable between a Roosevelt progressive like Simpson and a Taft conservative like Hilles. By the 1930s, Simpson considered Hilles to be his "political mentor and closest advisor."[93]

Also emerging as a mentor during these years was Keyes Winter, who became Republican leader of the 15th A.D. in 1927. Winter grew up in Indiana, where he was an inspiration to friend and author Booth Tarkington. After graduating from Yale, he went to law school in New York City and stayed. In the 1920s, as deputy state attorney general, he waged a campaign against unscrupulous securities dealers. As leader of the 15th A.D., Winter fought so hard against Tammany that a still-obscure Fiorello La Guardia convinced him to manage his first—losing—campaign for mayor. From these more experienced politicians, Simpson learned much, less by sitting at their feet than by working together with them as the Republican Party weathered some turbulent times.

Republicanism in the 1920s rested upon three interlocking ideas: that government should be strictly limited, that foreign involvements should be few, and that individual businessmen could best ensure prosperity. A nation disillusioned by the high ideals and experimentation that had led to war closed its eyes and embraced these pillars. The 1920 New York Republican platform pronounced it a time "not for timidity, but for caution" and "a time when if ever in our history we should discard theory and stick to fact."[94]

Calvin Coolidge found firm footing on this platform. He understood the value of public relations and he worked well with party stalwarts, few of whom were as humble as Hilles. Coolidge was also smart enough to leave the presidency after only one full term and while times were good. Rushing to fill the void, however, was a man who worked best on his own. Trained as a mining engineer, Herbert Hoover had traveled the world and earned a fortune before coordinating food assistance to Belgium at the outbreak of World War I. He replicated the feat in Russia after the war, and then as Secretary of Commerce was the most enterprising man in Harding's cabinet. Harding marveled that Hoover was "the smartest gink I know." Although Hoover toed the party line, unfortunately promising that under the Republicans "poverty will be banished from this nation," most old-line leaders suspected Hoover of being too activist and too technocratic. His cold exterior and tendency to view people as pieces of a puzzle worried them.[95]

Hoover did have his partisans, of course, among them 15th A.D. Republican co-leader Ruth Baker Pratt and the arrogant Ogden Mills, a former congressman and undersecretary of the treasury under Coolidge. Sarcastic and sartorially impeccable, Mills was also a member of the 15th A.D. Republican Club. Simpson was in the middle of the Carol Bodmer case when he traveled to Kansas City as an alternate in the New York delegation to the 1928 Republican National Convention. He was disappointed to find that the convention was "a foregone conclusion for Hoover." "It means a hard fight instead of a cinch as it would have been with Coolidge," he wrote Helen.[96] Simpson may have been thinking beyond the national election, for he had personal aspirations that Hoover had interfered with.

The rise of Herbert Hoover had a curious effect on the Republican Party: it led the party's reform and conservative wings to make common cause. Having built bridges to both, Simpson had some justification for high hopes in 1928. Keyes Winter had planned to put up his protégée for a New York congressional seat, but he had worried too loudly that "Hoover did not understand the people."[97] Charles Hilles had been counting on a Coolidge second term and so lost influence to Ogden Mills. After the Hoover forces swept the table, Ruth Pratt got the spot Simpson had been hoping for.[98]

There was always state office. Public relations man Snell Smith, whom Simpson had helped out in a legal case, advised him to run for the state assembly. Torn, Simpson sought counsel. Father-in-law Nathan Porter and senior partner Albert Barnes advised Simpson to build up his legal practice first. Both men acted out of self-interest but also voiced the prevailing assumption that deprived the Republican Party of many potential leaders: "gentlemen" did not enter the fray until they had made their first million—at which time they could be statesmen rather than politicians.[99]

Simpson had already found one outlet for his political aspirations more in line with these expectations, presidency of the 15th Assembly District Republican Club. It is likely that Simpson had been encouraged to take the position by Keyes Winter, who was club president under Frank Coleman. As Republican Leader of the 15th A.D., Winter needed a good staff man, an adjutant. That was something that Simpson could do well. For the next two years, Simpson wielded the gavel at club meetings and organized events of all types, from posh dinners at New York's best hotels to summer festivals in Central Park where good "Republican" children were expected to listen to speeches in between cups of ice cream.[100]

The club grew and prospered under Simpson's leadership. By late 1929, membership exceeded 3,000 and the club could afford to begin building a new home, a three-story $125,000 brick building on East 83rd Street near Lexington Avenue. Meanwhile, Simpson's friendships, instincts, and aspirations had led him to take on many new responsibilities. He also took a growing role in party matters. In 1930, he pushed for the designation of Keyes Winter as U.S. Attorney, arguing that "party loyalty and party service should be rewarded by recognition."[101] Ruth Pratt made sure the job went to a Hoover supporter. It was a familiar problem. Since Theodore Roosevelt's day, most activists in the 15th A.D. had been patrician reformers. Hoover had no use for them. Therefore, as one club member noted, Hoover's election put the 15th A.D. "in constant turmoil for quite a number of years."[102]

THE GREAT DEPRESSION

Turmoil, of course, is a relative term. The troubles in the 15th A.D. were small compared to those faced by a growing number of Americans as the Great Depression took hold in the early 1930s. The economy had been in trouble for years. America's wealthy and still small middle class enjoyed a rising standard of living, but agriculture lagged far behind. The international economy was in chaos, having never fully recovered from the world war. In the United States, the cutting-edge automobile and electronics industries propelled the economy ever higher, but there was trouble ahead. By the late 1920s, everyone who could afford a car had one; everyone who could afford a radio had one. In a still small consumer economy, the manufacturing miracle could not continue forever. This was an insight lost on investors, particularly the millions of new ones who entered the booming market in 1928. They bought stocks on credit so that in a rising market they would get returns far in excess of what they had invested. Should the market fall, they would be obligated to meet their "margin call" to make up the difference, which would also far exceed an initial investment. But everyone knew that the market never went down. Not, that is, until October 1929.[103]

The national economic crisis coincided with a profound personal crisis for Kenneth Simpson. They hardly faced homelessness, but the Great Depression did knock away the underpinnings of the Simpson's comfortable Park Avenue existence. Helen's income, earned from family investments, was particularly hard hit. Money never meant much to Simpson. It was a means to an end, and Simpson was nearly always focused on ends—he once admitted that he found collecting "the most unpleasant and embarrassing part of a lawyer's business."[104] When it came to cases, he could grapple with, if not master, the ins and outs of corporate finance. But when it came to personal finance, he usually let Helen take care of the details. Those details were soon overwhelming. The Simpsons were hardly novices to the stock market, but the crash wiped out experts and novices alike. By the spring of 1930, registered letters were arriving nearly every day, demanding that they meet a margin call on one investment or another. "I've been practically wiped out," he wrote to Helen, then in France.[105]

Then, in early May, sister "Sallie" died suddenly at age forty-four. Sarah Hamlin and her husband had settled comfortably into the life of New York intellectuals. But the Depression had hit them very hard; Simpson had even arranged for them to reorganize their finances. Her untimely death could not help but add to Simpson's growing despair about things undone in his own life. Shortly after Sallie died, a good friend of hers confided to Simpson that "she expected great things of you."[106] It was a lot to handle, and Simpson was not handling it well.

Simpson had spent a few years already as a heavy drinker. He knew that he could not master alcohol, only stay away from it. He stopped drinking at mid-decade but started again in 1927 or 1928. Word got around, and although he quit again in 1929, he had by then developed a reputation. After Sallie died, and while Helen was in Paris, Simpson began drinking again and ended up in what one physician called "a very mild nervous breakdown." Then there was another. Simpson dropped out of sight for a few weeks—"ill" to his friends and colleagues. Two-year-old Kelly went to stay with family friends and aunt Ada Saxton came to visit. The two talked over old times, he confided to Helen, and he reconnected with "Mother and Father and Sallie and the family."[107]

Simpson pulled out of that slump, but the financial problems continued. By early 1932 the family could not longer make the rent on the Park Avenue apartment. The landlord offered them a smaller apartment, but Simpson held him off through legal action. In late 1932 he began resigning club memberships, explaining to a friend that "I am going through a difficult period, financially."[108] It was particularly disappointing that Simpson had finally gained acceptance to the ultra prestigious Union League Club just as he became unable to afford it. By early 1933, Simpson had "found it necessary to retrench in every possible direction."[109]

Simpson needed to guard his health as diligently as his finances. Since youth he had driven himself relentlessly with no consideration for the consequences, and regular exercise ended with his Army days. In early 1925, the Porters undertook what Simpson called a "family conspiracy to improve my health."[110] A physician told him that he smoked too many cigars, drank too much coffee, and stayed up far too late. By the summer of 1929, when he was hospitalized with an acute kidney infection, all that had changed was that Simpson had traded cigars for the pipe that would become a trademark. Simpson favored briars and "Lord Bromley" tobacco mixture, and biting the stem and lighting and relighting the bowl of his pipe provided an outlet for copious nervous energy. Simpson adopted his other trademark at about this time as well. He had grown a short, clipped moustache briefly in the early 1920s. Hoping to look older, he grew another one in 1929 and kept it. By the early 1930s, Simpson did indeed look older. With growing frequency, illness—perhaps a cold or flu, perhaps alcohol—put him out of commission for up to a week at a time. Lack of exercise, depression, and chronic insomnia, made worse by overuse of sleeping pills, had also taken a heavy toll. In the summer of 1930, Simpson sent a photograph to Dorothy Harvey, then living in France. Distressed, she wrote back, "Don't you think it must be very bad for the looks to go into politics?"[111]

In January 1931, the Simpson's second child, a daughter named Helen Louise, was born. At about the same time, a physician told Simpson that he would have to take time off to rest. Helen rented a house in Eze, France. With a spectacular view of the Mediterranean, it was only a few kilometers from Villefranche, where the Harveys lived in a house that Helen had found for them. She began planning an extended trip. Simpson, characteristically, decided to tackle his problems—both mental and physical—head on, and he began a journal in which he intended to document what he called the "reorganization" of his life.[112]

The trip that spring began badly. The Porters paid for the trip and accompanied the Simpsons on the voyage over. This only underscored Simpson's growing sense that he was not in control of his own destiny—he felt that he was being "kept." Simpson was taking far too many sleeping pills, but his insomnia only got worse: Helen sat up with him nights reading French history. Things got better at Eze—Simpson finally began to sleep. The family also visited the Harveys, who had experienced their own financial reverses. Dorothy was still at work on her biography of Theodore Dreiser, but Henry Harvey had begun writing potboilers, which did not sell.[113]

Simpson was hopeful upon his return to New York. He disliked working for Albert Barnes—he felt as if he were being "kept" by Barnes also—and began actively looking for a new position. At the same time, he reviewed the proofs of Dorothy's book and helped her negotiate a publication deal. Both were soon disappointed. No new legal prospects appeared, and the reviews of Dorothy Dudley's *Forgotten Frontiers* were mostly merciless. One reviewer accused her of purveying "the half-baked notions that passed as the new gospel of freedom in the early 1920s."[114]

Simpson's work on an important case only left him farther from the courtroom than ever and made him further determined to leave the firm, since renamed Barnes, Richardson & Halstead. In theory, it was a fascinating case. In 1929, hoping to save his failing institution, a Denver banker persuaded the Chase Bank—which enrolled a group of six Manhattan banks as contributors—to issue his bank $495,000 in certified checks. It was soon clear that the Denver banker had used deception, and the tricky legal question of whether a certified check was a promise or a payment went all the way to the Supreme Court. Working with lawyers from Shearman & Sterling, Simpson logged in excess of 120 hours per month on that case alone during June and October 1932.[115]

Friends urged Simpson to leave the firm, but with no other prospects he felt trapped, secure as third partner in a firm that had grown to include four junior partners as well. One colleague urged him to go on his own, but Simpson had tried that before and was not eager to do so again. By the late winter of 1933, Simpson had sounded out nearly every law firm in New York, only to be told vaguely by some that they were "retrenching" due to the Depression and forthrightly by others that he was considered "irresponsible on account of the alcohol of the past."[116] Lacking what he called "exciting or useful work" and wanting desperately "only the opportunity to try cases in court," Simpson again slipped into depression. For the second or third time since giving up alcohol, he took an overdose of sleeping medication.[117]

Simpson had reached an impasse. He had early given up corporate law at a prestigious firm. His career as Assistant U.S. Attorney, despite its sensations, had not opened up the opportunities for trial work that he expected. Perhaps Simpson had begun to realize that he might never achieve his dream of being a great trial lawyer. Years ago he had readily jettisoned his acting aspirations, but he had invested too much to do that again. What was the alternative? Simpson still rejected the idea of pursuing his love for politics: instead, he considered it a "serious personal weakness" that had undermined his legal career.[118]

During the 1920s, Simpson had sought guidance and psychic sustenance from father figures such as Martin Littleton, Charles Hilles, and Keyes Winter. The relationship with Dorothy Harvey, many years his senior, also attests to a yearning for emotional guidance. But by the early 1930s, Simpson began to realize that no one could lead him where he needed to go. "Be KFS not MW Littleton," he wrote in his reorganization journal.[119] Parties, popping off to Paris, and dabbling in politics might have been attractive to a few New York dilettantes, but Simpson realized that this was a betrayal of the promise that he had shown in his youth.[120] In the early fall of 1932, Simpson went to the Adirondacks alone, where he hoped to complete the reorganization program. What he wanted most, he wrote Helen, "is the feeling that I'm living my life, not scratching around trying this and trying that to kill time." "Just to wait for breaks won't do," he wrote, "we've got to go out after them."[121] Dorothy Harvey offered a simple observation. "It appears," she wrote, "that you will never be quite happy until you are launched on that political career."[122]

CALLING FOR CHANGE

In the fall of 1932, more Republicans were thinking about ending a political career than beginning one. It seemed as if the political landscape that they had so confidently controlled became barren and hostile overnight. "Party plans," wrote Hilles in early 1932, "have been shattered, and men whom we had reason to count upon are no longer potential supporters."[123] It was a catastrophe of the party's own making: the Republicans had taken full credit for the prosperity and so received full blame for the crash. Although Hoover did more than any previous President to counter economic crisis, it was not enough, and his cold, undiplomatic approach only made things worse. "He met every situation with the directness of a rhinoceros," wrote one historian.[124] What disturbed Americans most was the existence of poverty in the midst of plenty. The realization that neither businessmen nor "free enterprise" were benevolent protectors of the public good led many Americans back once again to an idea that they had only recently rejected: the idea that only government—a powerful, activist government—could counter the depredations of the powerful corporations. Suddenly, the party needed progressives.

Franklin Delano Roosevelt shared with his cousin good political judgment and good fortune, but not party affiliation. It was the Democrats who kept the last sparks of early twentieth-century Progressivism alive, and although almost any Democratic candidate would have won in 1932, the magnitude of the victory meant that President Roosevelt was relatively free to kindle those sparks into a new flame—soon to be dubbed "liberalism." Simpson again considered a run for Congress in 1932, but lacking support from Hoover forces, he stayed out of the bloodbath. "Hoover or Roosevelt—the choice is so dismal," he wrote Dorothy Harvey. "I'm almost glad to be on the sidelines."[125] The Republicans were buried almost everywhere. Roosevelt won by 7 million votes and carried forty-two states to Hoover's six. The U.S. House and Senate were securely Democratic. In New York City there was only one outpost of Republicanism left: the 15th A.D. had put over the Republican ticket by a plurality of 5,000.[126]

New York Republicans had enough trouble even without the Great Depression. Capable and charismatic Democrats like Tammany boss Charles Murphy, Governor Al Smith, and Senator Robert Wagner rallied recent immigrants in the cities and native stock progressives everywhere. In New York City the Republicans were so unpopular that before every election, prominent Republicans habitually disavowed any intention to run for office and thus become a sacrificial lamb. In 1924, pen manufacturer Frank Waterman accepted the mayoral nomination after fourteen others turned it down and was overwhelmingly defeated.

Party leaders had for years discouraged any potential candidate who might challenge the business-friendly party orthodoxy enough to attract working-class and progressive voters, and the Republican State Committee, controlled by the utilities industry during the 1920s, abandoned New York City to the Democrats. When, in 1929, the enterprising and energetic Fiorello La Guardia snared the nomination, party leaders snubbed him as being too much of a radical. The Great Depression shook up even the hidebound Republican State Committee. A prosperous Long Island reformer named Kingsland Macy took over as chairman in 1930 and began trying to liberalize the party, replacing prohibitionists and "ten cent fare" supporters with candidates who might have a chance with the voters of New York. But Macy made too many enemies too quickly, and party regulars usually prevailed.[127]

That left the progressive Republicans of New York's 15th Assembly District alone on their political island considering how best to extricate the party from its difficult position. State leaders had written them off, and national leaders—Hoover faithful all—considered them to be little more than an annoyance. The 15th A.D. Republicans could do little about these things, but they could begin building in their own backyard. They could finally unseat the cautious, conservative Sam Koenig.

Walter Mack, who took over as president of the 15th A.D. Republican Club in 1930, was a businessman who specialized in corporate turnarounds. Like Simpson, he was born in 1895, had an Ivy League education, had served in the war, and had a penchant for fine clothing. He was also a firm believer that government had a role to play in ensuring a better life for its citizens. Mack, who later made Pepsi-Cola the number two soft drink in America, was also a great salesman, so in 1932 Keyes Winter talked him into running for the State Senate.[128]

Mack got off to a good start with an endorsement from Calvin Coolidge as "a businessman who knows the value of a dollar." But there was another endorsement that he needed. Three weeks before the election, two men visited Mack's headquarters and asked if he wanted to win. Mack replied in the affirmative, and they told him to meet them at the corner of 89th and Park Avenue. A black armor-plated limousine drove up, and Mack, perhaps against his better judgment, got in. He soon found himself in the back room of a billiard parlor face to face with gangster Dutch Shultz. "I was the only fellow there without a revolver in one armpit and another on the hip," Mack recalled. "You want to be elected?" Schultz asked. Mack again replied in the affirmative. Shultz told him that for $5,000 he would ensure victory in the problematic 17th Assembly District. Mack declined.[129]

It was Simpson who suffered the consequences of Mack's principles. He had offered to help his friend out on election day. He agreed to take on the tough 17th, which was just north of the 15th and included parts of Harlem. When Simpson showed up at a public school on 112th Street, he was beaten and tossed into the street. Nearby policemen turned their backs as Simpson brushed the dust from his suit—having seen enough, recalled Mack, to know that "they were just running up the votes the way they'd run an adding machine."[130] Mack ran ahead of his Democratic opponent everywhere else, but took only 5 percent of the vote in the 17th, and that lost him the election. Mack began gathering evidence of collusion between Koenig and the pro-Tammany election judges he had appointed in the 17th.[131]

Koenig's time had run out. About the only Republicans in New York City who stood by him were the district leaders, who, to a man, remained faithful. The crusade against Koenig, therefore, began as a series of skirmishes as each assembly district sought to unseat its pro-Koenig leader. By the end of 1932, six assembly districts were in open revolt. Things were more complicated in the 15th Assembly District. As a matter of principle and party regularity, Keyes Winter did not want to openly oppose Koenig. Neither did the membership want to depose Winter. Mack, Simpson, and other activists proposed that the club, rather than the assembly district leader, lead the drive against Koenig. Winter bristled at the idea and prepared to step down. In the interim, he absented himself from New York County Republican Committee meetings so as not to shore up Koenig.[132]

By the time the 15th A.D. Republicans began thinking about a successor, it was the spring of 1933 and Franklin Roosevelt had embarked upon his "Hundred Days." The question was, who would best help New York Republicans to deal with the consequences? Walter Mack was a possibility, as were blue-blood activist Newbold Morris and young alderman Joseph Clark Baldwin. But Keyes Winter took charge of selecting his successor, and he had set his sights on Simpson. Some of the groundwork was done in mid-May when Simpson went to Washington to meet with national party leaders— "arguing, fighting, and flattering them," he reported.[133] On June 2, Simpson was selected to represent the 15th A.D. on the County Republican Executive Committee. On the evening of June 5, New York's "silk stocking" Republicans gathered in their well-appointed clubhouse on East 83rd Street and unanimously elected Kenneth Simpson as Republican leader of the 15th Assembly District. Simpson then rose to move for adoption of a resolution calling for change in county leadership.[134]

The Great Depression had opened an opportunity for a new kind of Republican politician. Perhaps at the expense of his legal career, and certainly at some personal cost, Simpson was in place to take that opportunity. It was not the easy leap into national politics that a run for Congress might have been. Rising through New York City politics would demand agility, acumen, and the energy that few could muster. Energy Simpson still had in excess, but the long apprenticeship had drained away other reserves. Too many frustrations had been submerged in illness, despair, and drink. Some of the youthful idealism remained, but a new alloy of cynicism made it brittle. Disappointments had robbed him of his resilience and left him more likely to break than to bend. But this was Kenneth Simpson's moment and he knew it. As he rose to rally New York's Republicans behind changing their party, he rose to the challenge of changing himself.

CHAPTER THREE
A WELL-PLAYED HAND

Seven men sat at a green baize poker table in a smoke-sodden New York hotel room; it was early March 1937. The conversation was conventional, but the tone was above average—the Hoyle Club descended from the legendary Algonquin Roundtable, and these were men who worked in words. Marc Connelly, Arthur Kober, Alfred de Liagre Jr., and Theron Bamberger were all playwrights and producers. There was humorist Franklin P. Adams, his column read by millions of Americans daily, and Percy Waram, whose colorful Cornish personality made up for the fact that he was an actor. A telephone rang incessantly in the background, and it seemed always to be for the politician of the bunch. Kenneth Simpson had been invited into the Hoyle Club by friend Franklin P. Adams. Outsiders considered him an exception to the dramatic and literary cast of the club, but the players knew better. Simpson also put words into other people's mouths, and his job was tougher: there was no script, an ever-changing cast of thousands, and, as the telephone insisted, no time off.[1]

Five players had folded when Marc Connelly drew a flush. Although his métier was satirical comedy, Connelly took his cards seriously. He ran through the odds, ready to raise. Then he looked up. Simpson may have quit gnawing at his pipe stem, may have raised a brow. He definitely bet with a bit more "alacrity" than usual.[2] Connelly called, and Simpson produced a royal flush. Kenneth Simpson was on a winning streak. In recent years, he had worked his way from ward politician to chairman of the County Republican Party. The royal flush had put Simpson on the right side of 1 in 649,740 odds. But he would have to play his hand better next time—luck alone could not elect a Republican ticket in New York City.

NEW BEGINNINGS

Between 1933 and 1935, Simpson sharpened his journeyman's skills as district leader, his contacts increasing and his sphere of operations widening as his abilities grew. There was a new law firm, better cases, and a bigger place for his growing family. But he never put politics down for long because there was much at stake. New York City was just emerging from its own dark period, and Simpson was determined to see that it did not return. "There is one dominant issue in this campaign," he informed the Republican voters of the 15th Assembly District during the fall 1933 mayoral contest. "How can New York City free itself most completely from machine rule?"[3]

Tammany's grip had already been broken by Judge Samuel Seabury and the corruption investigation that drove Jimmy Walker from office. But reform had a handhold at best. Joseph V. McKee, a good-government Democrat, began to clean up the government but after only four months was swept aside by Tammany in a special election. The year 1933, accordingly, brought forth another of New York's dalliances with Fusion as Seabury brought liberal Republicans and Democrats behind a sparkplug politician named Fiorello La Guardia. The problem for Republicans was that La Guardia was populist, pro-labor, and hardly a Republican at all. La Guardia hoped to overcome that problem with an appearance at the 15th A.D. Republican Club.[4]

The members anticipated fireworks to outshine even their own sparkling cufflinks and glittering jewelry, but La Guardia confounded expectations, appearing even-tempered and humble. "I don't know whether you ladies and gentlemen have decided to admit me to the social register or whether you just wanted to go slumming with me," he told the crowd, and then went on to win them over. That fall, New York's Republicans backed Fusion for the first time since 1913, McKee split the Democratic vote, and La Guardia was elected. Although Tammany kept the district attorney's office and so kept the city's nose out of its business, La Guardia began rebuilding New York City. It was a welcomed victory, but not a Republican one.[5]

Meanwhile, Simpson was shaping 15th Assembly District Republicans into an effective force in anticipation of races for Congress, State Senate, assembly, and alderman and backed two municipal court justices in the fall of 1934. This district level work could be painstaking and exhausting, but the same fascination for organization that had made Simpson an enterprising adjutant helped him to master the mechanics of electoral politics. No detail was too small. Simpson conducted exhaustive registration drives, established precinct headquarters, and put sound trucks on the streets. It was Simpson who rented the storefront on 86th Street, where, he wrote Charles Hilles, "I have a dozen unemployed bond salesmen working on double shift."[6] All the while, Simpson kept close tabs on the district's fifty-six polling places, visiting every one of them on primary day.[7]

The 1934 election lengthened Simpson's list of credits. He got colleague Joseph Clark Baldwin elected to the State Senate and put confidante Newbold Morris into Baldwin's old seat on the Board of Alderman. He also got the 15th Assembly District behind Joseph McGoldrick, a good-government Democrat, for city comptroller. This was a substantial accomplishment because, after 1933, party regulars were once again reluctant to back Fusion candidates or other "irregulars." They had good reason: independent and "non-partisan" tickets, however good they were for New York City, robbed the parties of the city positions and government jobs that they needed to survive. Simpson considered his toughest task in 1934 to be "trying to keep a political organiza- tion together without patronage."[8]

The state party was dealing, less effectively, with the dilemma that Republicans everywhere confronted in the midst of the Democratic New Deal: accommodation or conflict? State Republican chairman W. Kingsland Macy chose accommodation and took on the Republican "Old Guard" for standing in the way of reasonable change. Stalwarts of the New York party, however, joined together to defeat Macy and build a platform that denounced the New Deal as "immoral." The result was electoral disaster. Republican gubernatorial candidate Robert Moses gained fewer votes than his predeces- sor had in 1932. The party even lost the state legislature, a difficult thing to do given favorable apportionment provisions.[9]

Larger forces were at work. Economic and population trends were undermining the old New York City business-upstate farming alliance that had been the lifeblood of the party for years. The rise of urban, industrial, immigrant America could not be rolled back. Americans now expected gov- ernment to act as a counterweight to the powerful, impersonal institutions that were changing their nation. Old Guard Republican Party leaders looked back instead to the days of small towns, small business, and small government. So the debacle of 1934 opened the way to a new generation of Republican leaders, less confrontational than Macy and more willing to adapt to changing conditions. Charles Hilles understood this, predicting that "the Republican Party cannot stagger to the Left. No . . . We are not going to stagger, but we are going to the left as sure as I am alive."[10] Hilles's protégé, Kenneth Simpson, went further. "Dressing up in sackcloth and ashes over the demise of the constitution and 'rugged individualism' is beside the point," Simpson wrote. He believed that the party had to "convince the man on the street that it is not against him."[11]

Simpson should have known what he was talking about, having lately spent time with some men on the street. Mayor La Guardia had inherited a host of controversies, including unrest among city taxi drivers. In February 1934, there was a strike that turned violent. Simpson served as a member of the first of a series of taxicab commissions established by the administration. Through the winter and spring of 1934, he studied the industry and "learned the inside of the business from the inside of many cabs."[12] Simpson believed that taxi rates must remain low for the good of the industry, but his colleagues disagreed and it was another three years before the problem was solved by the medallion system, which raised driver wages by limiting the number of taxicabs in the city. Although politics and public service like this cut deeply into Simpson's billable hours, his legal career was looking up all the same.[13]

The relationship with Barnes, Richardson & Halstead ended badly. Although the firm was dissolved amicably enough in July 1933, the agreement provided Simpson with further compensation upon conclusion of a sizeable customs case. But then Barnes refused to pay, leaving Simpson no choice but to take his former partner to court. Even the imperturbable Helen was "angry for the first time in her life," Simpson confided.[14] In early 1934, Simpson inked an agreement with the firm of Hunt, Hill & Betts. He again looked forward to doing litigation and trial work. His May 1 start date came and went in grand style, effective while he was overseas. In late April, the Simpsons had sailed for the Continent. In May, while Helen shopped in Paris, Simpson toured the countryside along the French and Spanish border with Dorothy Harvey.[15]

He arrived back in New York to resume his practice at one of Manhattan's most prestigious addresses, the forty-story Equitable Building at 120 Broadway. His window office commanded a bird's eye view of the city, the river, and the bridges below. He wrote Dorothy that he felt as if he were "starting life over again."[16] French diarist Anais Nin, who visited in the fall, confirmed the salutary effects of Simpson's new start, writing to Dorothy how attractive he was.[17]

Simpson had clearly established a reputation for dealing with all things French. This may have attracted Hunt, Hill & Betts, which had its own reputation for handling maritime business, including the *Titanic* and *Lusitania* claims. That expertise, along with influence at City Hall, gained Simpson a contract with the French Line to negotiate city cooperation in the construction and leasing of a new pier in the North River for the ultra-luxury liner *Normandie*. He was among the dignitaries who greeted the ship as it completed its maiden voyage in June 1935.[18]

French expertise also figured in Simpson's biggest case, a complex dispute over the estate of millionaire publisher and perfume manufacturer Francois Coty. The dispute began in April 1934, when Coty funneled $1.5 million of his company's assets into the United States in a thinly veiled attempt to keep it from his ex-wife. Coty died soon after and Madame Yvonne Alexandrine Cotnareanu, eager to get control of the company and cash in, hired lawyers on both sides of the Atlantic—her New York counsel was Samuel Seabury. The case expanded, catching up Swiss and American banks and spurring injunctions and multimillion-dollar counterclaims. When the American lawyers sought French expertise and the French lawyers, American expertise, Simpson's name came up. By 1935 he was assisting Paris lawyer Michel Brault for Seabury's firm in New York and for the Wilmington, Delaware, law firm of Biggs, Biggs & Lynch.[19]

Simpson also kept a hand in corporate law and divorce work. Surrogate court cases, involving the disposition of property on behalf of children, the elderly, and the indisposed, multiplied along with contacts at City Hall. If Simpson had a specialty, however, it may have been representing intellectuals and artists such as writer Edmund Wilson, pianist George Copeland, and composer Virgil Thomson, all of whom were friends. An undaunted Simpson also took a few more shots at entrepreneurship, despite his earlier bad call with *Time* magazine. In 1934, he lined up investors for the Hartford opening of an opera with music by Thomson and libretto by family friend Gertrude Stein. Although it shattered every convention, *Four Saints in Three Acts* went on to Broadway. But that was the exception. When good friend Norman Bel Geddes invited him to invest in a play called *Dead End*, Simpson declined, calling it "the surest way of emptying a theater I can imagine." The show was a hit, first on Broadway and then on the silver screen.[20]

Despite such lost opportunities, the Simpsons had by mid-decade left the straits of the early Depression behind. Helen's investment earnings rebounded, and Simpson's practice thrived. The family was doing well enough that, despite Simpson's claiming to love New York in the summertime, it opted to rent a house in Westport, Connecticut, during the summers of 1934 and 1935. Simpson spent weekends there whenever possible.[21]

By then the Simpsons had outgrown the Park Avenue apartment that they had occupied for a decade. Kelly was now eight years old. He had developed a surprising interest in the work of Gertrude Stein and a more conventional fondness for dogs. Helen-Louise was four, and Elizabeth, born in October 1932, was no longer a toddler. In the summer of 1935, the Simpsons bought a more spacious place, a five-story red brick townhouse, at 109 East 91st Street.

Just a few yards down a quiet, tree-lined street from Park Avenue, the Simpson's door opened to a wide marble stairway leading to a second floor salon replete with modern art. Its showpiece, surrealist Joan Miro's "Poetic Object"—consisting of a wooden woman's leg, a derby hat, and a stuffed parrot, among other things—was the hit of the Museum of Modern Art's late 1936 Dada and Surrealism show. The dining room featured rugs by French artist Lurcat as well as a glass-topped table designed by Simpson himself and built in France. Downstairs, in Simpson's study, the décor was different— heavy oak paneling surrounded an oil portrait of William Kelly Simpson.[22]

The Simpsons were hardly homebodies, of course. The regular trips to Europe continued, especially for Helen and the children—Simpson hoping that they would turn Kelly's interests from dogs to "history, geography and cathedrals."[23] In between times, visitors including Kerensky, the Harveys, and Bernard Fay stayed in the fifth floor apartment completely given over to guests and accessible by special elevator. Into this bustling household of family, servants, and guests was born, in November 1936, a fourth child, Sarah Pierpont Fleurnoy Simpson. "I hope she lives up to all those names," joked her father.[24] Meanwhile, Simpson's political stature was rising ever higher. Republicans were putting the future of the party in his hands, giving Simpson himself a great deal to live up to.

COUNTY CHAIRMAN

During the early 1930s, Republican assemblyman Warren T. Thayer wrote a letter that helped change Simpson's career. Thayer was secretly on the payroll of a New York utility, the letter just a line saying he hoped he had done well by the firm. Regulation of utilities—which were justly suspect due to their natural monopolies—was a staple of turn-of-the-century Progressivism and a popular cause. Nevertheless, New York Republicans continued to side with the power companies—all except state chairman W. Kingsland Macy. In his crusade to liberalize the party, Macy chose public utilities as a battleground and when, in 1934, the Federal Trade Commission discovered the Thayer letter, Macy set out after the Old Guard. Charles Hilles confided to a colleague that Macy's "desperation for an issue brands him as an unfit man to carry the party's flag,"[25] and within months conservative gatekeepers had blunted the attack and replaced Macy. But there remained a problem. New York County was led by a Macy man; the Old Guard wanted a capable and "regular" leader in place for the 1936 presidential election year.[26]

Chase Mellen Jr. was just thirty-six years old when he won the New York County chairmanship in the same fight that had made Simpson 15th Assembly District leader. He was a blue-blooded banker's son and a graduate of Harvard Law School. Mellen had lost a leg during the World War and was not afraid of a fight. He was, as one colleague put it, "thoroughly idealistic but knowing nothing about the art of politics" and not up to the job of building a countywide organization without patronage.[27] By the fall of 1935, Mellen retained the allegiance of reform Republicans, but no one else. As they did in 1933, district leaders began taking sides, some calling for "a more experienced person" not caught up in the spat between the Macy reformers and the Old Guard. Late in the morning of September 19, twenty-three of them met at the Hotel Astor to consider candidates. One suggested what Hilles had believed all along: that "someone like Ken Simpson" would be a good choice. By mid-afternoon it was unanimous.[28]

Mellen was a friend, so Simpson was reluctant to fight him, even though he knew that Mellen was not up to the job. There was also the matter of Simpson's reputation. He knew, as a colleague had emphasized earlier, that anyone who took on Mellen would be considered "a dummy for the Koenig crowd."[29] Predictably, Mellen made much of "back room conferences" and corrupt bargains. He claimed to have no problem with Simpson personally, but insisted that "by environment, by association, he typifies conservative Republicanism." Even the Board of Governors of the New York Republican Club split over the issue, some sure that Simpson was an arch-conservative, and others that he was the "most outstanding, able and liberal of our younger members."[30] This very ambiguity enabled Simpson to bring the warring

Chase Mellen, left, and Simpson at the Mecca Temple, September 25, 1935. *(Courtesy of the Yale University Manuscripts and Archives)*

factions in the party together. On September 21 Simpson agreed to run, stating that "I am doing this with one purpose in mind—to restore harmony, unity, and vigor to the party organization."[31]

There followed four days of constant campaigning and low-key lobbying in advance of the general meeting of the 2,500-member Republican County Committee. Mellen personally dealt out the tickets, subjecting delegates to one last appeal. On the night of September 25, when county Republicans poured into the Mecca Temple, a neo-Moorish Shriner's Hall on West 55th Street, they were all in a fighting mood.

Simpson delegates soon discovered that Mellen had relegated them to the foyers and balconies and packed the orchestra pit with his own noisy partisans. Mellen ensured that it was, as the *New York Times* described it, a "turbulent, disorderly convention" but could do little else. The sentiments of the delegates were clear from the start when Simpson backer Joseph Clark Baldwin trounced Mellen—his former roommate at Harvard—for temporary chairman. Hoping that time would turn everyone against what he considered a "prearranged deal," Mellen forced through a roll call of every single delegate.[32] As the tedious procedure dragged on, fistfights broke out, combatants threw oranges, tomatoes, and onions, and the policemen on duty called for reinforcements. Above it all in the balcony, some calmer heads of the 15th Assembly District played bridge. At 2:25 A.M. it was all over. Kenneth Simpson was elected Republican Chairman of New York County by a 1,640 to 752 vote. Mellen knew his opponent too well not to be gracious in defeat. He expressed hope that Simpson would "make it possible for progressive Republicans to give you their enthusiastic support." "I belong to no faction," Simpson assured everyone.[33]

In the aftermath, party leaders were hopeful at best. Upstate conservatives ventured that Simpson was one of them. The liberal *World-Telegram* cautioned that "whether or not Mr. Simpson would fill the bill only time and test could show."[34] Only Nathan Porter seemed certain about the result, assuring his son-in-law that he would surely be "dropped from the social register."[35] In early October, in an effort to unite a party described by the *New York Times* as "shot through and through with bitterness and personal grudges," Simpson converted the library of the National Republican Club into a casino and held a "breathing spell affair" for four hundred party faithful.[36] Although Simpson lost a stack of chips at the roulette wheel, he played the fall election better, helping state Republicans to win back the legislature. So far so good, but the real test of Republican Party strength—and the surest indicator of whether conservatives or liberals would guide it—came in 1936 as the party took on the New Deal for the first time.[37]

A LIBERAL EMERGES

As Franklin Roosevelt tried to restore the nation to prosperity, he also transformed the nation's economy and politics. He had no single, coherent plan, but in the wake of Hoover's seeming inertia most Americans welcomed Roosevelt's "bold, persistent experimentation." The first experiment, central to what became known as the "first New Deal," was an attempt to replace harmful economic competition with government-brokered cooperation. The National Industrial Recovery Administration, established in June 1933, brought businessmen together to write codes to stabilize industries and create jobs. It also encouraged unions in hopes that they would raise wages and increase American purchasing power. This attempt to broker a better economy, unfortunately, alienated both left and right. Conservatives in Roosevelt's own party created the American Liberty League to "teach the necessity of respect for the rights of person and property."[38] Populist demagogues Louisiana Senator Huey Long, California doctor Francis E. Townsend, and Detroit radio priest Father Coughlin made increasingly bold and strident challenges to the free market.

The Supreme Court killed the first New Deal, ruling the National Recovery Act unconstitutional in May 1935, so Roosevelt changed course, abandoning government-brokered cooperation for the creation of countervailing power that would protect the citizenry from the harmful effects of capitalism. This "second New Deal" truly changed the face of the nation: in July 1935 came the National Labor Relations Act, and in August came the Social Security Act, the Public Utility Holding Company Act, and the Revenue Act of 1935—levying what wealthy Americans dubbed the "soak the rich tax."

This programmatic about-face and flurry of legislation left most Americans confused. Republicans understandably were at a loss as to how to respond. When Simpson took over as county chairman, however, there was little time for reflection: the Republican Convention was coming up in June 1936 and it was up to party leaders to choose delegates.

The Republican Party had always won the presidency by bringing Western forces into play with a core coalition of businessmen and middle-class Easterners. The New Deal was undermining Republican fortunes in the burgeoning Eastern cities by creating from newly Americanized immigrants and working people a countervailing Democratic coalition. In 1936, therefore, the Republican Party hoped to throw Eastern support behind a popular Westerner who could pile up states beyond the Mississippi. Who that westerner might be, party leaders were not ready to say, but a few influential ones hoped that it might be Hoover. It was decided to send "uninstructed delegates" to the convention who could then back the most likely winner.

It was Simpson's job to assemble a group of New York County delegates who represented the city's Republican power brokers and would adhere to the "uninstructed" game plan. For every choice there were many hopefuls. The discontented could launch "delegate fights" within their own districts, so choosing was a delicate job. Simpson consulted early and often with Charles Hilles, but he did the work himself and passed successfully this test of his county leadership.[39]

By mid-February Simpson had assembled his delegates. The group reflected a good faith effort to compromise between the Old Guard who had earned the honor and the young Republicans who held the key to the party's future. Simpson tried to include representatives from most of the assembly districts, but since the preponderance of influentials came from the 15th, this was a difficult task. Simpson worked patiently and carefully and in the end won support for a list almost exactly as anticipated.[40]

There were still inevitable fissures that reformers allied with Kingsland Macy and Congressman Hamilton Fish Jr. sought to widen. Macy and Fish had allied with Idaho Senator William Borah who was trying one last time to reform the party along lines drawn by Westerners in the age of the first Roosevelt. At the heart of his unreconstructed Western progressivism was a resentment of bigness of all kinds. New Dealers recognized that big cities, "big business," and "big labor" were there to stay. Borah progressives wished to "trust bust" the country back to its rural roots. Trying for the Republican nomination against long odds, Borah had begun a guerilla campaign for delegates. On his behalf, Macy and Fish began enlisting Borah delegates to challenge the "silk stockings" that Simpson had representing other districts.[41]

At the Republican State Committee meeting, Fish, in an argument strained by his own backing of the seventy-year-old Borah, called for "new blood." Others criticized those who "don't control any more votes than their own, or of their maids and butlers."[42] But Simpson was not afraid to play tough; he started backfires to keep down the "incorrigibles" pledged to Borah and removed district election officials when necessary. In the end, Simpson's delegates all survived the early April primary. But those convinced by the delegate fight that Simpson was a conservative were soon again wondering.[43]

The phrase "social security" has come to have a somewhat bloodless connotation in the American lexicon. Few consider what it meant to a generation that had seen its very existence imperiled by a seemingly malevolent market— Americans who faced ruin if unemployment or illness struck and friends and family failed. Even in 1935, many among the wealthy did not understand how the idea that the nation owed its citizens a measure of "social security" galvanized working- and middle-class voters. It is to Kenneth Simpson's credit that he understood.

By early 1936, Simpson had signaled his intent not merely to accept, but to safeguard, what was good about the New Deal. As Roosevelt had done in Washington, Simpson began to enlist experts to boost the capacity of the county committee. He created a law committee in October 1935. In February 1936, he established a Legislative Advisory Committee on Social Welfare charged with shaping measures to benefit New York's citizens. He convinced such world-class experts as Louis Dublin and Lillian Wald to participate.[44]

In 1935, the Democratic state legislature passed a number of pro-New Deal measures including unemployment insurance, utilities regulation, and labor-friendly legislation. When the Republicans regained the legislature, they were not as eager to go along with Governor Herbert Lehman's New Deal measures. In March 1936, Lehman introduced a bill that lowered New York's pension age and provided greater assistance to handicapped children. The $4 million raised by a tax on liquor would have gained the state $20 million in federal funding. The Republicans in the legislature stood on principle. They had pledged to cut taxes and so stopped the bill in committee.[45]

Rural upstaters could see no reason for social legislation. Their chief spokesman, Representative James Wadsworth Jr., held that "there can be no such thing as social security in this world of ours today."[46] That left downstate Republicans at a loss as to how to make the party relevant to the lives of their constituents and afraid of a wholesale rejection of the party over social security. In May, Simpson assembled a coalition of five New York City area county Republican leaders and sent a telegram to the Republican speaker of the house asking that the bill be reported out of committee. To his frustration, leaders from his own assembly district helped kill the bill once and for all. Not surprisingly, the assembly also made short work of the recommendations sent up by the New York County Legislative Advisory Committee. This practical defeat put the New York County chairman on record as a "liberal" as surely as did a more principled pronouncement that came a short time later.[47]

For half a century, the poles of American politics had revolved around an axis of gold. Pro-business conservatives saw the gold standard as the way to keep the economy stable at home and trade flowing abroad. They also saw a gold-backed dollar as being about as inviolable as the law of gravity. Besides, as gold became scarce during the late nineteenth century, holders of gold grew richer. Western populists, on the other hand, believed a floating currency to be more equitable to farmers and working people whose indebtedness rose steadily as the value of gold appreciated. Roosevelt had buried that issue in 1933 when he abandoned the gold standard, but a few backward-looking Republicans threatened to dig it up again.

In late May 1936, as party leaders prepared for the convention, Simpson offered a few offhand remarks to a reporter. He said that the "platform should declare for the continuation of relief" and that it should back a "managed currency" rather than a return to the gold standard.[48] Simpson's remarks created a flurry across New York. In a variation of the "traitor to his class" charges being leveled against Roosevelt, an appalled Ogden Mills noted that this pronouncement was strange coming from the 15th Assembly District. Upstate farm organizations, in contrast, were pleased, as was liberal newspaperman Frank Gannett. Even Hamilton Fish Jr. congratulated Simpson, confiding that "I had begun to think that you represented the reactionary forces within our party."[49]

For all of his ideological and programmatic stands, what really mattered in a county chairman was the ability to get things done. And where previously Simpson had worked within the sphere of the city, he was increasingly influential within the state—especially as part of a group of young leaders who were steadily and surely taking over.

A number of other recently elected county chairmen were determined to adapt the party to a New Deal environment. The group, unimaginatively dubbed the "Young Turks," included John R. Crews of Kings County (Brooklyn), Russel Sprague of Nassau County (Long Island), Charles Griffiths of Westchester

County, and Edwin Jaeckle of Erie County (Buffalo). The latter soon emerged as something of a rival. Although he had only become Erie County chairman in 1935, Jaeckle had been on the State Republican Committee since 1926 and was the most seasoned—and also the most imperious—in a crowd of strong leaders. He had come up through ward politics in Buffalo, been in the Navy during the war, and then served as Erie County collector of taxes. Jaeckle was smart and a tough trench fighter, perhaps out of necessity since he was an upstater in a group of ambitious downstaters. For the time being, though, the Young Turks stuck together to take control of the party machinery.

Pharmaceutical executive Melvin C. Eaton had been installed as state chairman by the Old Guard in 1934. The Young Turks were willing to live with Eaton—provided, as one insider put it, that he was "placed strictly under guard."[50] But the fight over the social security bill presented the party with an embarrassment and the Young Turks with an opening. On May 16, 1936, the day that the assembly killed the bill, the Republican State Committee met. Simpson motioned to create an executive committee that would assume the powers of the state committee between meetings. Given his close relationship with Hilles, Simpson must have known in advance that the Old Guard would concede. The vote allowed control of the New York Republican Party to pass decisively from the Old Guard to the Young Turks.[51]

1936 CONVENTION

State Republicans had solved a few problems, but the national party was in disarray. At the heart of it was disagreement over whether the party should win elections or serve as a harbor for a set of "timeless" core values and principles. The New Deal's assault on the old certainties had been so profound that a surprising number of the old stock, middle and upper class faithful were prepared to lose until such time as the rest of the nation should come to its senses. Another problem was that the basis for the old farmer-business coalition had fallen apart. As small farms disappeared, there were not enough rural votes to go around, particularly since New Deal agricultural programs had converted a good many of the farmers that remained. As the 1936 election approached, however, there was little choice but to try to reassemble the old coalition one last time.

One man seemed to have at least a chance of pulling it off. Alfred Mossman "Alf" Landon of Kansas won that distinction by being the only Republican

incumbent governor to be reelected in 1934. He had other good qualifications: he was an oilman but supported reasonable regulation of business;
he had fought the Ku Klux Klan and had been a Bull Moose Progressive. It
also helped that to many it seemed that the only alternative was the former
President. It was hard to get excited about the bland Kansan, but far easier to
believe in his electability than Hoover's.

It was Simpson's job to get the New York County delegation—safely
"uncommitted" and Borah-proof—to Cleveland, Ohio. Once there, they
would find out what the West wanted and get behind it. Hilles had encouraged Simpson to bring Helen along and make a vacation of it. But Helen was
no fan of politics. She chose to take the children, join her parents, and set sail
for Europe instead. On Sunday morning, June 7, a delegation of two hundred
Republicans from New York and Westchester Counties gathered at Grand
Central Terminal to board a New York Central train dubbed the "Simpson-
Griffiths Special." The fact that the departing delegates were likely to go to
Landon was evident in their being serenaded by a band playing the Kansan's
campaign song, "Oh Susannah."[52]

The delegates arrived late that night to find accommodations less
than optimal. "The service has broken down almost completely," Simpson
lamented to Helen. The elevator took half an hour to arrive and it released the
weary travelers to rooms that were "microscopic." The political atmosphere
was as depressing as the accommodations. Party warhorse Sam Koenig told
Simpson that it was the "most listless convention" he had ever seen. Landon
was a sure thing, Simpson wrote Helen, if only because there was "almost as
little interest in stopping his nomination as in nominating him."[53]

In nearly every state delegation the story was the same. A faithful few
harbored hopes for Hoover, while up and comers were as intent on burying
him as on promoting Landon. On Monday, Simpson attempted to nominate
two of his most illustrious constituents to functionary positions, what would
have been pro forma under other circumstances. When Simpson put up
former Hoover cabinet member Ogden Mills for chairman of the Resolutions
Committee, he was met with stony silence. He had better luck renominat-
ing Hilles—an old Coolidge, rather than Hoover, man—for the Republican
National Committee. Only Jaeckle objected.[54]

The delegation soon settled into a seemingly intractable fight over
whether to back Landon immediately, as the Young Turks wanted, or to wait,

The New York delegates meet at the 1936 Republican Convention. Standing at left is Charles Hilles. To the right of Simpson is Brooklyn leader and staunch Simpson ally John Crews; Congresswoman Ruth Pratt is the second woman to the right of Crews. *(Courtesy of the Yale University Manuscripts and Archives)*

as the Old Guard wished. When reporters got wind of the story, however, the delegates acted quickly to quash the discord. They invited the reporters into the room, Simpson moved for the ballot, and the delegates—with Hilles dutifully voting first—backed Landon. Later that day, Hilles acknowledged the inevitable when he informed old Kansas Progressive William Allen White that "You and I are now the Old Guard."[55]

Thankfully, the convention picked up after a fiery nominating speech by Landon's campaign manager. "John Hamilton electrified the convention," Simpson wrote Helen. "I've never seen such apathy turned into such enthusiasm."[56] The enthusiasm carried Landon to a victory on the first ballot and carried the conventioneers back to New York. On the morning of Saturday the 13th, the delegates were met by another band and more reporters. "All the elements of the party got together," Simpson assured them.[57] But even then the spell was wearing off. The next day, Simpson estimated that the party had a "good chance to elect a governor and an outside chance to elect Landon."[58]

THE PARTY HITS BOTTOM

Two weeks later the "good chance" evaporated. State Republicans had been overjoyed to learn that popular two-term Democratic Governor Herbert

Lehman did not wish to run for a third term. With no clear Democratic successor, it was the first time since 1920 that the Republicans had a shot at the office. They put up William F. Bleakley, a Westchester County Supreme Court Justice well known around New York City, and a Catholic. When Bleakley won the support of Edwin Jaeckle—likely having promised him the state chairmanship—his nomination became certain. But after July 1, when Roosevelt convinced Lehman to reconsider, Bleakley had little chance of winning.[59]

Not long after the Convention, John Hamilton arrived in New York to lay plans for the fall.[60] On the afternoon of June 22, Simpson held an informal reception for him at East 91st Street ahead of a gala dinner for 3,500 at the Hotel Astor. It was an inspiring time because Hamilton, the power behind the Landon candidacy, was an inspiring man. The candidate himself was much less so. He was better in person than in public and his thin, reedy voice did not come across well on radio. It also did not help that Landon was virtually absent early in the campaign, leaving the field to the more charismatic Hamilton. This prompted the *New Yorker* to joke that the Republican ticket was headed by Hamilton with "Alf Moss Landon of Kansas for second vice president."[61]

Mostly, Landon was hobbled by the party platform and the imperatives of the campaign itself. In launching his second New Deal, Roosevelt had inveighed against "economic royalists" who threatened the common good, thus drawing a bright line between Democrats and Republicans. Landon could smudge but never erase it, and as the campaign progressed Landon moved farther to the right trying to gain traction. Roosevelt offered a bold, if inconsistent, effort to come to grips with modern America. The Republicans, on the other hand, with their sunflower emblem and "Oh Susannah" campaign song, offered rural nostalgia that appealed mostly to affluent old-stock Americans. Still, Hamilton expected a victory, because, he said, "every Rolls-Royce I see has a Landon sticker."[62] The *Literary Digest* also predicted a landslide for Landon in a straw poll based on telephone listings and auto registrations. The "haves" were talking to themselves and the "have-nots" were preparing to vote for Roosevelt.

Simpson dutifully campaigned through the summer and fall of 1936 and cast the city's first Republican vote early on the morning of November 3. But instead of a Republican resurgence, 1936 brought the cementing of the New

Deal coalition of working-class whites, African-Americans, and urban liberals that would rule politics for forty-five years. Their votes won every state except Maine and Vermont for Roosevelt. They gave the Democrats 80 seats in a 96-seat Senate and left the Republicans only 89 of the 435 seats in the House of Representatives.

In New York State, the Republicans won back the legislature, although entirely due to the rural vote; in New York City, however, the game had changed. The American Labor Party (ALP), formed to give working-class Jewish voters a way to vote New Deal without voting Tammany, swung the city to Governor Lehman by more than a half-million votes.[63]

Simpson learned three important things in 1936: first, the party had to accept the New Deal, in principle, if not in all its particulars; second, it had to rebuild from the bottom up; and third, it had to offer "a complete ticket that shall have the support of the plain citizens who have long since strayed from the fold."[64] After the election, Simpson attended opening night of a play by friend Norman Bel Geddes. He pronounced it a flop and it soon closed. Bel Geddes countered that while *Iron Men* may have lost $20,000, Landon had lost $12 million. "May we both have better luck next time," he wrote.[65]

Edwin Jaeckle was not counting on luck alone. Blaming Eaton for fumbling the governor's race, he sought the state chairmanship for himself. Simpson and John R. Crews of Brooklyn turned back that attempt in December. They accepted yet another placeholder, William Murray of Oneida County, and the Young Turks as a group remained in power.[66]

All in all, 1936 had been a year of mixed results. Simpson had become an effective county and state leader. He had strengthened his ties with Hilles while taking his place among the Young Turks. But too many party loyalists were content to be principled losers, and there would clearly be more trouble from the resourceful and resentful upstater Edwin Jaeckle. But by then Simpson had an even more pressing problem—and he was already getting plenty of advice about the 1937 New York mayoral race.[67]

It was a good time to leave town, and Helen heeded the advice of a friend who told her, "If you take Simpson on this vacation perhaps he'll be worth living with this winter." The two spent the better part of a week in Jamaica at one of Simpson's favorite pastimes—driving—through the jungle, over mountains, and along the beaches. They returned in mid-January to the much less hospitable terrain of 1937 New York City politics.[68]

THE RELUCTANT REPUBLICAN

Simpson's challenges and opportunities centered around two unassailable facts. First was that in 1937, New York City was home to 563,000 registered Democrats and only 122,000 registered Republicans. Second was the truculent, temperamental—though usually well-intentioned—Fiorello La Guardia. These obstacles were insurmountable on their own, but played against one another, there was much that could be accomplished.[69]

In 1937, Fiorello La Guardia was fifty-five years old and at the height of his power. An enormous store of energy was barely contained by his diminutive 5'2" frame, and his highly pitched but unfaltering voice could inspire or enrage in equal measure. He had other assets invaluable to a politician. There was, for example, his heritage. La Guardia's father was Italian, his mother was Jewish. He was born in New York but raised in Arizona. He had worked abroad in the consular service, held a post at Ellis Island, and could speak half a dozen languages. He was, in short, his own multi-ethnic ticket.[70]

La Guardia's career had been a series of crusades. As counsel to working-class New Yorkers, he learned to hate the Tammany politicians who slapped their backs and then picked their pockets. He served as deputy attorney general of New York State and in the U.S. Congress before joining the Air Corps and flying over the Italian front during the World War. After a term as president of the New York City Board of Aldermen, La Guardia went back to Congress where he attached his name to a landmark piece of labor legislation.[71]

During the 1920s, La Guardia continually harassed establishment Republicans and famously claimed, "I'd rather be right than Regular." As a mayoral candidate in 1929, La Guardia tried to shake New York from its Jazz Age torpor, insisting that Tammany was systematically sacking the city. But he was ignored, especially by Republicans who considered him a radical. He once appeared at the National Republican Club, but nobody came. La Guardia spoke anyway, to the clacking of the billiard balls as clubhouse stalwarts continued their game. Then the Great Depression hit, Judge Seabury began looking under rugs, and La Guardia, proven right, was ushered into the mayor's office. It is no wonder that he felt little allegiance to the Party of Lincoln and the people he called "clubhouse loafers."[72]

That was hardly Kenneth Simpson's fault, but it was his burden, and with his own strong personality, he was not inclined to accept such abuse. Putting the two together, said Walter Mack, could be an exercise in futility. "Get them in a room together, and they both start bubbling over and not listening to each other and end up by pounding the desk," wrote Mack.[73] Although either might loose pyrotechnics at a moment's notice, neither held a grudge for long. One fiery 1934 meeting ended with Simpson stalking out of City Hall, never expecting to speak to La Guardia again. Just a week later, however, the mayor arrived unannounced at Simpson's apartment for cocktails and settled in as if nothing had ever happened.[74]

Perhaps in part because of these similarities, Simpson was a rare Republican leader that La Guardia could respect. An hour-long meeting between the two at City Hall in early 1936 was newsworthy simply because La Guardia had always rebuffed previous party leaders. But La Guardia the opera aficionado was still very much the *prima donna*. In the summer of 1936, an unexpected death allowed the Republicans to pick a president of the Board of Aldermen. Most party leaders, angry because the insistently "nonpartisan" mayor withheld patronage, refused to discuss the issue. But La Guardia and Simpson met on common ground—at one of the regular summer concerts held outdoors at the Lewisohn Stadium in Upper Manhattan. In

Simpson (right) and Fiorello La Guardia (second from right) in the mayor's office. *(Courtesy of the Yale University Manuscripts and Archives)*

July 1936, the Simpsons and La Guardias had both come to hear Beethoven's Fifth Symphony and Wagner's "Das Rheingold." The two talked politics at intermission, although La Guardia admitted only that they had "talked about tonality, harmonics, and such things."[75]

No agreement was reached, and a few days later La Guardia laid out seven qualifications for president of the Board of Aldermen. Simpson countered that "the only man in the Greater City of New York who comes to mind as possessing all these is Fiorello La Guardia." If the mayor wanted to resign and run for the slot, said Simpson, the party "would support him enthusiastically."[76] All along, the mayor had wished to have Adolph Berle, a Columbia University professor, original member of Roosevelt's "Brain Trust," and now his closest advisor, take the spot. But Simpson put up Newbold Morris. Berle praised Morris's "great ability and unquestioned integrity" and turned down an office that he did not want.[77]

That Simpson was able to work with New York's greatest political force distressed some Republicans. No one could criticize La Guardia's stewardship. He had taken a corrupt and run-down city, cleaned it up, and built it up into the most modern and hospitable metropolis in the nation. But what might La Guardia do if his ambitions extended beyond the city? That was the question that Republicans—Simpson among them—always asked.

So as soon as Simpson returned from Jamaica in mid-January 1937, he began seeking answers. He sent letters to hundreds of city Republicans asking whether the party should back La Guardia in the fall. This seemingly innocent exercise touched off a postal landslide that piled up into the summer. Simpson's secretary, Gertrude Hess, dutifully labeled each letter "pro" or "vs." There were far more of the latter than the former, and some quite insistent, but Simpson responded to each one. Most of the "vs." letters put a premium on ideological purity. Typical is the woman who wrote that the party should "name a real Republican, even if he loses."[78] More helpfully, Simpson learned that conservatives rankled at La Guardia's constant displays of independence and were deeply disillusioned by the mayor's failure to get tough with the striking taxi drivers.

Among the early replies, though, was one that stood out for its insight. William Hard, a friend and progressive Republican journalist-turned Republican National Committee secretary, wrote, "I may be crazy but I think that the root of the answer to it is that municipal elections should not be national party elections." Hard also pointed out that it would be a "bold strike" for the Republicans to work with labor to bridge their age-old divide.[79]

Simpson was not inclined to make up his mind early, even if La Guardia made it easy, which he did not. Late every winter, statehouse reporters held their Legislative Correspondents Association show, the Albany equivalent of Washington's Gridiron Club, where reporters and politicians went off record and poked fun at each other in lighthearted—most of the time—skits and songs. At the March 1937 event, La Guardia went "out of his way to heap opprobrium on the Republican Party," Simpson reported to Stanley Isaacs. "I honestly think he feels he can get more votes by assailing the Republicans than otherwise."[80] A few days later, Simpson suggested to Dorothy Harvey that "if worse came to worse," he might "drive a bargain with Tammany."[81]

This was likely frustration talking. What Simpson really sought was to make La Guardia, the reluctant Republican, embrace the party. Some Republicans were threatening a primary fight; others had already endorsed La Guardia on "good government" principles. Late in April, while Simpson was still thinking, La Guardia summoned him to City Hall. It was another good time to get out of town. The Simpsons took a spring vacation in Virginia Beach and let the pot in New York simmer awhile longer.[82]

CREATING THE "HEADLESS TICKET"

For once, time was on the Republican side. Early in 1937, Franklin Roosevelt seemed to hold all the cards, but then trumps began to appear elsewhere. First, there was labor. Employers did not like the New Deal's pro-labor stance, which they believed obliged them to bankroll prosperity out of their profits. They fought the labor movement hard, but the unions fought harder. In early 1937, the United Auto Workers finally found a way to get General Motors to the bargaining table—through the "sit down strike." Few middle Americans noticed when employers violated labor laws, but they were outraged when workers began taking over factories.

Then came economic trouble. Throughout 1935 and 1936, business activity had crept steadily upward until, in the spring of 1937, it reached pre-Depression levels. But much of that growth had been generated by government spending, and when Roosevelt began reining that in, the cycle stopped. Beginning in April and worsening through the summer, another depression, dubbed a "recession" to distinguish it from the big one, set in.

But Roosevelt's biggest political problem was of his own making. In February, worried that the Supreme Court might dismantle the second New Deal just as it had the first, he introduced a plan—ostensibly to relieve aging Supreme Court justices of their workloads—that would have enabled him to appoint six more pro-New Deal justices. This too-transparent ruse pushed fence sitters into the opposition camp and provided long-time opponents with fresh and combustible ammunition.

But what appeared to be an opening could also be a trap. Had the reverses of 1937 really convinced Americans to abandon the New Deal and return to the Republican verities of the 1920s? If not, could the New Deal be co-opted or must it be combated? Those were questions that Simpson was asking himself while in Virginia—along with wondering, of course, just what La Guardia's plans were.

Some Republicans were afraid that in making La Guardia mayor, they might unwittingly launch him into the presidency. Others insisted that since La Guardia had backed the New Deal, they could not back him. Both arguments were made by a small group of Upper East Side conservatives in the spring of 1937. The group was led by twenty-six-year-old Bronson Trevor and included attorney Frederic Bellinger, a friend of Simpson's. The group hoped to rally Republicans behind an unlikely candidate, Democratic Senator Royal S. Copeland, whose two greatest achievements had been bringing air conditioning to the U.S. Senate and doggedly opposing everything that Franklin Roosevelt did. In mid-May, Trevor and Bellinger asked 15th Assembly District Republican Club president Hubert Thayer for permission to let them hold a referendum on the Copeland candidacy. Nothing was going to happen without the approval of the district leader, Thayer told them, and he was unavailable.[83]

The old bouts with depression seem to have ceased once Simpson found fulfilling work. He was still abstaining from alcohol and played some tennis at Westport, but otherwise Simpson had not done much else for his health during the 1930s. His hours were long and erratic, and stress levels were high, despite the solace that his ever-glowing pipe brought him. In April, Simpson had gone to a doctor, complaining about pain in his elbow—a fracture, he thought. A full set of x-rays found nothing broken. But the pain grew, and by mid-May Simpson was bedridden with acute arthritis in both of his arms.[84]

By May 24th Simpson was beginning to recover, so Thayer and Bellinger called at East 91st Street to discuss the Copeland resolution. They found the district leader and county chairman, visibly weakened but in good spirits, propped up in an elegant mahogany sleigh bed smoking his pipe. Simpson cautioned that before anyone could take up the petition, it would have to be mailed to the members for their consideration. Then he said there was something that he wanted to show them. Simpson had decided to make a bold move in the game with La Guardia—in a statement that he had decided to release to the press. Bellinger and Thayer gave their wholehearted approval.[85]

On May 26th, two shoes dropped. The Copeland forces had mailed their petition as instructed, and the issue was on the agenda for the Republican Club that night. The petition had struck a nerve. The ladies and gentlemen of the club were uncharacteristically unruly even before the festivities started. Thayer read instructions from the bedridden leader to discuss the issue fully and to vote according to conviction. Bellinger then opened his statement with the line "Dear clubhouse loafers . . ." and the crowd erupted.[86]

There were a few in attendance who considered backing La Guardia and "good government" as the party's best course for the fall, but they were only two dozen among scores and were "howled down" before they could make their case. The La Guardia backers may not have gained much, but neither did the pro-Copeland crowd. A parliamentary procedure—devised by Simpson in advance—ensured that the 15th Assembly District Republicans would not go on record supporting Copeland.[87]

That same night, Simpson sent his carefully crafted statement to the papers. They all carried it the next day, the *New York Times* on the front page. In words that were, as the *Times* put it, "franker than is the custom of political leaders," Simpson acknowledged that Republicans could hardly elect their own ticket. Republicans did, however, have "more than enough votes to elect or defeat any candidate for office on any other ticket."[88] Simpson then posed the question as to how Republicans should cast those votes. He pointed out that La Guardia had indeed allied himself with radicals and so betrayed the Republican voters who had elected him. He invited the Democrats to come up with a squeaky-clean, good government candidate that Republicans could fully support. Determined to use his leverage "for the progress of good government in New York City," Simpson concluded that "I do not intend to be hurried into a decision."[89]

Conservatives were ecstatic, while liberals criticized Simpson's "abdication of the Republican position to support a non-partisan Anti-Tammany administration."[90] Simpson was puzzled by both responses. His statement and news of the "stormy debate" at the 15th Assembly District Republican Club came out at exactly the same time, sending a subtle message that few besides La Guardia understood. The meeting demonstrated that, barring real compromise, La Guardia's prospects were hopeless in the city's most liberal Republican district. The statement signaled Simpson's desire to make good government— not the New Deal—the basis of the campaign. What most people missed at the time was that by setting unattainable expectations for the Democrats, Simpson had signaled that the Republicans would likely back La Guardia in the fall. He wished the mayor to pay attention, and he intended to do the same: "We are not going to lose anything if we wait and listen," he insisted.[91]

By the first week in June, Simpson had recovered from arthritis and had flown to the West Coast on legal business. When he returned, there was a new problem: Copeland was gearing up for a primary challenge. In his earlier statement, Simpson had tried to dismiss the Copeland candidacy, but now he had to take it seriously. Early in the third week of July, he drafted two different versions of the Republican position. At a Board of Aldermen outing on Long Island Sound, he ran them by Joseph Clark Baldwin. One backed La Guardia, the other, Copeland. Baldwin had been treasurer of La Guardia's 1929 campaign but had grown as tired of La Guardia's "independence" as anyone. "Fiorello La Guardia has used the Republican party for twenty-four years," he told Simpson. "I'd like to see the Republican Party use La Guardia for twenty-four hours to elect some of its own capable people."[92]

Baldwin did not even take the statement supporting Copeland seriously. Simpson was probably not taking it seriously either when, on July 24th, Frederic Bellinger asked him to back Copeland in the primary. Simpson said he would not, but that he wished someone would put him in anyway. By that time, Simpson's thinking on the subject was clear. He knew that if the election was about good government, La Guardia would win. He also believed that if the election was about the New Deal, La Guardia would just as certainly win. Given this inevitability, Simpson was determined to back La Guardia, provided he was "carefully surrounded by a straight Republican ticket or its equivalent." To accomplish this, Simpson suspected that he would have to deal with the American Labor Party.[93]

It was not hard to fill out the ticket. Newbold Morris had won big in the 1936 race for president of the Board of Aldermen. Since La Guardia had campaigned for him then, he could hardly refuse to do so now. Morris was also very popular with labor. Joseph McGoldrick was a registered Democrat, but highly independent. In 1934, he was drafted from Columbia University to right city finances, succeeded, and then was elected in his own right. There were some questions about those choices. La Guardia had tired of both men and was known to be looking elsewhere. They were also both from the 15th Assembly District. Simpson could always answer that there was no reason to balance the ticket as long as the 15th Assembly District polled 45 percent of the city Republican vote. As for La Guardia's preference, much depended on how the hand was played.[94]

Simpson and La Guardia both knew that they had to begin dealing with one another, but neither would make the first move. Finally, La Guardia gave in. He and his wife Marie invited the Simpsons out for the evening of July 22. Simpson had to miss poker at the Hoyle Club for a higher stakes game. The four had dinner at the Claremont Inn and then joined a crowd of three thousand upper-crust New Yorkers at the Lewisohn Stadium to hear Fritz Reiner conduct Wagner, Beethoven, and Strauss's "Don Juan." It was hard to know who was wooing whom, however, when Simpson invited the mayor back to his house for a nightcap.[95]

La Guardia feigned disinterest and told the chauffeur to "leave the motor running." The two men sat back in the wood-paneled study, La Guardia with a whiskey and soda, Simpson sipping a glass of White Rock. After an hour of pleasantries, La Guardia volunteered that he "assumed" the Republicans would back him in the fall. Simpson expressed surprise. He countered that, given La Guardia's New Deal sympathies, Republicans would only support him if they could command the rest of the ticket. "Who?" La Guardia asked. Simpson named Morris for council president; La Guardia acted disturbed. Simpson named McGoldrick for comptroller; La Guardia protested vehemently—so vehemently, in fact, that Simpson was convinced it was all a ruse. The two had been discussing labor, and La Guardia had detected some shortcomings. As he said goodnight, La Guardia mentioned that Simpson might gain a more "practical understanding" if he met with the leaders of the American Labor Party. "If you arrange it, I'll be delighted to see them," Simpson replied.[96]

The next day Simpson conferred with the other metropolitan area county chairmen at the Union League Club on Park Avenue and 37th Street. He was unable to assuage the anticipated resentments against Upper East

Siders Morris and McGoldrick. This could not continue, Simpson realized. Republican infighting only gave leverage to La Guardia. Simpson headed over to County Headquarters at 40th Street and Fifth Avenue to face reporters. As he walked the five blocks, he came up with a plan: he would write the ticket, La Guardia would sign on, and the county leaders would have to endorse it. Simpson went in the back door and asked Gertrude Hess to summon Morris and McGoldrick. Simpson's luck held up—although it was a late Friday afternoon in late July, both men were in town and soon at his office.[97]

Simpson found McGoldrick "excitedly agreeable."[98] Morris, on the other hand, was wary. He knew La Guardia wanted Berle in his place for the next administration and was dismayed to hear that the county chiefs were against them as well. "If they don't want us, who does?" Morris asked. Simpson did, and that was enough. He stepped out of his office and announced to the reporters there that the Republican Party would be making its ticket from the bottom up.[99] One of them asked who would run for mayor. "We don't know yet," replied Simpson. Another asked, "Does La Guardia know?" "Ask him," Simpson said mischievously.[100] Lowell Limpus of the *New York Daily News* got to La Guardia first. Every inch of the mayor's 5'2" frame bristled as he denounced the move as a Tammany trick. Limpus dubbed it "the headless ticket of Kenneth Simpson." But it was no trick, and Simpson did not intend to let it become a joke. He had a lot of persuading to do.[101]

ARM TWISTING TIME

First, there was more pressure to be put on the mayor to accept the ticket. In 1933, Samuel Seabury and his supporters had never come close to establishing a functioning Fusion Party. Now they were even more disorganized. La Guardia had to have Republican support, but Berle estimated his standing with party regulars to be so low that if he was not on the ticket he would "have a bad time of it in the primaries."[102] La Guardia nevertheless remained mute, convinced that his popularity rested on his independence. Then, at one highly public event, a passport "happened" to fall out of Simpson's pocket, starting speculation about whether the seasoned traveler could again be crossing the pond. Simpson did little to stop it—he wanted La Guardia to start talking soon.[103]

Republican newspapers helped pressure the mayor. One highly influential paper was the New York *World-Telegram*. Its publisher, Roy Howard, of the Scripps-Howard chain, was a prominent liberal Republican who earlier suspected that Simpson was aligned "with the old forces." "I did everything I could to plaster him," Howard admitted later.[104] But by 1937, the paper was solidly behind Simpson. Even more noteworthy was when the conservative Republican *Herald-Tribune* came out for La Guardia.[105]

Most of the arm twisting, however, was done at close range by Simpson himself. Frederic Bellinger wrote that "he addresses his audience, whether it be one or many, while walking up and down the floor with a pipe between his teeth." One Simpson technique was to "question his hearer, continue with his story, and repeat the last sentence of his conversation fully, word for word, after each question is answered by his listener." When he was most effective, Bellinger concluded, Simpson could "sell his idea to his listener as if it were the listener's own."[106] In making his pitch, Simpson drew on a vast store of information. He could talk at length with nearly every ward politician about the intricacies of his own block. Through the passage of twenty years' time, most of the energy that had once made Simpson the "uncrowned king of Yale" remained. He customarily worked fourteen hours a day—assisted for most of them by the faithful Gertrude Hess.[107]

Within a week, all of the arm twisting had paid off. On the evening of July 29, after one final negotiating session with Simpson and Seabury, La Guardia agreed to head up the Republican ticket. Simpson made a long and complex statement proclaiming that the ticket would ensure the mayor's reelection and sound the "death knell" for Tammany Hall. La Guardia's statement was shorter; he told reporters that Simpson "has always stood for good municipal government. He has a good ticket."[108]

There was more at stake that fall than municipal government, however. In the 1936 general election, New York State voters had approved holding a constitutional convention—the first since 1894—two years hence. This posed a particular hazard for the state Republican Party. In 1894, the assembly was apportioned along "rotten borough" lines: thinly populated upstate counties had the same representation as densely populated urban counties. This gave rural, traditionally Republican voters outsized leverage in the statehouse. Just in case, the constitution also stipulated that no two counties divided by a river—meaning the solidly Democratic Kings County (Brooklyn) and New York County (Manhattan)—could hold a majority in the assembly. The New York Republicans could lose these advantages in 1938 if they lost the delegate vote in the fall.[109]

Simpson hoped that the American Labor Party might help him solve this particular problem. He had already opened talks with the ALP during the drive to get La Guardia on the Republican ticket. At a meeting on Saturday the 31st, he hoped to accomplish more. Simpson asked Stanley Isaacs to come along. "You can talk their language and I can't," he admitted.[110] That morning, Simpson and Isaacs breakfasted with labor leaders Sidney Hillman, David Dubinsky, and Alex Rose. Over bacon, eggs, and coffee the Republicans agreed to back four ALP candidates for City Council. As the meeting broke up, Simpson raised an aside. If the ALP did not run its own delegates to the constitutional convention, would it at least refrain from backing Democrats? "What constitutional convention?" Dubinsky asked. Simpson explained— but not at length—and ALP leaders agreed to the "small favor."[111]

On the taxi ride home, Simpson turned to Isaacs and said, "I've got a question to ask of you, but I don't expect you to answer it. Will you run for Borough president?" "I'm not interested," Isaacs replied. "That's what I thought you'd say," said Simpson.[112] He had, in fact, already named Isaacs and several others as potential candidates, although he had yet to lock them in. Isaacs was the easiest. Theodore Roosevelt had been a childhood hero of his, and Isaacs had long been dismayed by the rightward drift of the party. Isaacs had a background in real estate and a keen interest in the low-income housing that was important to working-class New Yorkers. Upon learning that La Guardia was behind him, Isaacs said yes.[113]

As Simpson worked to fill out the mayoral ticket, an unexpected opening appeared. In 1932, Democrat Theodore Peyser defeated Ruth Pratt for the seat representing the 17th Congressional District in the U.S. Congress that Simpson had himself once coveted. On August 8, 1937, Peyser died, putting a congressional seat in play.

Republicans everywhere took notice. They knew that it would be one of a very few congressional races that fall and that it might be a dress rehearsal for the 1938 midterm elections. Simpson wanted a new face, someone who would help give the Republican Party a less hidebound, more streamlined look. It did not take him long to find someone who fit that description. Bruce Barton was a pioneer of the modern advertising industry. He also had penned dozens of paeans to personal improvement and business success in the 1920s. His most famous work was the 1925 bestseller *The Man Nobody Knows*, which depicted Jesus Christ as history's greatest organizer and salesman. A staunch

Republican, Barton understood before almost anyone else that the bases of American politics were changing: once voters cast their ballots almost entirely based on party loyalty. Now they were selecting individual candidates largely based on personality. Barton had recently been consulting with the Republican National Committee, and he and Simpson had a mutual friend in Roy Howard.[114]

It was at a dinner party at Emory Buckner's house that Barton first confided to Simpson that "he hoped someday to run for public office."[115] At the height of the summer, Barton was vacationing in cooler climes. But Simpson soon located him on a golf course in Canada. Barton repaired to the clubhouse to learn that he was wanted to run for Congress. It might be his first campaign, but Barton was no political novice. He called Roy Howard to make sure that La Guardia was on the Republican ticket. Then he called City Hall to confirm that La Guardia was also running on the Fusion ticket and that the ALP was also running a candidate, one who would split the Democratic vote. He got the answers he wanted, called Simpson back, and accepted.[116]

Simpson and Bruce Barton talk strategy. An electoral map of the 15th Assembly District is on the wall behind them. *(Courtesy of the Yale University Manuscripts and Archives)*

More reluctant than Barton, but first on Simpson's list of Republican "new faces," was Thomas E. Dewey. Born in 1902, Dewey was a newspaper editor's son from a small town in Michigan who had first come to New York City to sing. When his voice failed during a solo recital, Dewey decided not to trust his future to the vagaries of his vocal chords. He enrolled in Columbia Law School. As even his charitable biographer put it, however, the young lawyer retained an "instinct for drama, a tenor's temperament, and an inclination to take himself, and his work, with the utmost seriousness."[117]

Dewey began ringing doorbells in Greenwich Village in 1925 and served as president of the New York Young Republican Club. In 1931, he landed a spot as Assistant U.S. Attorney for Charles Tuttle's successor, George Z. Medalie. There, he made a close study of the criminal syndicates that plagued every aspect of New York's economy. He succeeded Medalie in 1933, the youngest U.S. Attorney ever, and took on gangster Waxey Gordon. In 1935, Governor Lehman took on the job that Tammany's venal district attorneys had shirked and appointed Dewey as special prosecutor to clean up organized crime in New York City. Dewey zealously began taking apart the "rackets," prosecuting Dutch Schultz and Lucky Luciano and becoming a hero of film and radio drama as New York's legendary "gangbuster."[118]

Dewey was a natural for district attorney, but his vanity and ambition got in the way. Simpson dangled the promise of a governorship or even the presidency before Dewey's eyes, but the young prosecutor claimed not to be interested, having received an offer from John Foster Dulles at the prestigious law firm of Sullivan and Cromwell. In reality, Dewey was reluctant to take the chance—even with someone as popular as La Guardia. Medalie had warned him that if he lost at this point, his political career could be over.[119]

Others noticed Dewey's potential. Seabury had tried to get Dewey to accept a spot on the Fusion ticket. La Guardia and Berle had also tried to persuade the prosecutor, but, recalled Berle, "Dewey's vanity, always disagreeable, was working overtime." He insisted on unprecedented full control of the police department and vowed not to run until there was a "public clamor" for his candidacy.[120]

Simpson had hedged his bets by convincing Irving Ben Cooper, who had worked on the Seabury investigation, to serve as a placeholder, but he never gave up on Dewey. Nor did La Guardia. The deadline for candidates to decline nomination expired at midnight on August 10th. If Dewey entered the race after that, he and Cooper would split the field. Cooper was willing to decline, but Dewey had to commit first. La Guardia reasoned with Dewey all through dinner on the 10th, but to no avail. Then Simpson took over. Gathering at William Chadbourne's apartment, Simpson and Chadbourne again went over all of the arguments with Dewey—and allegedly poured a few drinks—while Cooper ally Billy Hecht stood by with Cooper's declination in his pocket. Just in case, Cooper was also waiting in his office across the street from the Board of Elections. Dewey finally agreed to run, provided he would not have to announce for another forty-eight hours—he did not want to appear to have

Thomas E. Dewey in the mid-1930s. *(Courtesy of Dr. Kelly Simpson)*

snatched the slot from Cooper. This was at 11:45 P.M. Hecht got Cooper on the phone. Cooper crossed the street and took himself out of the race with minutes to spare.[121]

This excellent addition to an already strong ticket should have rallied Republicans, but the county leaders still held back. La Guardia did little to help matters. Through most of August, he was unusually silent—an Achilles "sulking in his tent because he hasn't got just the ticket that he wanted," complained Simpson.[122] Simpson took a week's vacation and left the mayor alone. Further confusing the situation was the Copeland candidacy. When Simpson returned from Maine, Frederic Bellinger informed him that he had indeed put Copeland in the Republican primary. "What else can I do?" Bellinger inquired. "Take him out!" commanded Simpson.[123] Simpson hoped that La Guardia and Dewey would focus the electorate on the popular fight against corruption instead of the unpopular fight against the New Deal. In his absence, he told reporters, "some of my friends here seem to have mixed things up and are now trying to hold a national election."[124]

Copeland was in the unusual position of being a candidate in both the Republican and Democratic primaries. But by early September, his momentum had stalled. The senator never got the business backing he had hoped for, and Republicans held their noses at his Tammany running mates. Democratic support eroded after James J. Dooling, the Tammany boss who had brokered his Democratic nomination, died suddenly. Then, on September 10, John R. Crews, the canny former prizefighter and Republican leader of Kings County, finally backed the Simpson ticket. Soon thereafter the rest of the counties— with the exception of the Bronx, which had already backed Copeland—fell into line.[125]

THE CAMPAIGN

There was far less strategizing and far more work involved in the campaign; Simpson described it as an "all day-all night grind."[126] Most of Simpson's days were spent at county headquarters, although when things got too hectic there, he retreated to his law office and worked the phone. Nearly every evening brought a personal appearance in which Simpson tried to convince city Republicans that building a strong, unified party from the bottom up was as important as electing the Republican ticket. Simpson customarily began by laying out the political situation as it existed. He then painted a picture of what the Republican Party could be in 1940 and how he expected it to get there. All the while, Simpson scrutinized the faces in the room and fine-tuned the message. In the end, one political activist reported, Simpson always imparted the sense that he "anticipated reaching a certain definite goal."[127]

Still, Simpson always had to answer the critics worried more about means than ends. When Simpson backed the ALP positions on housing and civil service, outraged Republicans decried his "sell-out of Republican and American principles to [labor leader] John L. Lewis and his communistic crew." Simpson countered that the ALP's attitude was "less communistic than the community property interest that Tammany Hall has in New York City."[128]

With a Democrat running for the Republican nomination and the Republicans backing labor, the 1937 New York municipal primary was, as the *Washington Post* put it, among the "most bizarre political events ever to take place in this country."[129] But Copeland won only the Bronx, leaving La Guardia to face hapless Tammany candidate Jeremiah Mahoney in the general election. It hardly mattered when a few days after the primary, La Guardia formally enrolled in the ALP. Simpson believed that the tumultuous primary "cleared the air like a thunderstorm" and drove out all issues but "good government."[130]

Fusion proved to be much weaker than it had been in 1933, leaving the Republicans and the ALP to vie for leadership in the general election and Simpson with the difficult task of giving the campaign "a Republican rather than a labor flavor."[131] Most Republican candidates worked well together. Morris, McGoldrick, and Issacs shared headquarters and established a strong *esprit de corps*. "I am delighted with the company I am in and the fact that we really stand for something," claimed Isaacs.[132] Barton's campaign made good use of what would one day be called "photo opportunities" and expertly appealed to New York's middle class—the small businessmen and white collar workers that Barton called the "forgotten man of 1937."[133] He was, Simpson thought, "pretty much the best campaigner of any of them."[134]

There was some trepidation about how Dewey, with his chilly public personality, would do, but the gangbuster proved to be an exuberant campaigner, and he won over working-class New Yorkers with Sunday night radio spots featuring true crime stories from his career. So although the recession and La Guardia's lack of popularity on Wall Street made fundraising difficult generally, Dewey had no trouble. But he kept the money to himself. Dewey built up a completely independent campaign, establishing headquarters in each of the city's twenty-three assembly districts. By the end of the campaign, he had $130,000 stashed away. Four days before the general election, therefore, Simpson asked Dewey to provide the "walking around money" needed to get out the vote in New York County's one thousand plus precincts. "You've sopped up all the money," explained Simpson. "If I can't get that money for the district captains, and if they don't have ten dollars apiece for the captain and the co-captain, there will be nobody at the polls on Tuesday."[135] Dewey took the appeal as a threat and a personal affront. He began nursing a grudge against Simpson that he would harbor for the rest of his life.[136]

The campaign closed with a radio broadcast rally at Madison Square Garden where Simpson served as master of ceremonies. The Republican-Labor-Fusion ticket was clearly bound for victory, but the event was not all exultation and charity. The borough president of Queens—a former staunch opponent of La Guardia's—was booed off stage, despite Simpson's otherwise successful efforts, as one in attendance put it, to keep the "big enthusiastic audience in line."[137] Every candidate made his own case, but Simpson spoke for the Republicans of New York when he stated that "by courage and faith we have reclaimed New York City. We have made it unsafe for Tammany."[138]

There was a touch of frost in the air, when, at five o'clock on the morning of November 3rd, Simpson arrived at the polls. "Fine Republican weather," he told reporters. "Victory is in the air."[139] It was indeed. La Guardia polled 1,344,500 votes to Mahoney's 890,750. He carried every borough in the city and brought out 200,000 more Republicans than had voted in 1933. Charles Hilles congratulated Simpson on his "body-blow to Tammany."[140]

The only note of discord rung on election night came from Dewey. At the end of the campaign, Berle wrote, Dewey "obviously has taken his own build-up seriously,"[141] and his resentments grew along with his self-importance. On election night, Dewey begrudgingly visited the chairman at County Republican Headquarters. "Where the hell is Simpson?" he growled.[142] He was less peremptory when Simpson introduced him to the crowd as the "people's duly elected District Attorney." Dewey cautiously noted that the votes had not yet been counted. When Simpson informed Dewey that his opponent had already conceded, Dewey shook his hand and announced, "That's all I've got to say right now."[143] As they were on their way out, photographers asked for an embrace. "None of that stuff," Dewey muttered.[144]

NATIONAL COMMITTEEMAN

The election of 1937 had been a tremendous achievement for La Guardia, the first New York Fusion mayor to win two terms. It was a critical first step for Thomas Dewey, who proved to be as good a politician as prosecutor. But their political star power did not outshine the spotlight turned on the county leader who had made it all happen. Simpson had indeed crushed Tammany—it was left with only one of the fifteen votes on the city's governing Board of Estimate. Barton turned a formerly Democratic congressional district solidly Republican, and Dewey outpolled even La Guardia in New York County. These sizeable gains in the city were mostly due to the Republican alliance with labor. Unusual circumstances and exceptional skill had enabled Simpson to get labor, the core of the New Deal Democratic coalition, behind the Republicans. The *New York Post* opined that "by using its brains, [the Republican Party] has obtained a new lease on life."[145]

The consequences of the accomplishment extended beyond city boundaries. The ALP accord had worked far better than expected. Attending the constitutional convention the next summer would be 102 Republicans and 76 Democrats—reapportionment was not in the cards. This was a rare move by city Republicans that upstaters could appreciate. "For the first time in years a sympathy and a real feeling of friendliness exists between the Republican organizations upstate and the party leaders in the city," wrote the *New York Times*.[146] Simpson's reputation suddenly even transcended state boundaries—national Republicans were taking the Barton and Dewey campaigns as blueprints for 1938. Some considered the New York election a fourth strike against the New Deal chalked up in 1937. By December 11th, when Simpson joined La Guardia, Barton, and Dewey among the New York contingent at Washington's annual Gridiron Club Dinner, his place in the national party was assured.[147]

Simpson had clearly earned consideration as a candidate for the New York seat on the Republican National Committee, and even earlier Hilles planned to yield the seat to his more liberal protégé. The day after the primary, Hilles resigned his appointment. "You are now launched auspiciously," he wrote Simpson the same day, "and I wish you every possible success."[148] Right after the general election, Simpson met with some upstate leaders who also gave him their "unanimous and enthusiastic approval."[149] Newspapers like the *Daily Mirror* commented that "a dose of what Simpson gave the local Republicans would be mighty good for the droopy nationals."[150]

After the 1937 election, the *New York Daily Mirror* suggested that Simpson's treatment for the ills of the New York party might work nationally as well.

Even at this late date, Simpson was not sure whether he wanted to be a political boss or not. On one hand, he felt duty-bound to build up his law practice. On the other, he still hoped for his own elective office one day. But Simpson took this new opportunity seriously. The Republican National Committee was undergoing a traumatic change, and Simpson believed that he could help it through. In mid-December, as he traveled to Albany for the Republican State Committee meeting, his appointment seemed inevitable.[151]

At the executive committee session prior to the meeting, however, Simpson learned that not everyone agreed with his inevitability. Edwin

Jaeckle had lately been preoccupied with making an unsuccessful run for mayor of Buffalo. But now he was back. "While New York does not have the Republican vote, they nevertheless demand the party," he fumed.[152] But even Jaeckle admitted that there was no better candidate for the Republican National Committee, upstate or elsewhere. Once the state committee convened, a representative from Kings County credited Simpson for the "revival of party spirit" and placed his name in nomination. Warren Ashmead, chairman of Queens County, seconded it. Even old Samuel Koenig lauded the "infusion of new blood, new ideas, in accordance with the times." The vote was unanimous. Simpson pledged to "devote myself, in season and out of season," to the party. He insisted that Republicans would prevail when they fielded candidates "in sympathy with the needs, legitimate aspirations, and hopes of the rank and file of our citizens in these troubled times." "Personally I believe in winning elections," he concluded. "That is what I think party officials are selected for."[153]

When the news came out, Emory Buckner sent a telegram that read simply: "The man for the job and the job for the man."[154] It seemed that Kenneth Simpson had finally found his place. In a few brief years, he had chalked up one success after another in the district, the county, the city, and the state. Each time, Simpson had played a difficult hand well. But with each victory the stakes went up and the going got tougher. And the game would go on.

CHAPTER FOUR
FIGHTING FOR HARMONY

The job of a political leader is to rein in countervailing forces and direct them toward a positive end—a difficult business, since at every step from the precinct club to Congress, conflict is far easier to achieve than cooperation. Because antagonism is institutionalized within the two-party system, politicians are as insistent upon preserving "harmony" within their own party as they are on calling their bitterest partisan enemies "esteemed colleagues." That political interactions often described in military or even street-fighting terms are usually conducted with the utmost decorum is just one of the contradictions of politics.

In the late 1930s, at the height of his political career, Kenneth Simpson exemplified this and other contradictions as well. He dressed impeccably and conservatively, yet he was one of the New York Republican Party's most mercurial and liberal thinkers. He was equally comfortable at luncheon in a patrician gentlemen's club or in a basement "beefsteak" thrown by roistering party regulars. For a time, Simpson's persuasive powers, along with respect for his ideas and accomplishments, enabled him to lead a discordant band of New York Republicans through scores of his own composition. But Simpson's world was too complex and too dependent on chance and circumstance to remain in balance, and he was not enough of a diplomat to keep either his enemies or his friends in line for long. Simpson soon found himself fighting for harmony and wondering whether it was worth the effort.

THE LIFE OF THE PARTY

Age had not mellowed the hard-charging former chairman of the *Yale Daily News*, but it had thickened him. Hundreds of party dinners and society gatherings had made Simpson stocky and taken away some of his agility—he was more likely to stand firm and fight than to employ fast footwork and what

Cartoonist Leo Hirschfield captured Simpson's trademark dress perfectly, to Simpson's amusement. Hirschfield gave him the original. *(Courtesy of Dr. Kelly Simpson)*

Edmund Wilson once described as his "fast-talking Irish line." As he aged, even some of the "Irish" wore off as well. The hair that had earned Simpson the prep school nickname of "red" now showed its tinge only at the temples, although Simpson's trademark moustache still flamed—and bristled—when he was angry.[1]

If Simpson's frame showed the passage of time, his wardrobe did not. That he was a deeply conservative man, despite his politics, is evident in that he never made the transition, along with most other American men of his generation, to the sporty shirt, broad tie, and wide shouldered, double-breasted suit that marked the man about town in the thirties. Throughout the Depression decade, he kept the patterned silk shirts, high collars, and woolen suits of the Roaring Twenties, and when nearly every other American male had taken up the fedora, Simpson still sported the bowler of an earlier age. He had his clothing custom-tailored, and he was meticulous in the details—he kept his silk tie neatly fastened with a pin and his Phi Beta Kappa key draped across his vest.[2]

This fastidiousness in dress contrasted with an easy and natural sociability that was among Simpson's chief assets. He was, wrote good friend Norman Bel Geddes, "one of the most amusing men around a dinner table that I know."[3] This interpersonal virtuosity was never more evident than during early 1938 when, the triumph of the 1937 elections and a mostly united New York party behind him, Simpson worked tirelessly to consolidate the progressive gains already made. His life would not allow for a routine, and he certainly had no typical day, but Tuesday, June 7, 1938, may be considered representative at least.

The morning was cloudy, cool by the standards of a New York City June, and a breeze made the wait pleasant as Simpson caught the bus from 91st Street downtown. After putting in a few hours at his law office on Wall Street, Simpson visited with Winthrop Aldrich, the president and chairman of the board of the Chase National Bank. Rain threatened, but never came, as he stopped at the University Club for lunch and then headed back to Wall Street to call on Morgan partner Thomas W. Lamont. These conversations with the rich and powerful all had the same end: to create "a money raising committee for the party."[4] Among the many services that Simpson's mentor, Charles Hilles, had provided was to serve as a Republican fundraiser on Wall Street. Now it was his turn.

After his meeting with Lamont, Simpson went back uptown. Just days earlier, he had moved the New York County Republican headquarters from a spacious, but expensive, suite on Fifth Avenue to more affordable quarters at 54 West 40th Street, just south of Bryant Park, in an office building shared with the National Republican Club. A visitor there was surprised to have his conference with the party leader continually interrupted by phone calls that were as likely to be about books, plays, and art as they were to be about politics. That left the caller with plenty of time to study the photographs of Helen and the four Simpson children prominently displayed on the desk.[5]

Later that afternoon, eight blocks away, Simpson met with State Republican Party chairman William Murray at the Roosevelt Hotel, where topics likely included the slate for the fall elections and the New York State Constitutional Convention, then in progress. Helen and the children were traveling in Europe, so Simpson came home to a house that was empty—save for the servants—and dined modestly on fried eggs and bacon before finishing up paperwork related to the convention and then going to bed.[6]

Simpson was happier in a full house than in solitude, however, and his dinner parties provided good copy for the society pages. At a March 1938 reception for Alexander Kerensky, notables in attendance included *New York Herald Tribune* publisher Ogden Reid and New York State Supreme Court Judge Ferdinand Pecora. As a New Deal Democrat and counsel to the United States Senate Committee on Banking and Currency that had investigated Wall Street, Pecora had paved the way for the Securities and Exchange Commission and helped blacken the reputations of Wall Street financiers. "What are you doing with these economic royalists?" someone asked Pecora, using the pejorative that Franklin Roosevelt had coined in 1936. Without speaking, the judge reached to a shelf in Simpson's walnut paneled study and took down three magazines—the liberal *Nation*, the progressive *New Republic*, and the radical *New Masses*.[7] Elsewhere, a woman partygoer inquired of the host, "Isn't it strange that you should entertain a Russian Revolutionist?" "No, it isn't," Simpson quipped. "After all, Kerensky and I are almost the only Republicans left."[8]

If the political alignment of their dinner parties was difficult to discern, it was well known, as one society columnist wrote, that the Simpsons put on "one of the best and most different suppers in New York." Guests were equally impressed by then-exotic dishes like chicken chow mein and Simpson's ability to play the affable host while keeping his "pipe clamped firmly between his teeth."[9] From Simpson's perspective, such social graces paid their greatest dividend later that year when, after six months of maneuvering by his card-playing companions, Simpson won admission to New York's prestigious Players Club. He had hoped to win admittance to the exclusive theatrical club on the premise that he was a producer of sorts, claiming that "my latest show (La Guardia-Dewey-Barton) was a wow."[10] In October 1938, he was finally elected, although as a "patron of the arts."[11]

An observer may have granted some of Simpson's premise, however. During the summer of 1938, he was indeed working on some very big "shows," particularly the constitutional convention. A host of issues were under consideration as New York brought a constitution devised for a nineteenth-century agrarian state into line with twentieth-century realities. Since Simpson's 1937 victories had secured control of the convention for the Republicans and made him the single most influential Republican in the state, politicians from Buffalo to Long Island weighed in with him as they sorted through the fine print that summer. At the outset, Simpson persuaded them to put a progressive in as chair of the convention.[12] He also insisted that the Republicans not stand in the way of reasonable reforms. By far, the touchiest subject was that of reapportionment. Party leaders were understandably intent on preserving their electoral advantages, but Simpson believed that some reforms, making the assembly more reflective of recent urban and suburban growth, were inevitable and that the party would be better off guiding than fighting them. In the end, Republicans gave very little ground in the area of reapportionment.[13]

A tempest did arise when the convention considered banning the use of wiretap evidence, pitting advocates Governor Herbert Lehman and the American Labor Party against opponents Dewey and LaGuardia. Simpson worked closely with Dewey rallying Republican forces against the ban—the two manned the telephones and strategized late into the night at county headquarters. After so much time in the public spotlight, Simpson was happy to work behind the scenes during the first half of 1938. And publicity could do nothing to solve the most elemental—and frustrating—task that Simpson faced, that of providing patronage to party workers.[14]

New York City Republican Party activists were accustomed to living on crumbs, but after the 1937 election, Simpson began fielding requests from many who believed "that there would be a different attitude toward the party

than has existed for the last four years."[15] But there was not: La Guardia controlled more than 90 percent of the city's patronage, and he joined the American
Labor Party shortly after the 1937 primaries, leaving Simpson to despair that
he could provide no patronage because he did not "know any Communists
or A.L.P. members."[16] "To win an election in theory and actually have no
jobs to distribute is the worst possible pass to be in," Simpson lamented. To
complicate things, the La Guardia administration stubbornly adhered to its
"good government" promises. Stanley Isaacs, for example, insisted on putting
qualified engineers into posts that Tammany had always staffed with politicos.
The district attorney's office also raised the bar to officeholders. The idealist
in Simpson understood this, but the practical politician in him was no less
frustrated. Simpson estimated that it would take two or three hundred jobs
to satisfy loyal party workers. "He never got a quarter of what he though he
ought to have as a minimum," recalled Dewey.[17]

NOT A SECOND TIME

Having already established a reputation as the smartest of city politicians,
Simpson now had to prove that he was much more than that. The 1938 "midterm" congressional elections were critical for both parties because they set
the terms for the 1940 presidential race. The party in power usually lost some
ground in the mid-terms—for the Democrats it was most important not to lose
too much. The Republicans, on the other hand, hoped not only to gain seats
in Congress but to do so in a way that established some principles and a viable
national electoral strategy for 1940.

Simpson had already laid down some fundamental principles for the
party. These were essentially a modified form of populism that blended
the "common man" ethos of the New Deal and the "self-reliance" tenets
of Republicanism. Orthodox Republicans assumed that voters had been
deluded by New Deal sophistry, but Simpson insisted that they were "a whole
lot smarter than some politicians give them credit for."[18] He argued that party
leaders had extended the idea of rugged individualism to the point that it
hurt, rather than helped, working people. He believed that the party itself had
been "betrayed" by "those in whose hearts and minds there is no compassion
or thought for the man on the street."[19] Voters, Simpson believed, had justifi-
ably abandoned the hidebound, slavishly pro-business Republican Party for
the only viable alternative.

On one occasion, standing at the window of county headquarters and looking down at workers in Bryant Park, Simpson commented that "those men are worth more to us than all the millionaires I know who live on Long Island half the year."[20] Whether the "us" he referred to was the nation or the party is not clear, but it could well have been the latter. In the late 1930s, most political analysts took for granted that working-class votes would go to the Democrats. Simpson believed that this might not be the case and could cite precedent. In the late nineteenth century, British Prime Minister Benjamin Disraeli had created a majority coalition for his Conservative Party by taking the unlikely step of enfranchising working people who, despite assumptions to the contrary, turned out to be tories at heart. Simpson believed that old-stock American working people were no less conservative and so encouraged legislation that would bind working people to the Republican Party. In early 1938, for example, he backed a bill providing for low cost insurance to be sold through New York State savings and loans. But Simpson was still new to the larger political arena—in early 1938 he had yet to set foot inside the state-house in Albany—and if his principles were universal, his electoral strategy was not.[21]

Simpson had good reason to believe that utilizing the Republican-American Labor Party alliance a second time might be a viable option. Statewide, the Democrats badly needed labor votes to win offices, but in the convention and in the legislature the ALP was still working with the Republicans. "Not in many years, indeed, has the outlook in a campaign year seemed less favorable to the Democrats," wrote the *Christian Science Monitor*.[22] But others saw trouble ahead. In May, Republican National Committee secretary William Hard warned Simpson that party regulars would not stand for continued cooperation with the ALP. A year earlier, Hard had believed that local alliances and national issues could be successfully compartmentalized. But now, he maintained, the situation had changed. Simpson shrugged off the advice, assuring Hard that any alliance with labor would be "made for the duration of the campaign."[23]

More than anything else, Simpson wished to preserve the gains made in 1937. He hoped to ensure that Bruce Barton, who had won only an interim congressional seat, would get his own full term. Simpson also wanted to help his friend Frederic Coudert win a seat in the State Senate. At the time, Simpson could see no reason not to enlist the help of labor. He opened talks in

June, and by the end of July, he had made arrangements covering twenty-five assembly districts and seven senatorial districts in Manhattan and Brooklyn. Simpson described them privately as amounting to "armed neutrality" in districts that were in play for the Republicans and outright cooperation only in overwhelmingly Democratic districts.[24]

But the ALP drove a harder bargain than Simpson realized. Labor agreed to run a New Deal candidate against Coudert—that would split the Democratic vote. It promised to do the same in the 17th Congressional District—that would return Barton to the House. In exchange, Simpson promised to cooperate with the ALP in the 16th Congressional District, where it hoped to make short work of Democratic Representative John J. O'Connor. Simpson might have seen this as an advantageous exchange of two seats for one. He did not count on Franklin Roosevelt putting the O'Connor race in the national spotlight.[25]

By the late 1930s, Franklin Roosevelt's toughest opponents were not Republicans but conservative Democrats dismayed by the growth of national power at the expense of the states. A series of setbacks, culminating in the defeat of his Executive Reorganization Bill in 1938, prompted Roosevelt to tackle the problem head on. In June 1938 he set out to work for the defeat of opponents within his own party. This unprecedented and politically unpopular move was quickly branded—in terms that evoked the tactics of European dictatorships—Roosevelt's "purge."

All but one of the Democrats targeted were Southerners and therefore unlikely to fall. The national spotlight, therefore, quickly turned to New York's John J. O'Connor. Roosevelt was particularly troubled by O'Connor who was from his home state, was the powerful chairman of the House Rules Committee, and had declared himself at odds with almost all recent Roosevelt initiatives, particularly the Reorganization Bill. The New Dealers put their own candidate, James H. Fay, into the race against O'Connor and required only that the Republicans split the conservative vote by running their own candidate as well.[26]

Simpson called the decision to go along "a tough one," and he waited as long as he could to make it. He claimed to have weighed a number of factors. For one thing, Simpson insisted, the Republican Party could not "present a constructive and intelligent opposition" on the basis of "hate Roosevelt."[27] There was also the opportunity to launch another political career. In mid-

July, Simpson asked conservative Republican John Burke to make the run against O'Connor. This could have been seen as a friendly gesture, for Burke was an opponent of Simpson's. More likely, Burke considered it an affront, since his enmity was based on the alliance with labor that Simpson asked him to be a party to. Burke refused, voicing the widely popular sentiment that Republicans should support O'Connor.[28]

By the end of July, O'Connor was under attack and appealing to Republican voters for help. Simpson was clearly not going to offer any, somewhat gratuitously insisting that despite his recent opposition to the Reorganization Bill, O'Connor was "100 percent New Dealer."[29] Letters from resentful Republicans began pouring into Simpson's office, and it became clear that the rank and file Republicans refused to be party to the purge and would support O'Connor. In August, Simpson tried to put a good face on a bad deal. He persuaded Allen Dulles, partner in the prestigious law firm of Sullivan and Cromwell, to join his stable of hand-picked candidates. Dulles was a fine choice, a Princeton-educated former diplomat and international lawyer destined to become the first civilian director of the Central Intelligence Agency. But it was an empty gesture: the 16th was a solidly Democratic district, and Dulles never had any intention of serving in Congress. Perhaps admirably, perhaps foolishly, Simpson kept up his end of the bargain. "It was a very difficult decision for Ken to make and I hope he will not suffer in consequence," wrote Charles Hilles. "I know he is striving to do the right thing."[30]

Intentions meant nothing to Simpson's critics, however. A *Daily Mirror* editorial threatened that "by knifing O'Connor, you'll go down with him, Mr. Simpson."[31] During the late summer, in fact, Simpson became a rallying point for diverse groups of conservative Republicans. In mid-September, one of these, calling itself "The Women's Rebellion against New Deal Taxation," described by one newspaper as a handful of debutants and "socially prominent young matrons," picketed Simpson's office. They remained just long enough to get their pictures taken and then they picked up their lap dogs, got in their limousines, and went back up town.[32]

Dulles also went back up town rather than to Washington, for although O'Connor lost the Democratic primary, in a stinging rebuke to Simpson, Republicans elected him over Dulles in the Republican contest. The 16th was a Democratic district, however, and O'Connor's career was over. Simpson's complicity in this defeat was all the more distressing because everywhere else in the nation, the President's purge had failed. Ever the optimist, Roosevelt described the outcome in terms that Simpson would have well understood: "Harvard lost the schedule but won the Yale game."[33] Simpson had made a fatal mistake for a political leader—he had gotten too far ahead of his constituency. And despite repeated insistence that standing with the ALP on local issues was not the same as standing with it on national issues, he had failed to realize that a senatorial race, particularly one involving such an important senator as O'Connor, was a national issue.[34]

A *New York Daily Mirror* cartoon comments on Simpson's ill-fated compliance with the purge of Congressman John J. O'Connor.

The fact that the ALP deals were secret—if only open secrets—elicited resentment over Simpson's highhanded approach: he was looking too much like a "boss" for Republican tastes. The deals also revived old concerns about Simpson's reputation for radicalism, one that threatened to detach him from the constituency that he needed most—the financial elite. "It would seem that the articulate elements of the party from Wall Street to the National Republican Club feel that I am studiously trying to turn the party over to the sinister forces of communism," Simpson wrote to Alf Landon, only half in jest.[35] After the election, Simpson ended up resigning from the National Republican Club and was blackballed from the super exclusive Union League Club, both bastions of Wall Street conservatism. At the outset, the labor deal seemed far too easy not to make; in the end, it was far too costly to live down.[36]

FIGHT IN THE 15TH

Simpson could survive outside the rarefied atmosphere of the Union League Club as long as his grassroots were secure. But critic Bronson Trevor had been hard at work pulling them up. Trevor, a backer of Royal Copeland in 1937, was the well-to-do grandson of an investment banker and a nephew of U.S. Senator Bronson Cutting. Trevor acquired his uncle's taste for politics but seemed to prefer sniping from the sidelines to elective office. In September 1938, Trevor's well-financed fingers knit the diverse and growing ranks of Simpson opponents into an opposition slate of delegates to the Republican State Committee: Trevor himself challenged Simpson for his spot on the state executive committee.[37]

Trevor launched his campaign with an open letter to Simpson that attacked his "secret deal" with the American Labor Party and his opposition to O'Connor. Mass mailings were expensive, but Trevor could afford it. "He simply flooded the district with literature, telegrams, and letters denouncing Simpson," recalled Frederic Bellinger.[38] Among the signatories to Trevor's missives were such groups as The Republican Committee for John J. O'Connor and American Principles of Government, the New York Chapter of the National Republican Builders (headed by John Burke), the Republicans against LaGuardia Committee, and the Women's Rebellion against New Deal Taxation.[39]

Simpson joked that voters "don't know what to think when they get a letter from the Committee for Republican Virginity, or whatever it is," but he also began mobilizing to resist the challenge.[40] Bellinger, Trevor's erstwhile ally in the Copeland cause, took charge of Simpson's primary effort, doing his best to counter the flood of adverse publicity. Simpson also counted on support from the influential friends that Trevor had written into his ticket. Bruce Barton, Charles Hilles, State Senator Abbott Low Moffatt, Frederic Coudert, and Walter Mack all publicly disavowed any support for Trevor, and as the primary approached, each of them worked behind the scenes to convince New York County voters to stick with Simpson. Simpson got 2,400 votes to Trevor's 1,900—it was a surprisingly close vote, with Simpson losing twelve precincts in his own 15th Assembly District.[41]

The fall 1938 primary had been exhausting, and it helped convince Simpson that he had to lighten his load. On September 27, he announced his resignation as leader of the 15th Assembly District. It was "the only political job I ever really wanted," he confided to a colleague, "and the first one I had to give up."[42] Overwork was one factor: about that time he wrote a friend that "the discharge of my many political obligations has required virtually all of my time and efforts, frankly to the impairment of my health, my disposition, my family life, and my law business."[43] But it is also likely that Simpson hoped that this would be seen as a gesture of good faith by at least a few of his critics. In January 1939, Simpson was succeeded as leader of the 15th Assembly District by Frederic Coudert.[44]

Two months later, dignitaries and friends presented Simpson with a plaque recognizing his leadership during "five of the hardest years in the history of the Republican Party" and signed by 125 members of the 15th A.D. Republican Club. The inscription stated that under Simpson's "leadership the Republican Party has been reborn. It is again the progressive, militant organization that its founders hoped it would be."[45] Attending were an illustrious assembly of people who owed much to Simpson. City Councilmen Newbold Morris and Joseph Clark Baldwin were there, as was State Senator Moffatt and U.S. Congressman Barton. The district attorney, however, was absent. Busy with a "solid afternoon of engagements," he sent a telegram instead.[46] It was a sure sign that by then much had changed between Ken Simpson and Tom Dewey.

KINGMAKING AND ITS COST

In the fall of 1938, a great deal happened very quickly. Simpson had been wounded in the primary, but he remained the single most influential

Simpson with family in March 1938, after receiving an honorary plaque from the members of the 15th A.D. Republican Club. *(Courtesy of the Yale University Manuscripts and Archives)*

Republican leader in the state and believed that one big win would make most Republicans forget all about O'Connor. Simpson still hoped to capture the governorship and extend his liberalizing program statewide, and he believed that he had the candidate to do that. It was a matter of mutual convenience. Thomas Dewey wanted the office very badly, and so long as Simpson appeared to hold the key to electoral success, Dewey was happy to throw in with him. It was a precarious alliance, however.[47]

Dewey's meteoric rise from special prosecutor to national hero had made him difficult to live with. That summer, vacationing in the mountains of Virginia, Dewey was incensed when only one of the locals recognized him and no one asked for an autograph. Comfortably back in New York, Dewey began planning next steps. As early as June, he confided to Simpson that he hoped to run for governor.[48]

Most party insiders considered Dewey too inexperienced. Further, influential lawyer Richard Scandrett wrote Simpson, it would be "extremely bad politics" for Dewey to abandon the district attorney's office so soon.[49] Party leaders also had qualms about Dewey's character. "I think Dewey may go fairly far in public affairs, unless his political ambitions should warp his judgment," Hilles wrote, clearly implying that the latter was a distinct possibility.[50]

Through the first half of 1938, Dewey concealed his aspirations and kept on gang busting. In late May, he formally charged Brooklyn Tammany boss James J. Hines of conspiring with gangster Dutch Schultz, content in the knowledge that the case would make his star shine all the brighter. Dewey had little choice but to wait: popular New Deal governor Herbert Lehman was considered unbeatable. That changed in mid-July when Royal S. Copeland died, opening up a U.S. Senate seat that Lehman would almost certainly go after. There began almost immediately a carefully orchestrated "draft" campaign, and the *Christian Science Monitor* announced that, should Dewey convict Hines, "he can get any political office in New York State that he wants."[51]

By early September, Hines appeared to be on his way to conviction, and Republicans were confident that Dewey could win the governorship. Then, while cross examining a minor witness, Dewey made reference to a subject that Judge Ferdinand Pecora had ruled out of bounds. Pecora declared a mistrial, and suddenly Dewey's prospects were in doubt. Simpson was sympathetic. He had done almost the same thing in 1926 during the Daugherty trial, although a mistrial had been narrowly averted. Two days working the telephone convinced him that New York voters were also sympathetic towards Dewey, blaming the mistrial on Pecora instead. Buffalo boss Edwin Jaeckle agreed. A few days before the Republican Convention convened at Saratoga Springs, he pronounced Dewey "stronger with the people now than he was before."[52]

Dewey may have been the star of the Saratoga Springs Convention, but it was mostly a Simpson production. On September 27, a train carrying the New York County delegation headed north to the upstate resort town. Simpson spent the five-hour trip strategizing with Dewey mentor and former States Attorney George Medalie, who was managing the Dewey campaign. When the train arrived that evening, Simpson emerged wearing a three-inch "Dewey for Governor" button. The delegates formed ranks behind a band and paraded across Saratoga Springs to the Grand Union Hotel, a gilded age edifice in the middle of town that served as convention headquarters.[53]

The next day Bruce Barton opened the convention and Jaeckle, chairman of the rules committee, presented a moderate party platform, establishing early that the reformers would direct the party that fall. The real work of the convention, however, was done that night as Simpson darted from room to room—occasionally hunkering down for a time in his own suite—cutting deals with the state's most influential leaders. The convention was rife with rumors that Lehman, under heavy pressure from Roosevelt, might decide to run again, but Simpson ignored them and put through his entire slate of candidates, with Dewey at the top. In his exuberance, he promised to hold the Democratic margin in New York City to 500,000 votes.[54]

On September 29, Dewey arrived at the convention hall under motorcycle escort. That evening, Simpson stood before the assembled delegates and, under floodlights and flashbulbs and over shouts, cheers, and ringing cowbells, introduced the 1936 nominee, Judge William F. Bleakley who, by tradition, was to nominate Dewey. The exultations of the convention delegates were audible to Republicans statewide as Dewey's acceptance speech was broadcast live over the radio. It was a bad sign when the broadcasters dropped the feed from Saratoga Springs to run news of British Prime Minister Neville Chamberlain's agreement with Nazi Germany regarding the annexation of Czechoslovakian territory. It was worse news when the next day, just as Chamberlain was announcing "peace for our time" on the tarmac at London's Croydon Airport, Herbert Lehman announced that he would run for reelection as governor.[55]

Plenty of Republicans, therefore, left Saratoga Springs more concerned than optimistic. Dewey resented what he saw as Simpson's attempts to share the glory that was rightly his. "He embraced me to the point of almost choking me," Dewey recalled.[56] Other Republican leaders bristled under Simpson's heavy-handed management of the convention. "Simpson failed to handle the standpatters very tactfully," wrote columnists Joseph Alsop and Robert Kintner, who predicted that if Dewey lost, "the standpatters will gang up on him."[57]

The campaign, heavy on confidence and light on substance, set the pattern for all subsequent Dewey efforts. Dewey used radio skillfully and, as he done the year before, kept a tight focus on Democratic incompetence and corruption, although his running mate allowed some veiled anti-Semitism—directed at the Jewish Lehman—to creep into his campaign. The night before the polls opened, Simpson, perhaps a bit worried, wrote to Dewey that "win, lose or draw, I want you to know that I think you have put up the most intelligent, as well as the most dramatic and dynamic campaign that I have ever been associated with."[58]

Statehouse reporter Warren Moscow was closer to the mark when he called it a "cute campaign" that paid no attention to actual issues.[59]

The 1938 midterm election was a great event for the Republican Party nationwide. The sit-down strikes and the court-packing incident helped, but it was the "Roosevelt recession" that convinced middle-class voters that the Democrats could not deliver on their promise to restore lasting prosperity to the nation. The result was a midterm bounce much larger than usual, as the Republicans cut the Democratic majority from 229 to 93 in the House and from 56 to 42 in the Senate. Some new Republican faces emerged, like Senator Robert Taft and Governor John Bricker in Ohio and thirty-one-year-old Governor Harold Stassen in Minnesota, who seemed to promise a way out of the party's dead end. Thomas E. Dewey also made the news, but not for winning.

Relatively speaking, the New York Republicans did very well. In 1932, the Democrats won the governorship by an 850,000 vote margin. In 1936, they won by a 525,000 vote margin. In 1938, Lehman's margin was a razor-thin 64,000 votes. The Republican Party actually polled more votes than the Democrats; it was the American Labor Party that elected Lehman. And— almost immediately—fingers began pointing at New York County where the vote for Dewey had been unusually low and the margin for Lehman, at 681,000 votes, had been higher than Simpson promised.

Simpson, hard pressed to explain the vote, condemned La Guardia's failure to support Dewey, complained that the anti-Semitism charges had lost the Jewish vote, and noted that many New Yorkers preferred to have Dewey as district attorney rather than governor.[60] Later, Simpson offered yet another explanation: Republican weakness on international issues. "Very frankly," he stated, "what lost us the election was the emergence on the international scene of another man with a moustache."[61]

There was some validity to all of these explanations, but a growing majority of New York Republicans cared more that Simpson had been unable to carry his own backyard, and had allowed their candidate to be defeated by the very group—the ALP—that he had cooperated with in other races. And no one could forget Simpson's pledge to hold New York City's margin below the 500,000 vote mark. If he had done it, Dewey would have won.

Upstaters who had taken little notice of the O'Connor debacle held Simpson personally responsible for Dewey's loss. That, as one scholar put it, "shattered the brief era of good feelings" and ended the expansion of

Simpson's influence in New York State.[62] Having decided that Simpson's usefulness was at an end, Dewey went looking for someone else to help him. He had met Ed Jaeckle for the first time on the stage at Saratoga Springs, and he was impressed.[63]

COMMITTEEMAN

For Simpson, everything was suddenly more difficult, and clarifying his status on the Republican National Committee (RNC) had been difficult enough already. Very little had happened since Simpson was nominated in late 1937. In June, his membership, along with that of two other replacements, Californian William F. Knowland and Connecticut businessman Samuel F. Pryor, was approved—pending action of full committee. By fall, that action had not been taken. Simpson was annoyed and let RNC chairman John Hamilton know it.[64]

Simpson's standing with the party veterans on the RNC plummeted as opposition in New York increased. On November 15, the *New York Times* gave coverage to a letter that John Burke sent to Simpson accusing him of "stupid leadership."[65] Simpson tried to maintain his equanimity in the face of such remarks, attributing them to "extremists, 100 per centers and viewers with alarm." They would always be there, Simpson insisted, and "perhaps we couldn't do without them."[66] Although the charges and the critics were many, the issue was fundamental. As Dewey observed later, Simpson "was asserting leadership for the whole city which was traditional in Tammany Hall, but the Republicans regarded themselves as barons in their own bailiwicks."[67] Trying to bring the party together in such a highhanded way—and failing—helped ensure that Simpson would be torn apart.

While the architect of the ticket took a beating, the losing candidate came out ahead: journalist William Allen White even likened Dewey's 1938 defeat to the 1858 Senate loss that helped make Abraham Lincoln President. Dewey wasted no time in jettisoning his liberal baggage. As recently as the summer of 1938, he had hoped to get ALP backing in the gubernatorial contest; now Dewey began looking farther to the right for support. Everywhere he found cooperative Republican leaders alienated by Simpson's lack of diplomacy, resentful about perceived patronage slights, or just keenly aware of the new realities. He also began meeting once a week with Jaeckle.[68]

Having failed as a kingmaker and saddled with a radical reputation,

Simpson no longer appeared to be New York's best choice for the RNC; some worried that the committee might reject his nomination entirely. A few were determined not to give it the option: a group of county leaders intent on rescinding the nomination called a state committee meeting for November 28. But when the executive committee met in Albany, the consensus was by no means clear; instead, Sprague, Jaeckle, and Griffiths bargained with Simpson, who vowed not to stray from the party line should he be seated on the RNC. Jaeckle placed a call to John Hamilton in Washington, D.C., informed him that the Republican State Committee planned to nominate Simpson, and asked if he would be seated. Despite concerns that he might be a "trouble-maker," Hamilton gave his assurance.[69]

At the Republican State Committee meeting that followed, upstaters Rolland Marvin and Thomas R. Broderick moved to rescind the Simpson nomination. This was defeated by downstate county leaders John R. Crews and Russel Sprague, who moved that the State Committee recommend Simpson for a spot on the RNC executive committee. New York had usually merited a seat on this committee: Simpson mentor Charles Hilles had sat on it for decades. That initiative was turned back as the majority—but not Dewey backers Sprague and Jaeckle—joined Marvin and Broderick in opposi-tion. The issue of Simpson and the RNC seemingly resolved, Jaeckle took his reward. Reporting that Dewey had requested it, Simpson, Sprague, and Crews put Jaeckle through as the new chairman of the executive committee.[70]

The turn of events in Albany strongly suggests that Jaeckle had made a deal with Simpson. Although there was inevitably some rivalry between the state's strongest county leaders, Simpson had little reason not to back Jaeckle—a fellow progressive—for executive committee chairman. As he rode an early morning milk train back to New York City, Simpson thought little about that deal. Instead, he thought about that RNC executive commit-tee seat that it seemed he might be denied.[71]

Herbert Hoover had not been happy when Hilles resigned from the RNC and tapped Simpson to succeed him. Now stronger politically than he had been since leaving office, Hoover appeared to be intent, if not on regaining the presidency, then on engineering the nomination of a conservative who would redeem his reputation and his legacy. As Simpson put it, "he is not apparently content with waiting for the vindication which he deserves and which will one day come to him from the pens of historians."[72] It appeared to Simpson that Hoover—a New Yorker—had been lobbying the state committeemen and perhaps national committeemen as well. This was not as outlandish as it might seem. As one Republican leader wrote of Hoover, "He's like a red Indian. You never see him. All you see is a flickering in the bushes, and you know he's been there."[73] Back in New York City on the morning of November 29, Simpson caught a plane for Washington, D.C., where the RNC was to meet in just hours. He had been up all night.[74]

The RNC leadership found the situation just as perplexing as Simpson did. Long-time member Ruth Pratt was also up for the open seat, but a contest between her and Simpson would have created the spectacle of an outright test of whether the RNC was liberal or conservative. Pratt did not force the issue, but Simpson posed a bigger problem. Party regulars were griping about his so-called radical ties, and if he might be troublesome on the RNC, what would he be on the executive committee? The obvious solution was to put off Simpson and give the seat instead to party veteran Daniel Hastings of Delaware who had been waiting for it. Simpson appears to have understood that this might be the case. That, the pressures of the previous day in Albany, and a night spent worrying might explain what happened next.

The meeting was set to begin at 10:00 A.M. Simpson arrived a few minutes before ten out of breath and ran into reporters in the lobby of the hotel. He granted them what he called a "hasty interview" that was really more of an inflammatory statement. The Republican Party, Simpson told the delighted reporters, must rid itself of "reactionary influences of the past," naming specifically Herbert Hoover and the American Liberty League. "If we turn toward reaction we might as well fold up. If we look forward we cannot miss in 1940," he insisted. Then a reporter brought up "party harmony," a theme that Hamilton and other RNC leaders had been emphasizing. "We'll have harmony, damn it, if we have to fight for it," Simpson snapped.[75]

The contents of Simpson's "hasty interview" were unknown to RNC leaders, who delayed the opening of the meeting so that they could convince him to drop his bid. Simpson may have had some supporters, but he bowed to the inevitable and did as he was asked. The RNC awarded the executive committee's "Eastern" opening to the conservative Hastings, who was "balanced" by a South Dakota liberal. After the meeting, Hamilton called it a "happy medium." A chastened Simpson told reporters that "what was done was done in the interest of party harmony."[76]

Simpson in fighting stance during the late 1930s. *(Courtesy of the Yale University Manuscripts and Archives)*

The RNC made something of a prophet out of Simpson and indicated that Republicans had learned nothing during their years in the wilderness. Hastings, nicknamed "Du Pont Dan" in recognition of his subservience to Delaware's biggest business and ruling family, stood "as far to the right as the American political front extends," commented the *Washington Post*.[77] Columnist Arthur Krock called him "a heritage from the Harding-Coolidge era."[78] In truth, ideology probably had little to do with the choice. Hastings had been promised the seat—and in a conservative organization the conservative thing to do was to give it to him. This made Simpson no less determined to shake up the party for its own sake. "I went down there looking for a seat on the executive committee and came back without a seat, but with an issue," he wrote Richard Scandrett.[79] Hoover had an issue as well. A few weeks later, at a party given by councilman Joseph Clark Baldwin, Simpson spotted the former President sitting among admirers and walked over to shake his hand. Hoover expected Simpson to apologize first—he sat on his hands and looked the other way.[80]

THE BREAK

Politicians need friends—the more influential the better. It was bad enough that out of pique and principle Simpson had alienated Herbert Hoover, the most influential of the old party leaders; he had also become increasingly estranged from Tom Dewey, the most influential of the young. Knowing Dewey's temperament, Simpson should have been more careful, but he considered Dewey to be a political lightweight and showed it. In a condescending letter sent right after the 1937 election, Simpson told Dewey that "you have won a great victory and I am confident that you will not temper it with inadvertent errors of judgment."[81] Although letters like this can hardly have helped further the friendship, the two worked well together through most of 1938.[82]

But the hard feelings emerged again after the nomination at Saratoga Springs where Simpson, complained Dewey, "accepted full credit for it and was, as usual, out in front in the newspapers."[83] After the election, Dewey nursed a grievance similar to the one over "walking around money" in 1937, claiming that at the last minute Simpson had demanded appointment as district attorney. This is highly unlikely, however. New York's governor seldom appointed district attorneys, and Simpson had never expressed any interest in such an office. Dewey, on the other hand, had confided to others that he might try to buy Simpson's cooperation with such an offer.[84]

Simpson had made a lot of mistakes in 1938, and he evidently numbered furthering the aspirations of Tom Dewey among them, particularly when Dewey, having failed in his gubernatorial bid, decided to run for President. The possibility had been raised as early as the November 1938 RNC meeting, and it was assumed that Simpson would back Dewey. Instead, he pointedly reminded reporters that Dewey was still district attorney and that "he will do that job exclusively for the next four years."[85]

Dewey had no such intention. He was intent only on winning the Hines retrial and positioning himself for a presidential bid. He accomplished the former in February 1939, and in furtherance of the latter vowed privately never to jeopardize his reputation again by trying another case in court. Hearing this made Simpson all the more determined to find someone besides Dewey, and word got around. At a March 1939 "Inner Circle" dinner at the Waldorf-Astoria, New York City reporters staged one skit focusing on Dewey's presidential aspirations and another portraying Simpson and upstate publisher Frank Gannett in search of another, more suitable presidential candidate. This split in the New York ranks was troubling, so a New York congressman sponsored a "harmony dinner" in Washington intended to "settle differences" between the two. Dewey did not attend.[86]

During the last year, Simpson had continued to develop a political position well to the left of the Republican mainstream. Along with insisting that Republicans should respect the good that highly rational "average voters" found in the New Deal, he also elaborated a coherent critique of the party's deeper ills. He saw the problem as being with the "Republican psyche." Party leaders, he believed, were preoccupied with trying to convince the American public that they had not been responsible for the Great Depression. Emblematic of this, he believed, was Hoover's attempt to reassert his influence. Simpson was convinced that until the Republicans gave up this fruitless quest, theirs would never again become the majority party. As he put it in a well-publicized upstate newspaper exchange in January 1939, "since 1932 a lot of water has gone over the dam and some of it is never coming back."[87]

Simpson was alarmed, therefore, when during the first week of February, he returned from a two-week cruise with Helen to find a circular waiting in the mail. The flyer, which had gone to Republicans nationwide, featured both

Dewey and Hoover and the theme "The March to Victory in 1940 Starts." "It looks like a campaign document," Simpson wrote to Dewey. Simpson told Dewey that Hoover remained politically unpopular and that he was more interested in personal vindication than in building up the party. Simpson also reminded Dewey what the New Deal had accomplished and how much the electorate—even potential Republican voters—valued its reforms. "Should a course of conduct be followed now," he asked, "which would give these millions the possibility of speculating that a Republican victory in 1940 would mean—a return to 1932?"[88]

Dewey's answer was to join Hoover at the head table at the National Republican Club's annual Lincoln Day dinner, where the conservative crowd reserved its only standing ovations for the new and unlikely duo. Later in the evening, Ruth Pratt, who did not confuse personal relationships with politics, escorted Simpson over to "meet" Hoover. The former President "very graciously" shook Simpson's hand, although he was careful to see that no reporters or photographers were around. The press continued to chronicle the unlikely alliance of the old war horse and the young Galahad: Dewey dined at home with Hoover on March 13.[89]

Dewey had already ended his dalliance with Simpson "liberalism." He now believed that it was time to decisively end Simpson's brief leadership of the New York State Republican Party. Characteristically, Dewey did it by indirection, choosing as his venue the annual Legislative Correspondents' Association dinner in Albany. On March 23, 1939, New York State politicians and journalists gathered to poke fun at one another off the record. At a table near the head of the room sat the most distinguished of the guests—Herbert Lehman, Fiorello La Guardia, and Tom Dewey among them. At the next table over were the big county leaders: Ed Jaeckle, Rolland Marvin, Russel Sprague, John Crews, and Simpson. The politicians provided speeches, but the journalists provided the skits that were usually the most memorable features of the dinners. The year 1939 was obviously Dewey's—the reporters entitled the program "Knighty-Knighty—or a Michigan Yankee in King Herbert's Court" and told a humorous story of a Boy Scout hitchhiker's odyssey from Owosso, Michigan, to Washington, D.C.[90]

Dewey was universally disliked by reporters, so the skits portrayed him as conceited and dictatorial. One parody song, ostensibly sung by Dewey, carried the refrain, "arrogance, that's me."[91] Dewey took the jabs with the requisite good nature and then stepped to the dais to deliver a few jabs of his own, directed not at reporters but at Simpson. Like all of his speeches, this one had been the result of hard labor—Dewey had personally revised a number of drafts, and although he usually crafted an impressive presentation with as little substance as possible, in this case he drafted some deceptively light remarks that actually said a great deal.[92]

Dewey started with a few lighthearted digs at Lehman and La Guardia before getting to Simpson. A joke about Simpson's kidnapping La Guardia's American Labor Party was entirely within the bounds of propriety, but then Dewey got personal. He established the premise that "Ken is really a very nice fellow—in between his speeches" and then observed that "the only trouble with Ken is that he doesn't suffer from laryngitis at the right time." He referred to the attention that the newspapers had given his alliance with Hoover and said, "As a matter of fact, we were negotiating a deal. Mr. Hoover finally agreed to send all of his old collars to Ken Simpson. We both hope they don't choke him."[93]

Statehouse reporter Warren Moscow watched as the dignitaries shifted uneasily in their chairs and Simpson "sat silent, white with rage."[94] Later that night, Simpson took another long and dejected train ride down the Hudson. He was in the habit of leaving late night notes for Helen, who could hardly have been expected to keep his nocturnal schedule. In the early morning of March 24 he wrote, "Believe it or not, Tom Dewey went out of his way, in his speech last night, to make particularly unfriendly if not hostile cracks at me—under the thinly veiled guise of humor."[95] Simpson went to bed believing that Dewey had done it just to get in with upstaters—he was not yet willing to admit that Dewey had tried to read him out of the New York State party that night.

UNEASY PEACE

As the full import of Dewey's remarks became clear, New York Republicans began to choose sides. Within the week, leaders of New York City's 11th A.D. Republican Club put through a resolution endorsing Simpson for reelection to the county chairmanship "in case anyone wanted to start a primary fight."[96] Early in May, the 17th A.D. Republicans followed suit. These were skirmishes in a coordinated counteroffensive; the first battle came in the highly conservative National Republican Club. In late April, Simpson ally Walter Mack ran for president against incumbent John R. Davies, a veteran municipal court judge who stood for "100 percent Republicanism."[97] Columnist Arthur Krock noted that Republicans nationwide seemed to take an interest all "out of proportion to the apparent political equation"—but not when it was understood that this was really a contest between what Krock called "Hoover Republicans" and "Simpson Republicans."[98] Unfortunately, in this hotbed of Hooverism, Mack was soundly defeated.

It was more auspicious when, in late May, the New York County Republican Committee passed a resolution validating the labor party alliances of previous years and giving its leader a personal vote of confidence. Simpson took the opportunity to make yet another plea for liberal Republicanism. "Let's not fool ourselves," he said. "We must accept as sound and valid many of the major principles of social reform that recently have been established."[99] Simpson did what was necessary to shore up his base, even shutting off patronage—what patronage there was—to the 5th Assembly District, one of two that continued to consistently vote against him. Having shown some strength, Simpson held out an olive branch of sorts, suggesting that he would back Dewey in the upcoming presidential race.[100]

Bronson Trevor was not paying attention though. He prepared once again to go after Simpson, who seemed far weaker now than he had been a year earlier. Trevor formed a "1940 Republican Victory Committee" and by the first week in June had sent out 15,000 circulars announcing an anti-Simpson slate to represent the 15th Assembly District on the county committee. A few days later, opponents in the 23rd Assembly District launched their own primary fight against Simpson forces.[101]

Influential Dewey backers had already begun laying plans for Simpson's demise. State chairman Murray, a figurehead friendly to Simpson, was to be replaced by Jaeckle. Sprague, meanwhile, was to replace Simpson on the RNC. Even New York County leaders who had formerly backed Simpson, discouraged by his inability to provide much patronage and afraid of ending up isolated, sent out word to the Dewey camp that they would break when the word came. But it never did. There were two reasons for this. First, it was still unclear who could effectively take Simpson's place in New York County. Three strong district leaders were willing to take the county chairmanship, but each one preferred Simpson over one of the other two.[102]

Most importantly, Dewey simply could not decide whether to take the decisive step or not. By this time, he was among three top contenders for the Republican presidential nomination. Whether a break with Simpson would hurt him or help him, no one could say, and Dewey did not like to take chances. It was also still not clear how effective Simpson's counteroffensive might become. On June 23, Oswego County Congressman Francis D. Culkin delivered some remarks in Congress about the conflict in the New York Republican Party and had a statement inserted into the *Congressional Record*. These were unambiguously pro-Simpson, putting him squarely in the tradition of Lincoln and Theodore Roosevelt, also Republicans "willing to break with the past when they felt it necessary."[103] The remarks got wide press attention, and Culkin followed them up with a public call for Dewey to support Simpson as county chairman. "Simpson's hand never showed publicly," wrote Warren Moscow, "but Dewey understood, and recognized he was engaging a dangerous opponent."[104]

By one account, Dewey at first believed that he could buy Simpson off with promises of an appointment to the federal bench. Jaeckle and Sprague, well aware of Simpson's continued influence, encouraged compromise as well. By early summer, though, the foundations of the New York Republican party were badly fractured, allowing liberals, conservatives, and the generally discontented to drive wedges wherever they found a crack. Perhaps most importantly, Dewey became convinced that the ongoing conflict was a detriment to his presidential prospects. Simpson's problems were also coming to a head as Trevor's primary challenge made much of Dewey's refusal to back him. It was time to make a deal: Simpson accepted an invitation for dinner at Dewey's house on June 28, 1939.[105]

Simpson informed Dewey that he would need three things: to be reelected county chairman, to remain on the Republican National Committee, and to be made a delegate at large to the 1940 Republican Convention. Dewey agreed to all of these requests, provided Simpson would deliver the votes of all twenty-four New York County delegates to the convention. Simpson explained that the delegates would have to reflect the sentiment of the county. Dewey insisted that as New York's "favorite son" he would be entitled to all of them, and the meeting broke up inconclusively. A few days later, Dewey, accompanied by Jaeckle, Sprague, and others, visited Simpson again. This time Simpson agreed to "consult" in making up the convention delegation. But he remained far from happy, confiding to an upstater that "he would prefer to have anybody except Dewey nominated."[106] Still, according to Dewey, Simpson signed an agreement promising that he would support Dewey through the first ballot at the convention, and the two settled into an uneasy peace.[107]

Throughout the summer and into the fall, Simpson continued, as he described it, "gallivanting around the state paying parochial calls, and preaching the gospel to various county committee picnics."[108] Simpson's "gospel" hardly conformed to conservative expectations. In his set speech, he insisted that "we must accept as sound and valid many of the principles of reform that have been recently established," naming them as: collective bargaining, social security, regulation of the securities markets, unemployment insurance, and wage and hour regulation. Simpson avoided using the word "liberal," but it was less ideology than specificity that irritated Dewey. He was convinced that the way to the White House was to say as little as possible, and he did not appreciate having Simpson put so much on the record.[109]

On September 19, Simpson swamped the Trevor ticket in the primaries. It became official at a meeting of the Republican County Committee on the 28th, where 95 percent of the 4,000 delegates voted for Simpson. Dewey had honored the agreement, backing Simpson all along the way, and Simpson did his best to keep up his end of the bargain. On the night of the 29th, he appeared at the National Republican Club and, under the watchful eye of John R. Davies, delivered a speech attacking the New Deal and papering over any previous significant disagreement in party principle. Meanwhile, Simpson and Hoover had worked out their own agreement and the crisis seemed to be over when, in early November, the Simpsons joined the Hoovers at a party given by investment banker Lewis Strauss. Wide-eyed reporters spotted the unlikely group a few hours later at the Army-Notre Dame game at Yankee Stadium. But it remained to be seen whether Simpson would be constitutionally capable of keeping up the peace with Dewey and Hoover.[110]

PERSONAL PRICE

It was fortunate that while Simpson's political life grew tumultuous in the late 1930s, his personal life became more stable. There does not appear to have been any recurrence of the old bouts with depression, and the Simpsons continued to draw support from a wide network of friends and acquaintances. There was one exception, however, and it was a big one: Helen Simpson had become deaf.

For reasons that are not clear, Helen's hearing had begun to noticeably deteriorate by the early 1930s. Even as the loss grew greater, she resisted taking any remedial steps and so became increasingly isolated from friends and family. Helen's hearing was almost gone by 1937, but nevertheless, Simpson wrote to Dorothy Harvey, "she is so proud or sensitive that she doesn't recognize it."[111] They had bought the best of hearing aids but Helen refused to wear them, and in February 1939, after one particularly unfortunate dinner party, Simpson issued an ultimatum. In one of his late night notes, he pleaded with Helen to open herself up to the people who loved her and informed her that he would not be going to dinner or anywhere else with her again unless she agreed to use her "ear machine."[112] Helen responded by writing up an agreement in which she promised to wear it when she went out or entertained. Lightening a tense and sad situation, Simpson signed the agreement over the title "former colonel, Knickerbocker Greys."[113]

Simpson had halted his affair with Dorothy Harvey during 1937, much to her regret. But within a year, the two had rekindled the relationship, with Dorothy, as before, providing a worldly engagement with culture and politics that Helen did not. For most of the late 1930s, Dorothy and her husband were in Chicago building up a real estate business, and the two met occasionally for what she called "perfect days and nights." But also as before, the relationship was strongest at a distance, and it cooled noticeably after 1939 when the Harveys moved to New York—living just a block away from the Simpsons on 92nd Street.[114]

Despite this long-term affair, the passion and tender resolution of the ear machine incident indicates that the Simpson's marriage remained strong. And if Helen was by nature always a bit distant and dispassionate (by one account she always called her husband "Simpson"), the two had much to share. They traveled alone together at least once a year. In February 1938 they vacationed in the Georgia Sea Islands and the next winter took a cruise in the Caribbean. Helen continued her yearly trips to Europe, which centered on shopping for clothing in Paris. In the summer of 1938, Helen took the two older children along, and Kelly wrote faithfully to his father every day.[115]

And then there were the dinner parties that usually occurred somewhere along the boundaries of society and culture. The Simpsons spent an evening just before Christmas 1939, for example, at Sherry's in the company of notables including conductor Andre Kostelanetz and pianist Arthur Rubenstein. Simpson continued to take pride in his knowledge of music and literature

Kenneth and Helen Simpson in a rare moment of relaxation. *(Courtesy of the Yale University Manuscripts and Archives)*

and enjoyed telling the story of one dinner party when a young woman approached him and said "I have wanted to meet you for years, there are so many questions I have been wanting for years to ask." Simpson anticipated the usual inquiries about city or state politics. Instead, mistaking him for party host Edmund Wilson, the young woman asked about Proust. Simpson fielded the questions so well that she did not discover her error until much later. But it was not only of his own cultural achievements that Simpson was proud. Displayed prominently at the house on 91st Street was a framed letter from Gertrude Stein, with thanks for the comments on her play *Four Saints in Three Acts*. Simpson liked to see how long it took for guests to realize that the letter was not to him but to Kelly.[116]

Somewhere among his political and personal engagements Simpson managed to keep a law practice going. His political connections had enabled him to pick up a steady stream of cases in New York City Surrogate's Court, where special guardianships for minors or incompetent persons had become something of a specialty. Bronson Trevor tried to make an issue of the favoritism that the Surrogate's Court seemed to show Simpson, but the fact that he failed completely suggests that in the 1930s it was still an accepted practice for the courts to provide employment for notable politicians. By this time, Simpson had given up any prospect of making his mark as a trial lawyer. His biggest corporate case, the complicated and tedious Coty litigation, finally wrapped up in early 1939. On May 1 of that year, Simpson left Hunt, Hill & Betts and along with David Brady, with whom he had worked closely in the Coty case, and former U.S. Attorney Gregory F. Noonan, established his own general practice firm, Simpson, Brady & Noonan, with offices at 48 Wall Street.[117]

With his personal and professional life seemingly running in comfortable grooves, one might have expected Simpson to relax a bit. Instead, the cyclical pattern of exhaustive work and ultimate collapse that he had established earlier in life continued. Anecdotes describing Simpson's relentlessness were commonplace in social circles, political gatherings, and even the newspapers. In one instance, Simpson even wore down a major corporation. In 1938, Simpson embarked for a cross-country airplane flight only to learn that he would not be allowed to smoke his pipe. The pipe long ago having become standard rather than optional equipment (he had fifty-six of them), Simpson indignantly cancelled his trip and began petitioning the airline. Eventually, he persuaded United Airlines to provide him with a special permit allowing him to smoke his pipe on board so long as other passengers did not mind.[118]

Smoking was a pleasure that Simpson would not deny himself, but overeating was something that came with the job. In early 1939, reporter Joseph Mitchell spotted Simpson presiding over a "beefsteak" dinner thrown by the 20th Assembly District Republican Club at the Odd Fellows Hall on East 106th Street. Simpson did not speak much. His duties appear to have been limited to standing before the crowd of middle-aged Republicans, nodding, bowing, and, along with his constituents, consuming as many steaks, chops, and kidneys as possible. "When you go to a beefsteak, you got to figure on eating until it comes out of your ears," said the butcher who provided the beef. "Otherwise, it would be bad manners."[119] Simpson had excellent manners— and he went to a lot of "beefsteaks." In this and other matters, what was good politics was not necessarily healthy. Frederic Bellinger, who ran Simpson's 1938 primary campaign, began to be concerned that summer when Simpson appeared "overworked, tired, and all in." Bellinger became frantic when, in September, Simpson dropped out of sight for a week and the faithful Gertrude Hess would say only that her boss was sick. Simpson did not emerge until the night before the primary. Bellinger later wrote that "he told me he had just risen from his sickbed and he looked it."[120]

These episodes could only have been made worse as Simpson again turned to drugs for some relief. By early 1939, his old problem with insomnia had returned, and Simpson was using Benzedrine to overcome daytime drowsiness and keep going through his long hours of work. By late 1939, the pattern was clear: after every struggle came a collapse, when Simpson would disappear from sight for a time. In another indicator of trouble, Simpson's speech had become "jerky and monosyllabic," as one journalist put it.[121] Talking politics had always made Simpson animated—but now it was also leaving him red in the face and out of breath. As 1939 turned to 1940, Simpson's political predicament provided scant relief for his troubled constitution.[122]

THROWING BRICKS

Kenneth Simpson grappled as closely with Thomas E. Dewey as anyone ever did, but it was not the voluble political leader but his laconic wife Helen who left posterity the telling epigram: "You have to know Dewey very well in order to dislike him."[123] These puzzling words were instantly understood by those who did indeed know Dewey, and they explain better than volumes could his strange path through American political history. Primary voters, who knew Dewey least, voted for him with alacrity. Veteran politicians who knew him well worked for him out of duty or opportunism, never passion. And voters—at least on the national stage—always seemed to come to their senses just in time. By the time of his legendary loss to Harry Truman in 1948, the entire nation knew Dewey, but in 1939 he was a fresh face—and as much comic strip character as credible candidate.

Republicans everywhere were heartened and the party finally seemed to be on the rebound in late 1939. Democratic standard bearer Franklin Roosevelt was not expected to violate the two-term presidential tradition, and the Democrats had no one else waiting in the wings. This good political weather gave rise to the first bumper crop of Republican contenders since the

1920s. Michigan Senator Arthur Vandenberg was the veteran in the field, although surprisingly unenthusiastic about the run. Robert Taft, son of the former President and one of the new Republican faces to sweep into office in 1938, was widely admired for his principles and intellect, although he lacked charisma. And finally there was Dewey, who was neither a veteran nor a principled intellectual. He was, however, charismatic—at least from a distance.

By then, most of New York State's influential county chiefs had signed on with Dewey because he looked like a winner. That made Simpson's seeming reluctance to support him all the more peculiar. But Simpson was not the only Republican troubled by Dewey. Herbert Hoover, Charles Hilles, and John Hamilton all reported coming away disturbed from intimate meetings with Dewey. For one thing, he appeared to be more than just a calculating politician. Even for such a tough breed, he seemed incredibly ruthless: "cold—cold as a February icicle," as an aide put it later.[124] Almost as disconcerting was Dewey's continued refusal to engage with issues—he ran on his prosecutorial skills rather than policies and programs, and the public let him. Syracuse Mayor Rolland Marvin, no political friend of Simpson's, condemned Dewey's personal attacks on Simpson at the Legislative Correspondents' Association dinner out of principle. As the presidential primaries approached, Marvin complained that "what I am concerned about more than anything else is to have Tom come out and definitely state his views on major issues. The role of prosecutor is not enough to my way of thinking."[125]

But reservations on the part of the professionals did little to diminish Dewey's popularity with voters in New York State and elsewhere. In late November 1939, the *Washington Post* announced that Dewey would soon make his candidacy official and that Simpson would sign a proclamation making him New York's "favorite son." But New York already had another favorite son, publisher Frank Gannett, backed by upstaters Broderick and Marvin. Simpson had to decide.[126]

Characteristically, he put off the decision. He was not there for Dewey's campaign kickoff in Minneapolis on December 6, nor did he attend the opening of Dewey's New York headquarters. Although Simpson had been friendly with Gannett, he chose not to back that favorite son either. Instead, in late December at a dinner in Boston with Massachusetts Congressman Joseph Martin, one of Simpson's staunchest out of state defenders, Simpson told reporters that he would "go down the line" for Dewey, but "as this is still a free country" he believed that he had "a right to attend dinners to other presidential aspirants."[127] Accordingly, in mid-January 1940, he attended a dinner of the Ohio Society of New York to hear "dark horse" candidate Governor John W. Bricker. This would not have been significant except that Dewey was speaking at the Pennsylvania Society of New York that same evening. Simpson would only tell reporters that he "could not attend two dinners at the same time."[128]

Late in the month, Simpson and Dewey campaign manager Russel Sprague both attended a Republican conference in Topeka. Simpson learned that voters outside New York were not staunchly "for" Dewey—they just seemed to like him. Sprague learned that other Republican leaders were skeptical about a candidate for national office who could not control his own state. Simpson was convinced that the Republicans still had time to find a better candidate. Sprague was starting to think that it was time to do something about Simpson.[129]

Back in New York State, preparations for the convention were under way. Dewey was furious that Simpson had broken their agreement but as of yet was following the path of compromise, allowing Simpson—who still had the support of Brooklyn leader John R. Crews—to keep his RNC seat and go to the convention as a delegate at large. The Dewey group also let the Gannett supporters field a few convention delegates. These efforts at compromise had important implications, however. Eight delegates at large were chosen from among the state executive committee, and of these, four were opposed to Dewey. In the unlikely event that a floor fight arose at the convention, it would be these "independents" who would vote first. Dewey's backers were confident that would not happen, however.[130]

Simpson was, meanwhile, devoting much time and travel to derailing Dewey's presidential aspirations. He went straight from the state executive committee meeting to Knoxville, Tennessee, where he spoke at a Lincoln Day Dinner. On February 21, the *New York Times* printed the obvious—that Simpson would "bolt the candidacy of District Attorney Thomas E. Dewey at the first opportunity."[131] Just over a week later came the annual Legislative Correspondents' Association dinner, and while Dewey was again the star of the show—one skit was entitled "Mr. Myth Goes to Washington"—Simpson's standing was now quite different. In the parody "Sing Something Simpson," the reporters had Simpson warn Dewey:

"No listen, Tom, and get it straight—
It is my fond intention;
All other things to relegate
And give to you the well-known gate
When I travel out as delegate
To the G.O.P Convention
Beware, take care, my knife is out,
And I will sheath it never—
Of that there is no manner of doubt
No probable, possible shadow of doubt,
No possible doubt whatever!"[132]

Early in March 1940, Simpson brushed up his stump speech at the National Republican Club. No longer on John R. Davies's leash, he lambasted Hoover and Dewey partisans in equal measure, insisting that the party should not "disinter old platforms" and observing that the point of election was "not to put the president in jail but to relieve him from office."[133] Then Simpson took to the road again. After a speech in Ohio, the *Columbus Dispatch* called him an "inspirational exhorter who talks cold turkey to the precinct vote hustlers." The Republican *Dispatch* agreed that the party could not repudiate the New Deal and survive. "If on the other hand there is a sincere desire to win on the basis of justice, Mr. Simpson has shown the way."[134] Closer to home, the Troy, New York, *Times* was more critical, claiming that a purely personal disagreement had put Simpson and Dewey "on edge so long that it has been a metropolitan scandal."[135]

By early 1940, however, the differences between Dewey and Simpson were far more than personal: for the first time since his years at Yale, international affairs were beginning to preoccupy Simpson. The preceding months had brought a succession of frightening crises and sad resolutions. Nazi Germany occupied Austria in March 1938 and the Czech Sudetenland in September. Despite the agreement he made with Neville Chamberlain while the New York Republicans bargained in Saratoga Springs, Hitler annexed all of Czechoslovakia in March 1939. The European nations drew the line, and on September 1, 1939, when Nazi Germany invaded Poland, Europe plunged back into all-out war.

By the 1930s, most Americans had decided that entering the First World War had been a mistake. The staunch isolationism that pervaded national politics at mid-decade had even compelled the Roosevelt administration to pass the Neutrality Act, forbidding the sale of arms to belligerents. By 1940, Americans were only beginning to understand that sooner or later they would have to stand with the embattled free nations of Europe. They still wanted, wrote *The Nation*, "to be as unneutral as possible without getting into war."[136]

Simpson, like most other elite Easterners, was an internationalist in an isolationist nation. His familiarity with international trade and finance underscored the interdependency of the world's economies. As someone who had made the Atlantic crossing many times, he understood that the oceans were neither the barriers nor bastions that they appeared to be to Midwesterners. Throughout the decade, however, the Republican Party remained in the thrall of Main Street isolationism, and not surprisingly, all of the Republican presidential candidates carried isolationist credentials. For Arthur Vandenberg and Robert Taft, it was a matter of high principle. For Dewey, it was a matter of sheer expediency—he was never more insistent upon avoiding European entanglements than while campaigning in heavily German Wisconsin.[137]

Simpson was not averse to political expediency so long as what was gained was greater than what was given away, but he took a firm position on principle almost from the moment the war began. Early in September, he had gained newspaper attention for backing—along with Congressmen Bruce Barton and James W. Wadsworth Jr.—an immediate amendment of the Neutrality Act to permit the sale of munitions to any foreign country on a "cash and carry" basis, a stand that was about as far on the edge of internationalism as was possible at the time. Dewey's refusal to seriously consider the question made Simpson all the more convinced that he was ill-suited to lead the nation in such troubled times.[138]

Dewey watched Simpson's barnstorming trips and his deviation from isolationist orthodoxy with undoubted exasperation. Nor could it have been gratifying when, in October 1939, the *New Yorker* carried an extensive and highly flattering profile of Simpson dubbing him New York's Republican "Boss without Cigar." Dewey knew that there could be only one boss in New York, and it would not be Simpson.[139]

In retrospect, Dewey's next move seems inevitable, and the question arises: how could as sharp a strategist as Simpson end up so exposed? Simpson's chief mistake was believing that the liberal wing of the party was stronger than it was. He saw three more or less evenly matched forces in the state: Hoover conservatives, the personal followers of Dewey, and the liberals aligned with himself downstate and Ed Jaeckle upstate. He hoped that the liberals would gain adherents over time, as it became clear that neither Dewey nor Hoover offered viable leadership. But Simpson had miscalculated. He knew that despite every politician's obligation to compromise, he would never jettison his commitment to the liberalization of the party, and he assumed that Jaeckle felt the same. Even after Jaeckle made the jump to the Dewey camp, Simpson evidently expected him to return when the liberal forces were rallied.[140]

Up in Buffalo, however, Jaeckle was hemmed in not by liberal Democrats but by conservative Republicans, so his perspective was different. He recognized that, through 1938, the vast majority of upstate New Yorkers remained strongly conservative and deeply opposed to downstate domination of the party by what they called the "Simpson-Dewey forces."[141] By cutting his ties with Simpson, Dewey had removed Simpson liberalism as a liability. By cozying up to Hoover, he further underscored his conservatism. By 1939, upstaters were ready to consider Dewey one of their own, a transition made complete when Jaeckle became Dewey's top advisor. It was a marriage of politics rather than principle, but Jaeckle did not let that bother him.

Dewey had already privately asked Simpson to resign as county chairman, complaining, as Simpson put it, that his continued advocacy of progressive causes was an "embarrassment to his candidacy for the Presidential nomination."[142] In the spring of 1940, while Dewey stumped primary states in the Midwest, his advisors debated what to do about Simpson. On April 2, Dewey won the Wisconsin primary. A week later, he prevailed in Illinois and Nebraska. Dewey staffer and pioneer of presidential polling George Gallup confirmed that his candidate was on solid ground.[143]

Dewey decided at last to clean house. His top priority was to diminish Simpson's influence as much as possible before the convention and to keep him in check while it was going on. Some suggested simply kicking Simpson out of the convention delegation. But Simpson still had friends in the Dewey camp and on the state executive committee—notably Brooklyn's John R. Crews—who kept that from happening. Instead, the Dewey forces decided to check Simpson's influence by challenging his seat on the RNC. The election of committeemen was traditionally done at the convention, and should Dewey dominate there, Simpson would be removed as a matter of course. But Dewey's men were not taking any chances—they wanted to make Simpson a lame duck and undermine his authority immediately. The county chiefs began by drawing up resolutions rebuking Simpson for "ignoring prevalent sentiment" and "conspiring with outsiders," among other things.[144] Simpson's

Buffalo Republican leader Edwin Jaeckle who, as Dewey's top strategist, became Simpson's toughest opponent. *(Courtesy of Dr. Kelly Simpson)*

friends toned down every draft until they had a resolution that was—in appearance—innocuous.[145]

When Simpson arrived in Albany for the Republican State Committee meeting on April 12, he probably knew that something was up. He brought along with him Gabriel Kaplan, a close assistant and an expert in election law. But the executive committee meeting—where the real business of the state committee was usually done—passed relatively uneventfully. At 2:30 that afternoon the general meeting began. With the exception of Jaeckle's replacing William Murray as state chairman, an indicator of Simpson's waning influence, the agenda was mostly routine. Attendance was low, therefore, and most of the votes were proxies cast by just a few county chiefs. The proceedings apparently over, Jaeckle concluded with a plea for "harmony" within the state party. Then, he asked, "Is there any other business to come before this meeting?"[146]

Warren Ashmead of Queens rose and introduced the painstakingly crafted resolution. It stated that since RNC members were "expected to reflect the views of their constituents," it was "desirable" that the selection of National Committee members "be not deferred until the busy days of the Republican National Convention." Ashmead moved to have the chairman call a meeting to select RNC members in advance of the convention.

The few delegates in attendance who had not been party to the plan feverishly tried to figure out what was really going on. A delegate from Steuben County took issue, charging that this was clearly an attempt by members of a faction, "by whatever manipulations and maneuvers they see fit, to come to such conclusions as they desire." He motioned that the resolution be tabled. Gabriel Kaplan spoke up, noting the irony of this move following Jaeckle's plea for party harmony and charging that "the resolution is entirely illegal." Even upstate leader and sometime Simpson opponent Thomas R. Broderick suggested that the resolution be tabled.

At length, Jaeckle recognized Simpson. "Mr. Chairman and members of the State Committee," he stated. "At least I was not the one to throw the first brick." Simpson claimed that the move was a complete surprise and completely illegal. He insisted that part of the state could not impose its favorite son on the whole. "All I have done is the best I can," Simpson told the group. "I, frankly, have been very disappointed in some things that have developed, and my enthusiasm has cooled as the enthusiasm of most of the delegates and most of the members of the rank and file of the party in New York by many things that have happened." Later, Simpson tried to address the specifics of the charges, but Jaeckle, insisting that there was "nothing personal" about them, would not allow it. Despite the warnings of a few that any appearance of party harmony would vanish when the story hit the papers, Simpson lost a vote to table the resolution 69 to 209.

The division having been made clear, Jaeckle called for a rising vote on the main question. The majority stood. "You had better take a look, Ken," Jaeckle barked. "I don't want any questions later, now. Are you satisfied to have the motion carried?" "I am not going to court about it," Simpson growled. Dewey, of course, was also fighting for harmony. He later dismissed the unpleasant task of stripping Simpson of his power as just "part of the business of cleaning up the organization and getting a united group."[147] Simpson had watched the Republican Party almost destroy itself in 1916, so he well understood the importance of unity. And he certainly believed that his course of action, so destructive of Dewey's prospects, would eventually bring party harmony about. But Simpson was done worrying about that: henceforth, he would fight for things even more essential than harmony. A few days later, Simpson wrote to an old Yale friend: "The problem now to be resolved is whether or not you can tell the truth in politics and still stay in politics. As soon as I get the answer I will let you know."[148]

CHAPTER FIVE

"WITH A FIGHTING SPIRIT"

On Saturday night, April 13, 1940, questions flew as the nation's political elite gathered at Washington's Willard Hotel. Could Tom Dewey, characterized as little Lord Fauntleroy spoiling for "a chance to wear long pants and give the New Deal hell," really win the Republican nomination? Would the sphinx, Franklin Roosevelt, ever utter a word about a third term? At intervals, a chorus of reporters dressed as owls flapped across the stage asking "Who, Who Who? Whom will they nominate?"[1] The inquiries were in earnest, for just weeks before the major party conventions, no one could tell who the nominees might be. But at least one man in attendance was getting some answers. Before, during, and after the Gridiron Dinner, Kenneth Simpson was flitting from party to party, table to table, and from one hotel room to another, gathering allies for a battle in New York.[2]

Tom Dewey was indeed as petulant as the reporters depicted him, and Kenneth Simpson was the cause. Presidential contenders, after all, were expected to have the solid backing of their home states. Dewey had tried to bind the Manhattan leader with a bargain, but in an otherwise sturdy New York platform, the Simpson plank refused to stay nailed down—Dewey's only recourse was to fight for control of the state.

Or was it? Within days, Dewey was reconsidering. Slipping in the presidential polls for the first time, it looked as if the last thing he needed was an outright battle in New York. Arch conservatives egged Dewey on, however. If he could not handle Simpson, they asked, how could he handle the presidency? Then Simpson forced the issue. On May 15, he announced that he would not acquiesce to being voted off the Republican National Committee. Simpson promised to stump the state, put his own case before the voters, riddle Dewey's full of holes, and otherwise make "a hell of a fight."[3]

THE FIRST BATTLE

In politics, few things earn respect like electoral success. Dewey had demonstrated remarkable vote-getting ability, but still Simpson was not impressed. Reminded that 100,000 people had turned out for Dewey at just one western whistle stop, Simpson countered, "What of it? Five times that many tried to crash Rudy Valentino's funeral."[4] Simpson declined to be caught up in the boy prosecutor's ballyhoo and hoped to convince other Republican leaders to side with him instead of the popular prosecutor. He started by issuing a pamphlet that emphasized his recent achievements. Simpson also made the most of his wide and influential political network. He was being courted by nearly every potential Republican presidential candidate, except for Dewey, and he invited them all to his house on Saturday, April 20, for a reception prior to a New York political dinner. Attending were Robert Taft, the Ohio senator whose principled gravity contrasted sharply with Dewey's youthful expedience, and Joseph "Joe" Martin of Massachusetts, House minority leader and one of the party's strongest "dark horse" candidates. Also attending was a more recent acquaintance, utilities executive Wendell Willkie.[5]

Simpson with Joe Martin, left, and Robert Taft, right, the evening of New York's Inner Circle Dinner, April 20, 1940. *(Courtesy of the Yale University Manuscripts and Archives)*

Not yet ready to make a final choice, Simpson gave nominal support to Rochester publisher and New York "favorite son," Frank Gannett. This was clearly a marriage of convenience: Simpson was a liberal, Gannett a conservative. Simpson was looking for a serious, principled, and progressive candidate. Gannett was something of a dilettante. He was paying for his campaign out of his own pocket, and although he was in earnest he was hard to take seriously—a *Washington Post* columnist noted that, when speaking, Gannett gets "so angry, indignant, and outraged in the first 30 seconds that the general effect is somewhat comical."[6] Simpson promised Gannett, as he had Dewey, that he would back him on the first ballot. For Gannett, that was enough. He did not mind when Simpson announced that "instead of the New York delegation being hell-bent for Dewey as a favorite son, a large group will now go to the convention with open minds."[7]

As he stumped the state for Gannett, Simpson made the case for his own continued leadership in the party, did his best to torpedo Dewey, and laid down some principles for open-minded Republicans to follow. In a speech before the Columbus Circle Republican Club in late April, Simpson noted that even if a Republican won the presidency, the Senate would remain Democratic. The President, therefore, would have to be willing to cooperate with his opponents—there would be "no room for the principle of the purge."[8] When it came to foreign policy, Simpson told the New York Women's Republican Club in mid-May, the President had to have firm principles: he could not "advocate one thing in Wisconsin and another in New York." In general, however, Simpson stuck to the principles he had been promoting for more than a year. The Republican Party, he said, had to accept the basic elements of the New Deal, eschew isolationism, and pick the best qualified candidate for the presidency.[9]

As Simpson stumped, Dewey strategist Ed Jaeckle puzzled. Should he call the Republican State Committee meeting already approved and attempt to oust Simpson? Failing would be worse than doing nothing, and the *New York Times* had warned that the effort "was not assured of success."[10] If the picture was mixed for Dewey, it was mixed for Simpson as well. On April 19, the New York County Executive Committee met. Republican heavyweights Sam Koenig and David Costuma both agreed to back Simpson but also insisted on reaffirming their earlier endorsement of Dewey for President. A month later, the New York Young Republican Club also backed both Simpson and Dewey.[11]

The Dewey forces reasonably assumed that everyone would eventually have to take one side or the other. When that time came, they believed, the majority would jump on the Dewey bandwagon. They did not count on the wheels coming off the cart. During May, Dewey's standing in the polls continued to slide. Finally, Simpson forced the issue when, in late May, he attempted to short-circuit Jaeckle's carefully planned pre-convention process.[12]

Republican National Committee chairman John Hamilton had asked all state delegations to meet and select a member of the convention platform committee. A meeting was something that Simpson did not want. Gambling that Dewey might not want one either, Simpson sent out a letter asking the delegates to ballot by mail. Jaeckle quickly called the meeting, set for less than two weeks before the convention.[13]

In Albany on the morning of June 12, Simpson met with some of his most influential backers, including Congresswoman Ruth Pratt, Congressman James W. Wadsworth Jr., New York City corporation counsel Paul Windels, and Charles Hilles. By then it was clear that Simpson's campaign had not succeeded. "We organized our forces as best we could," recalled Windels, "although we knew we did not have the votes."[14] Syracuse mayor Rolland Marvin had tried to broker a deal between Simpson and Dewey a few days earlier; now he tried again. The delegates waited while the leaders argued, but finally the meeting convened.[15]

Simpson backers moved for postponement. "Kenneth Simpson does not deserve to be publicly chastised," Charles Hilles insisted. "Here is a young man," Hilles told the delegates, "who was persuaded to get into politics, who got in with a fighting spirit, with college enthusiasm, and with ability."[16] The motion was defeated, and Simpson lost to Russel Sprague 55 to 37. "It was my own fault," he told the press. "I never should have compromised with them any more than Chamberlain should have compromised with Hitler." Dewey now had almost complete control of the New York State Republican Party— with the very large exception of New York City. Simpson planned to use this fact to full advantage. "We have lost the first battle," he said. "We will win the next at Philadelphia and the final victory on election day."[17]

Viewed in terms of the presidential contest, the fight over the Republican National Committee seat seems to have been rash and vindictive. Emotions were high, and Simpson's boyhood friend George W. Perkins Jr. was moved to write, "I'm proud of you."[18] There was unwarranted elation in the Dewey camp.

International lawyer and future Secretary of State John Foster Dulles wrote to Jaeckle: "Dear Ed: You did a swell job on Simpson. Congratulations!"[19] It was a gratifying move perhaps, but it alienated New York City conservatives who might otherwise have gone along with the Dewey crusade, and it put New York City solidly against Dewey on the very first ballot—which could have serious consequences. Why did they do it? Dewey and Jaeckle had already begun to shift their focus from the national level, where Simpson's dismissal made little sense, to the state arena, where it made a great deal of sense indeed. International events left them little choice.

"All signs point to a Republican victory this year," crowed Republican National Committee chairman John Hamilton in February 1940. Indeed, common sense suggested that a change in the oval office was inevitable: Republicans everywhere were making headway with voters fatigued by the stalled reforms of the Democratic Party and willing to let the opposing party back into power. The incumbency argument was among the Republicans' strongest. Ever since George Washington had rejected a third term, no President had dared try for one. When Franklin Roosevelt refused to explicitly renounce a third term, even some of the President's former admirers were troubled. Hamilton, therefore, challenged the Democrats to renominate FDR—the Republicans would still win, he crowed. But then everything changed.[20]

Hamilton spoke in early 1940, when the world, after a succession of frightening upheavals, had seemed to settle into a new equilibrium. Parts of Europe had been swallowed up, but the great powers of Britain and France stood fast and Hitler seemed content. Many were even calling the conflict touched off in September 1939 a "phony war." In that light, the old political certitudes seemed likely to hold, and Dewey enjoyed a series of victories in the Republican presidential preference primaries. Robert Taft was shrewd enough to stay out of these non-binding primaries, but Senator Arthur Vandenberg's hopes were crushed by the young New Yorker who told crowds in isolationist Wisconsin and Nebraska that the United States must "resist every entanglement in the affairs of Europe."[21]

Republican confidence began to crumble on April 9, 1940, and the "phony war" became all too real as the German Army invaded Norway and Denmark. Influential Americans, followed reluctantly but surely by the voters, began to reject isolationism. Columnist Arthur Krock wrote that it was time that front-runner Dewey publicly state his foreign policy views. Dewey declined. Things got worse when, on May 10, the Nazis invaded Holland and Belgium. Suddenly the talk about a third Roosevelt term assumed a positive rather than a negative tone—who better to see the country through the coming storm than the man who had already taken it through the Great Depression? Roosevelt remained silent, but Ed Jaeckle believed that the game was up. On the night of May 10, he told his colleagues that the party would never nominate "a 38-year-old kid."[22] Dewey could not win the presidency in 1940, Jaeckle declared, but he could win the governorship in 1942. He would still have to curtail Simpson's influence in New York, however, and he would have to do it before the convention could increase it. It would soon be a well-worn joke that Tom Dewey was the "first American casualty of World War II."[23] Few realized that Kenneth Simpson was the second.

A MAN FOR THE TIMES

In 1937, when the nation seemed headed for prosperity and the public thrilled to Dick Tracy comics, Tom Dewey was the man for the times. But the glamour was gone by late May 1940, when Dewey intoned that "this has become a gangster world. I know something about gangsters."[24] That knowledge did not keep Dewey from continuing to flatter the Republican Party's isolationists, and to accuse Roosevelt of "edging the country toward participation in the European war to cover the utter bankruptcy of his domestic policies."[25]

Bruce Barton was not a staunch internationalist, but on June 13, 1940—the day after Simpson was voted out as Republican National Committeeman—he wrote to Dewey. "The war situation has introduced a wholly new and overwhelming factor into the Republican picture," wrote Barton. Now "many people are feeling that your years are a handicap in spite of your talents. I share this view."[26] The timeliness of Barton's letter was underscored the next day when the German Army occupied Paris.

It is likely that even in 1940 Franklin Roosevelt did not intend to run for a third term. The President had inked a deal to write a series of magazine articles in his retirement, just as his cousin Theodore Roosevelt had done before him. But he kept his options open, knowing that circumstances could change. When they did, and the fall of France left only Britain between a Nazi Europe and a free America, it is likely that Roosevelt decided to run.

If the fall of France brought Roosevelt into the race and helped edge Dewey out, it did little to clarify who, in the end, would carry the standard for the Republicans. In an unusual situation, an unlikely hero emerged, helped along by the New York County Republican chairman.[27]

Socialite and social activist Mary Lasker later insisted that she had been the first to introduce Wendell Willkie to Kenneth Simpson at a party thrown at her East 42nd Street apartment in the summer of 1939. She was clearly captivated by Willkie's charisma. She claimed to have considered him presidential timber and to have hoped that Simpson would too. Simpson himself credited Yale classmate Lyttleton B. P. Gould with being the first to propose Willkie to him as a presidential prospect. Whichever it was, like everything else in Willkie's political career, it happened very fast.[28]

Wendell Lewis Willkie grew up in the medium-sized town of Elwood, Indiana, the child of liberal German parents. He attended Indiana University, taught high school for a time, and then earned a law degree, eventually landing a job in Akron, Ohio, with the Firestone Tire and Rubber Company. Willkie distinguished himself at Firestone, came to the attention of a local power and light company, and in 1929 accepted a position as counsel to the Commonwealth & Southern Corporation, a newly formed public utilities holding company. He moved to New York with his wife and settled down on the Upper East Side, just a few blocks away from the Simpsons. In New York, Willkie somehow managed to hang on to his disarming Indiana charm, even as he rose to become president of the Commonwealth & Southern and make a fortune in finance, serving on the board of the Morgan-dominated First National Bank of New York. Political opponent Harold Ickes later described Willkie as "just a simple barefoot boy from Wall Street."[29]

The New Deal transformed the successful but unassuming New York lawyer into a public man and potential politician. The Roosevelt administration assaulted the utilities industry on two fronts. In 1933, the creation of the Tennessee Valley Authority, with its regional network of dams and power plants, put the federal government in direct competition with the nation's private power producers. Two years later came the Public Utilities Holding Company Bill, which threatened to set strict limits on the structure and activities of holding companies like the Commonwealth & Southern. Due to some spectacular collapses at the onset of the Great Depression, public utility holding companies—and their executives—were viewed with suspicion by most Americans. They were little concerned with the bill's "death sentence" provision, which allowed the government to wipe out holding companies that did not comply with regulations. Willkie was outraged, however, and spent most of 1935 in Washington, D.C., fighting the bill.[30]

The legislation passed, but it gave rise to an influential opponent of the New Deal. In 1937, Willkie, helped along by friends in the publishing industry, began writing articles in the intellectual *Atlantic*, the mainstream *Saturday Evening Post*, and the partisan Republican *Herald Tribune*. By the end of the decade, Willkie had emerged as a sharp and articulate defender of private enterprise who was all the more effective for his Midwestern charm. His eyes sparkled, his hair was tousled, and his suits hung loose and rumpled on his bearlike frame. Women were understandably attracted to Wendell Willkie, but potential voters were as well—he was one of the few sympathetic and likeable champions of business to emerge during the 1930s.[31]

There was one catch, however: Willkie was a Democrat. But neither Willkie nor the growing cadre of idealistic Republicans championing his cause let that bother them. That included Connecticut businessman Sam Pryor, who had been appointed to the Republican National Committee at the same time as Simpson. Other early converts included the man who had once "heeled" under Simpson at the *Yale Daily News*, *Time-Life* titan Henry Luce. Closest to Willkie by the summer of 1939, however, was Russell Davenport, a poet, novelist, and Yale man who worked for Luce at the helm of *Fortune* magazine. Davenport made a practice of inviting people to his Upper East Side apartment to meet the man that Mrs. Davenport said could "charm a bird from a tree—if he wanted to."[32]

By the fall of 1939, Simpson's search for a 1940 presidential candidate was well known, and Mary Lasker's party had apparently failed in its purpose. So Frank Altschul, a banker and Republican fundraiser, urged Simpson to take another look at the improbable Midwesterner. Simpson expressed his reservations with humor and only a bit of hyperbole. "So I am supposed to go back to the clubhouse and tell the boys that we will all have to pull together now to get the nomination for Wendell Willkie. They'll ask me, 'Willkie, who's Willkie?' And I'll tell them he's president of the Commonwealth & Southern. The next question will be, 'Where does that railroad go?' And I will explain that isn't a railroad; it's a public utility company. Then they will look at me sadly and say, 'Ken we always have thought you were a little erratic, but now we know that you are just plain crazy.' And that would be without my ever getting to mention that he's a Democrat!"[33]

In short order, Willkie took care of two of these problems. That fall, he registered as a Republican. He also sold the Commonwealth & Southern to the TVA—at his asking price. Willkie then focused completely upon getting the Republican nomination.[34]

A turning point came on April 9, 1940, when the Nazis invaded the Scandinavian countries, making Willkie's internationalism more palatable than before and sending frontrunner Dewey's polling numbers into the slump from which they never recovered. On the same day, Oren Root, a member of the 15th Assembly District Republican Club and grandnephew of former Secretary of State Elihu Root, launched a grassroots movement of "Willkie Clubs" that soon swept the country. That evening, Willkie himself put in an appearance on the radio quiz show *Information Please* and performed with impressive wit and grace.[35]

Within a week, Kenneth Simpson was pitching a tent in the still-sparse Willkie camp. At a meeting of the Republican National Committee in mid-

A clearly thrilled Simpson greets the charismatic Wendell Willkie. *(Courtesy of the Yale University Manuscripts and Archives)*

April, in what was apparently a prearranged move to raise Willkie's profile, Simpson proposed him as the convention's keynote speaker "to define the party's policies in the campaign."[36] Up to then, Willkie's plan had been to wait for a deadlock at convention and then step into the void. But as the event approached, his advisors convinced him to get out and speak. On May 11 in Minneapolis, Willkie read a few uninspiring prepared remarks and then threw the speech away and proceeded to electrify the audience. The boom had begun, and Simpson was already preparing to swing his delegates Willkie's way when the right time came.[37]

MIRACLE AT PHILADELPHIA

In her classic history, Catherine Drinker Bowen describes the Constitutional Convention as the "Miracle at Philadelphia." Lesser known is a miracle that followed 153 years later. The circumstances were similar—a sense of crisis, a deeply divided populace, and a nation that seemed economically and politically broken. In 1940 as in 1787, a sense of opportunity led a cast of outsized personalities toward compromise. In doing so, they helped unify the nation as it faced its greatest external threat in history. Had the Republican Party remained mired in isolationism during these crucial months, Americans would have wasted time and energy fighting among themselves instead of preparing, if reluctantly, for war.[38]

When they arrived in Philadelphia, Tom Dewey's campaign managers needed a miracle of their own. They had the promises and primary victories won weeks earlier, but that was all. Because his ranks were full of pledged but unenthusiastic delegates, "Trojan horses" liable to bolt to the opposition at any moment, the experts agreed that Dewey would have to get at least 400 votes on first ballot. Only if he started out within reaching distance of the 501 votes needed for nomination would those delegates stick.[39]

With confidence in short supply in the Dewey ranks, Simpson made sure to sow discouragement. On Tuesday, June 18, as the Republican National Committee members prepared for the next week's events, Simpson told everyone in town that the Dewey boom had definitely "collapsed."[40] Still, few of the Republicans in Philadelphia were willing to call themselves internationalists, and when, on June 20, Franklin Roosevelt appointed Henry Stimson as Secretary of War and Frank Knox as Secretary of the Navy, party regulars exploded. Both were prominent Republicans: Stimson had served as

Secretary of State under Hoover, and Knox had been Landon's running mate in 1936. Their agreeing to serve in Roosevelt's "coalition cabinet" seemed a clear betrayal, and enraged Republicans "read them out of the party." Undaunted, Simpson returned to New York that evening to attend opening night of his beloved Lewisohn Stadium concert series. For once, New York provided a respite from political rancor.[41]

On Saturday, June 22, when Wendell Willkie walked from Philadelphia's Broad Street Station to his headquarters at the Bellevue-Stratford Hotel, the party chiefs had yet to take his campaign seriously. Willkie had decided to run as an amateur, and in a gesture that he hoped would prove his sincerity, had skimped on hotel space. Taft had 101 rooms for his headquarters; Dewey had 78. Wendell Willkie, in contrast, had two. It made for close quarters, but Willkie had, as yet, a small team.[42]

At midnight that night, Simpson joined Bruce Barton, Rolland Marvin, Sam Pryor, Indiana Congressman Charlie Halleck, and Minnesota "boy governor" Harold Stassen in a strategy session. By 3:00 A.M. they had divided up the convention hall floor into zones of responsibility, created an organization, and drawn up a blueprint for victory. Their plan was the opposite of Dewey's. All agreed that there would likely be several ballots. They would start small and build momentum, seizing every opportunity to create the kind of psychological impact that would jar wavering delegates out of an opposing camp.[43]

By way of creating such impact, Simpson—exercising his authority as Republican Committeeman, which he retained until the end of the convention—resolved not to poll the New York delegation until the balloting actually began. He believed that the best time for the Dewey forces to know that they were short was when they could do nothing about it. Instead, he told reporters that he expected to conduct a delegate poll during the balloting itself so as to show the delegates what kinds of influential New Yorkers were behind Willkie. Stassen later cautioned against such a move, however, warning that it might appear to inject the Simpson-Dewey feud into the proceedings. Simpson reportedly acquiesced.[44]

Politicians are masters of simple addition. Shortly before the proceedings began, Simpson sat down with Texan R. B. Creager, Robert Taft's floor manager, and tallied up numbers on a pink Bellevue-Stratford laundry list. The most important number for everyone at the moment was how many votes

Dewey would get on the first ballot. Simpson came up with 363. Both men expected Dewey to come up short, but Simpson hoped for an opening that Willkie could fit through.[45]

By the time the convention opened on Monday, June 24, nearly every influential delegate had his own version of Simpson's laundry list. Few believed as yet that Willkie stood much chance. The conventional wisdom was that Taft and Dewey would strike some kind of bargain and the two top Republican vote getters would sew the ticket up tight. Others believed that the old war horse, Herbert Hoover, might captivate the convention in his Tuesday night speech, sweep all before him, and go on to vindication with the voters. Either seemed more likely than a Willkie victory for reasons that Indiana Senator Jim Watson indelicately laid out in the lobby of the Bellevue-Stratford. "Jim, I hope that I'm going to have your support," Willkie said. "I think it's a wonderful thing to welcome a whore into the church," Watson replied, "but I don't think she should be allowed to lead the choir the first night."[46] Willkie did not lead the choir on the first night of the convention, but from the galleries, during a delay in the program, came the first strains of music to liberal Republicans' ears—a few scattered cries of "We Want Willkie."[47]

On Tuesday night the speeches began. Immediately after having delivered the keynote address that kicked off a long and frustrated political career, Harold Stassen came out for Willkie. Next it was Herbert Hoover's chance to start up the road to redemption. Delegates waited expectantly. Even those who had long since moved on could not help but root for the man who had led the party during its darkest days. Hoover was up to the task. He had written a very good speech, perhaps his best ever, but before he had gotten far into it, cries from the audience came: "Louder." As *Time* magazine put it, "hot words of his finest address got lost in his bulldog chops."[48] What *Time* did not say was that Sam Pryor, who had only at the last minute become chairman of the committee on arrangements, had apparently switched microphones before the speech, ensuring that Hoover's comeback never happened.[49]

That night, with Hoover out, the delegates added up the numbers again. Offers and counteroffers flew between the Dewey and Taft camps, but with neither willing to take second place, no convention-clinching deal emerged. Simpson, meanwhile, went to work on the New Jersey delegation. Dewey had won a primary there in May. Now Arthur Vanderbilt, leader of the New Jersey delegation, was determined to hold all 32 votes for Dewey. But there were discontented in the ranks. At 2:00 A.M. on Wednesday morning, Morris Mogelever, a friendly columnist, brought the Republican chairman of Passaic County to visit Simpson. By 3:00 A.M., Simpson had a New Jersey floor manager for Willkie and there was another "Trojan horse" in the Dewey ranks.[50]

By Wednesday, nomination day, Willkie looked like the only interesting candidate in Philadelphia. Frank Gannett remained content in knowing that Simpson, although working for Willkie, was nominally committed to him. "Ken will stay with me until I release him," he said.[51] Gannett's nomination fell into the convention crowd with a thud, ensuring that Simpson would not have long to wait. Even among the front runners, disillusion was setting in. The Dewey delegates mustered up some dutiful enthusiasm as their champion entered the running. The man who nominated Taft believed it somehow to be a compliment to call the tight-lipped Cincinnatian "common as an old shoe."[52] The ennui flashed into anger when Indiana Congressman Charlie Halleck stepped up to nominate Wendell Willkie. From the floor came hoots and boos so insistent that Halleck wavered until convention chairman Joe Martin urged him back to the rostrum. On the floor, New York delegates Frederic Coudert and Rolland Marvin wrested the state standard from Dewey partisans and began a triumphant march around the hall. Twice the Dewey partisans fought to get the standard back, and Philadelphia policemen ultimately intervened.[53]

There may have been hostility on the floor, but there was jubilation among the spectators in the gallery, already being referred to as "the people" by sympathetic members of the press. By then, the gallery seemed destined to become legendary in Republican lore. As cries of "We Want Willkie" grew ever more insistent, the professionals on the floor began investigating the phenomenon. Behind it was, again, Sam Pryor. Pryor never disputed that he had ordered extra gallery tickets. As head of the committee on arrangements, that seemed to be his prerogative. He claimed to have done it because he was worried that the galleries might turn up empty. It was by pure chance, he said, that a pro-Willkie University of Pennsylvania student found out about the tickets and began distributing them to his friends. Joe Martin called the packed gallery an "open scandal," but friendly reporters likened it to the soul of the convention. The spectators agreed. When Martin cautioned them to be quiet since they were guests of the convention, someone yelled, "Guests, hell. We are the convention."[54]

Thursday began with bleary-eyed New York delegates waking to find the first editorial ever to grace the front page of the *Herald Tribune*—for Willkie. By late afternoon, the conventional hall was sweltering. Sixteen thousand were crowded into a hall built for fourteen thousand, and bright lights set up for newsreel cameras gave the place a surrealistic atmosphere. As the polling began at 5:30 P.M., the worst fears of the Dewey delegates materialized. On the first ballot their man polled 360 votes, three less than Simpson had predicted. The state of New York gave its most illustrious favorite son only 61 of its 92 votes. Then New Jersey, confidently expected to deliver all 32 votes, came through with only 20. Had it not been for Kenneth Simpson, Dewey may have clinched both delegations, and those extra 43 votes would have put him over the 400-vote psychological tipping point.[55]

On the second ballot, five more New York delegates switched over to Willkie, building a slow but steady momentum. It was a platitude that no Republican candidate had ever won the nomination after losing ground in a ballot, and when the second count showed a loss of 22 votes for Dewey, everyone knew it was over. The die-hard Dewey delegates sat glumly while Simpson and Marvin kept working the New York delegation for Willkie. Some believed that Taft had been holding back and would surge ahead on the second ballot—instead, he only edged forward incrementally. The big gainer was Willkie, who tallied 171 votes, just 32 votes short of Taft's count.[56]

At 6:30 P.M., the delegates broke for dinner. Those who returned to their hotels found mailboxes stuffed with telegrams sent out by the Willkie Clubs. The third ballot began two hours later. When New York was called, Dewey partisan Judge William Bleakley announced only 17 votes for Willkie. Walter Mack had likely known of Simpson's earlier plan to poll the delegates. Now, convinced that the Dewey forces were still undercounting the Willkie vote, Mack demanded the poll. There were "groans from the gallery," wrote a *Chicago Tribune* reporter, but they subsided as one of the most dramatic moments of the convention unfolded.[57] Simpson was the first member of the delegation to be polled. In full voice recognizable to radio listeners, he went on record for Willkie. Jaeckle later maintained that Simpson had held back the Gannett votes until just that moment. These, along with the votes of several other delegates determined to go on record for Willkie, gave 27 votes to Willkie, ten more than Bleakley had announced. The New York delegate poll did not make Willkie, but it undid Dewey. Many years and many conventions later, Dewey remained bitter about it.[58]

On the third ballot, the Willkie vote climbed to 259, Taft crept up to 212, and Dewey dropped to 315. Still, Dewey remained in the race. Not until after the fourth ballot, after Willkie had gained another 8 votes in New York, did the Dewey loyalists revolt. After Bleakley warned that he could no longer hold his Westchester County delegates, Dewey released them.[59]

By then, the contest was between Willkie and Taft. The correspondent from *Time*, who exaggerated the supposed "idealistic amateur" versus "cynical professional" nature of the contest, described the floor fight: "At every turn, bulked Boy Scout Stassen, bland, imperturbable [or] Boy Scout Simpson, sweating, a dead cigar or dead pipe alternately gripped in his mouth."[60] Simpson's work in New York was done on the fifth ballot when New York gave 75 votes to Willkie and a roar went up from the gallery. The ballot closed with Willkie ahead of Taft 429 to 377.[61]

By that time, Simpson was ranging widely through the convention hall, ferreting out delegates and watching for spots in the Willkie machine that might need a little oil. By the time New York put in those 75 votes, he was up on the platform as the convention reached its dénouement. After Alf Landon threw all 18 Kansas votes behind Willkie, Taft partisans and Hoover men clamored for a break in the proceedings. Everyone was sure that if the balloting could be postponed until morning, they would find a way to stop Willkie. But the Willkie men saw that coming. According to the *New York Daily Mirror*, Stassen shot up to the platform and conferred frantically with Simpson. Simpson consulted with national chairman John Hamilton, and Hamilton spoke with convention chair Joe Martin. "If we recess now," each man was heard to say, "you'll never convince the country it wasn't to stop the convention's free choice."[62] As Martin made the decision to proceed, Simpson stood nearby, his collar wilted, a dead cigar in his mouth, and a broad smile on his face.[63]

On the sixth ballot, Michigan gave up on Arthur Vandenberg's candidacy and went for Willkie. Then Pennsylvania, which had been holding out for its own unlikely favorite son all this time, also went to Willkie. The Ohio delegation moved that the vote be made unanimous. Dewey was on his way to the hall, but too early to peak, he was now too late to speak: Sprague stepped to the dais and pledged Dewey's full support for Willkie. Most of the exhausted delegates crept off to drink and to sleep. Simpson and the rest of Willkie's inner circle, however, sat up until dawn choosing a running mate. They finally

Simpson on the floor at the 1940 Republican Convention celebrating good news for the Willkie cause. *(Courtesy of the Yale University Manuscripts and Archives)*

settled on Charles McNary. He was a Westerner, an old-line Progressive, an isolationist, and immensely popular in the nation's farming regions. Franklin Roosevelt's advisors privately acknowledged that it was the "strongest possible ticket."[64] "For the first time since Teddy Roosevelt," wrote *Time* magazine, "the

Republicans had a man they could yell for and mean it."[65] And Simpson, for the time being at least, was determined that they would all yell together. "We don't hold any animosity toward those who opposed us," he told a reporter. "We will all work together."[66]

LOSING GROUND

There was good reason to be exhilarated. Very rapidly in the spring of 1940, from a series of seeming defeats came a victory of incredible proportions. The most engaging and politically progressive Republican in a generation was on the campaign trail, and Simpson had helped put him there. Willkie seemed to acknowledge this debt when he appointed Simpson to his campaign advisory committee. But would the bearlike Willkie follow in the footsteps of the Bull Moose Roosevelt? Would Simpson attain the influence that his achievement seemed to merit? He must have known that the odds were against it.

Among Willkie's top priorities was repairing the damage done in vote-heavy New York State by the Simpson-Dewey feud. He had two choices: accept the reigning conservative-upstate Dewey coalition intact or build a new political coalition based on Simpson's Manhattan-based progressive faction. The latter, of course, would take time and money, and Willkie did not have much of either. Soon after the convention, it became clear that the campaign would have to fall in line with the Dewey group. Even Simpson's appointment to the campaign advisory committee apparently meant little—it soon appeared to be more of a dumping ground for loosely allied Republicans rather than a tight cadre of like-minded strategists. Simpson's predicament was underscored in mid-July when the press revealed that Dewey had made the price of cooperating with Willkie "the political annihilation of Kenneth Simpson."[67]

After the surreal success of June came a dispiriting summer for Simpson. Instead of immediately taking to the hustings, Willkie wasted five critical weeks vacationing in Colorado. In Chicago, the Democrats, worried about world affairs and apprehensive about the popularity of the charismatic Willkie, nominated Franklin Roosevelt for the unprecedented third presidential term. Some Republicans were pleased, believing that Roosevelt's "power grab" would be an ideal issue to run against. Simpson worried that it might be all that Willkie would have to run against, but he soldiered on, establishing a Manhattan Campaign Committee for Wendell Willkie headed up by his long-time ally councilman Joseph Clark Baldwin and managed by top aide Raymond Fanning.[68]

Simpson's health deteriorated quickly after the convention—the old pattern of boom and bust seemed to be speeding up. By July 1, Simpson was, as he described it, at home with a cold, leaving Gertrude Hess to deal with the chaos at Republican County Committee headquarters created by latecomers scrambling to join the Willkie cause. He did not reappear until mid-month. It is unclear whether it was the pressure of the convention or the letdown during the weeks that followed that brought on the slump, but recovery was elusive: Simpson's physician, Dr. Leander H. Shearer, insisted that he rest for a few weeks more. On August 10, he and Helen registered to vote early as usual and soon afterward left for a vacation in Nova Scotia. A week later, Willkie returned from Colorado to begin the campaign and promptly fumbled the ball—giving a dull and tedious radio acceptance speech on August 17. Even worse for Simpson, back in New York City, more critical campaign positions were going to Dewey partisans.[69]

After giving the acceptance speech, Willkie stayed on his farm in Rushville, Indiana, to undertake a variant of the old Republican "front porch" campaign pioneered in the Gilded Age by William McKinley. It was not clear, however, that what worked in the balmy summer of 1896 made sense in crisis-ridden 1940. By the second week of September, when Willkie invited him to Rushville, Simpson was deeply disappointed. "He had the feeling," as Stanley Isaacs put it, "that Willkie was not grateful enough for the support he gave him in Philadelphia."[70] Simpson drafted a letter of refusal. Considering that Willkie had clearly given in to what he described as a "conspiracy of state bastards," Simpson believed that he would be left to talk about the weather—"or else tell you my opinions, which would be worse."[71]

Simpson filed the letter away and on the night of September 11 left for Rushville. Willkie, who had spent the 12th in Indianapolis with Joe Martin, arrived in Rushville about the same time as Simpson. The two spent the dinner hour sitting around the radio on an old-fashioned sofa in the parlor of Willkie's Rushville home, listening to La Guardia announce his support for Roosevelt. They discussed the situation in New York, with Willkie doing most of the talking, although Simpson managed to crack a joke for reporters.[72]

Willkie, who was turning out to be a much better talker than listener, expressed to Simpson some strong opinions about the New York senate race. He was determined to have the best ticket possible in New York and worried about a weak spot in the U.S. Senate. A formerly Republican seat had been won by Democrat James Meade in 1938. Now Willkie wanted Bruce Barton to mount a challenge. This race had been the subject of much discussion. Jaeckle and Sprague had urged Dewey to take it; Simpson had earlier favored Rolland Marvin but had lately come around to Barton.[73]

The problem was that it was unlikely that any Republican besides Dewey could have won that seat and Barton would have to give up his own safe congressional seat to try. Willkie let Simpson know that he wanted Barton—who had seconded his nomination at the convention and was a popular Republican moderate—to make the run out of party loyalty. Simpson put the word out on Willkie's behalf, calling Barton "an energetic and inspiring candidate."[74] Simpson, of course, had influence, but Dewey had control, and not until the eve of the New York State convention in late September did Willkie begin leaning heavily on Dewey lieutenants Jaeckle and Sprague. Finally, the night before the convention, Willkie called Barton personally and told him that he was his "first, second, and third choice." Barton dutifully accepted the job.[75]

The Republican State Convention opened on September 27 at the Westchester County Community Center in White Plains. Most of the day was devoted to the filling of minor candidate slots. Dewey gave a keynote speech, and the delegates began filing out of the hall. James Bruno, a district leader from Harlem, lagged behind, upset that one of his constituents had been refused a congressman-at-large nomination. As he left the hall, the 200-pound Bruno stopped Simpson and complained that he had "double-crossed" him. "I did nothing of the kind," Simpson retorted, turning away and beginning to fill his pipe. Bruno jumped him, and with what one newspaper described as a "mighty smash on the mouth," knocked Simpson to the ground.[76]

Bruno's assault did not slow Simpson down. A more painful rebuke came the next night when the convention met at the Empire City Race Track in Yonkers to hear a speech by Wendell Willkie. Dewey made the introduction. Simpson got no recognition from Willkie himself—he was even denied a seat on the platform. Simpson was not the only one slighted by the now gaffe-prone candidate. Willkie left the dais without mentioning

Bruce Barton, who was sacrificing his own political career for the good of the party.[77]

A PLACE ON THE TICKET

Even as he was being sidelined by state and national Republicans, Simpson was gaining a higher profile with the public. One of the sources of his celebrity was the radio show that had helped launch Willkie's candidacy, *Information Please*. The show was started in 1938 on a simple premise: a panel of personable wise men would answer, in entertaining fashion, questions sent in by listeners and put to them by the urbane Clifton Fadiman. It was unabashedly highbrow—"sort of an Algonquin roundtable of the air," as one writer put it, but listeners delighted in hearing each week's visitors match wits with regulars like columnist and Simpson confidante Franklin P. Adams, sportswriter John Kieran, and pianist Oscar Levant.[78] Simpson first appeared on the show in mid-May, just a few weeks after Willkie, and he did well. After all, the on-air gatherings were much like the private card games that Simpson frequented.[79]

He was invited back again on August 13 for a widely publicized match with New Dealer Harold L. Ickes. It was Ickes who had dubbed Willkie the "barefoot boy from Wall Street" and had condescended that Dewey had "thrown his diaper into the ring," but in that match, Ickes made some spectacular mistakes on political topics. Simpson missed his own question on presidential succession, but in another on the Constitution he came up with the right article number, and throughout he needled his Democratic counterpart relentlessly. In response to one remark by Ickes, Simpson countered that "the minority has some rights, including the right to read the Constitution."[80]

Simpson was well positioned to realize a dream of more than a decade and run for elective office. He had not created the opening but recognized it when it appeared. True, the prospect of jumping from city to national politics must have seemed daunting, and Simpson particularly looked forward to the 1941 mayoral race. But there were better reasons to take the opportunity. The Dewey machine was drawing an ever-tightening noose around Simpson's New York base. Even if there was a Willkie victory, Dewey would control the state. From his congressional seat, perhaps Simpson could build back his influence in New York State.[81]

On October 7, New York's 17th Congressional District held a convention at the National Republican Club and nominated Simpson for Congress.

Simpson in a reflective mood in his office at New York County Republican headquarters, about the time of his run for Congress. *(Courtesy of the Yale University Manuscripts and Archives)*

He accepted, making his first priority to elect Wendell Willkie and his second to elect Bruce Barton. His third priority, he said, was winning the congressional seat, since "never before in the history of our country will the Congress of the United States have a more vital part to play in guiding the nation to a cause of peace in a world of chaos." The meeting adjourned after only thirty minutes.[82]

With less than a month to campaign, Simpson acted quickly. He appointed aide Mark Maclay to be his campaign manager and made Walter Mack his campaign treasurer. Simpson set up formal headquarters in three rooms on the 6th floor of the National Republican Club, but his real headquarters were at home on 91st Street where newly hired secretary Esther Hogue handled correspondence and associates showed up for strategy meetings over breakfast.[83]

As a liberal internationalist of long standing, Simpson had no trouble winning some very solid backing. Influential newspapers like the *World-Telegram* and the *Herald Tribune* promoted his candidacy, and influential friends provided funds. Yale classmate and Brown Brothers Harriman partner Knight Woolley gave $50. Clare Luce donated $2,000. A less conventional campaign contribution came in the form of pipe tobacco. At no time was the Simpson for Congress campaign fund in short supply.[84]

Upon the backdrop of crisis in Europe, Simpson as candidate continually sharpened his positions on mobilization and international affairs. Like Willkie, Simpson supported the institution of a draft—an unpopular position with rock-ribbed Republicans. The Battle of Britain was also raging that fall, and Simpson condemned the Roosevelt administration's failure to provide the British with the assistance needed to resist the Nazi attempt to bomb them into submission. In a *World-Telegram* article, Simpson stated bluntly that he was for "giving all possible aid" to John Bull. "If there are any flying fortresses that we don't need for our individual defense then, for God's sake, let the British have them as fast as possible."[85]

In his speeches, Simpson demonstrated concern for more than geopolitics, however. On humanitarian grounds, he backed relaxing immigration laws so that refugees from occupied Europe, many of whom might be bound for concentration camps, could come to the United States—another idea unpopular among Republicans. If Simpson was at home with the educated and internationalist voters of the Upper East Side, he was less effective appealing to the middle- and working-class populace of the Upper West Side. His tendency to make historical analogies and offer complex arguments led one voter to caution him that his speeches were "beyond the capacity of the average person in the audience to understand."[86] "It is always well to be sometimes 'one of the boys,'" another voter reminded him.[87]

Simpson took at least some of this political advice to heart. He paid careful attention to issues like public housing and late in October made personal tours of the 17th Congressional District, especially on the West Side.[88] Small businessmen in particular were receptive to Simpson's more orthodox pledge to "give the inventive and productive genius of the United States a chance," yet also to "take care of the folks who need help."[89] On October 31, boxer Joe Louis campaigned in New York for Wendell Willkie. Stopping by the New York County headquarters, Louis posed with the candidate and signed a photograph for Simpson's son, Kelly. As the boxer left, Simpson called out, "Fighting is easy compared to campaigning, isn't it, Joe?"[90]

For Wendell Willkie, getting nominated turned out to be easier than campaigning. His first misstep came on the day after his nomination, when he called the convention delegates "you Republicans," confirming to skeptics that his conversion had been halfhearted.[91] Willkie's limp August 17 acceptance speech, broadcast nationwide on the radio, did nothing to redeem him with Republicans, nor did oversights like his failure to recognize Barton in his Yonkers speech. Barton was understandably convinced that "Willkie was contemptuous of the party and had no desire or willingness to accept advice."[92] Willkie's amateurs were also prone to make costly mistakes. Willkie staffers at the Republican National Committee had tried to elbow old-timer Charles Hilles out of the way—until Joe Martin gave Hilles an office next to his. One day a Willkie fund raiser came in from Wall Street with a handful of checks worth $5,000. Hilles looked at the signatures on the checks, took them away, and returned with new ones worth five times as much.[93]

But his problems as a campaigner aside, world events had made Willkie's candidacy, and in the end they unmade it as well. As Democrats and Republicans fought, the fate of Great Britain hung in the balance, making campaign rhetoric—particularly the Republicans' protestations against a Roosevelt third term—seem paltry. Despite the trouble abroad, most Americans hoped to stay out of the war, and Willkie—unable to play the interventionist to the extent that Roosevelt could—increasingly played to the isolationists. When Roosevelt managed to undercut those claims as well, assuring voters that "your boys are not going to be sent into any foreign war," Willkie knew that he was sunk.[94]

It was only near the end of the campaign, at a rally in Madison Square Garden on the night of Saturday, November 2, that Simpson was to reprise the leading role that he had taken in Philadelphia. At the rally, Simpson played the political impresario, making the opening speech and introducing speakers as varied as Clare Luce, Robert Moses, and Bruce Barton. At 10:30 P.M., Simpson introduced Willkie to a national radio audience. He had compared Willkie with his boyhood hero before, but now Simpson made the connection more explicit, invoking a famous speech made by Roosevelt in his "Bull Moose" run for the presidency in 1912. "Once we Republicans, or some of us," Simpson said, "stood with Theodore Roosevelt at Armageddon. Tonight we stand on the battlefield of a whole world in a life and death struggle for democracy." Simpson seemed convinced that the Republicans might finally win. "In previous years," he said, "we have all too often had everybody with us—but the voters. This year the people are on our side."[95]

More of the people than ever were indeed on Willkie's side. But in a time of crisis, the majority stuck with the reassuring Roosevelt. Willkie got 22 million votes, more than any other Republican in history. But he lost the popular vote and lost the Electoral College to Roosevelt, 449 to 82. Because the west side precincts returned first, things looked equally bad for Simpson on election night, but only for a short time. With an American Labor Party candidate splitting the Democratic vote, Simpson's 50.6 percent majority was a comfortable win. Barton went down to defeat as expected, but his efforts and Simpson's helped spur a record Republican turnout in New York City. Upstate was a different matter, however, and even though the election had launched Simpson on a new career, he could neither forget about New York politics nor that upstate vote.[96]

LAST STAND IN NEW YORK

After this latest challenge to Simpson's constitution, the familiar cycle recurred. Simpson was, in his own words, "laid up" for about a week after the election. Then, in order to get away and recuperate, he took Helen on a driving tour of New England, where, in the chilly autumn woods and hills, he came down with influenza that kept him home through the last half of November. Simpson accomplished a great deal, nevertheless.[97]

Simpson's celebrity status and political progressivism made him an ideal profile for the liberal illustrated New York newspaper *PM*. As a photographer snapped away, Simpson vented some post-election resentment to a person that he later claimed he thought was a photographer's assistant. The assistant turned out to be a reporter, and the County Republican chairman's remarks were soon known citywide. "All that the Jaeckle crowd did was to use Willkie money to build up a state Dewey organization to grab the governorship in 1942," Simpson grumbled. He concluded confidently that "I'm going to do my best to throw out Jaeckle, and I'm going to begin right now."[98]

Arthur Ballantine, the law partner of Simpson mentor Emory Buckner, asked in dismay, "Why would anyone think at this time of making a declaration of civil war within the party?"[99] Simpson explained about the photographer's assistant but still asserted that the state leadership was deplorable and that with the election over, "I believe the time has come for a housecleaning."[100] About the time of the *PM* interview, Noel Busch, who had written Simpson's flattering *New Yorker* profile a year earlier, asked him to pen a brief article for *Life*. The premise was that with Roosevelt having won nearly every big city in the country, Republicans had to learn how to win urban votes. The *Life* article came out on November 18 and told a nationwide readership what

New Yorkers had discovered a week earlier: Kenneth Simpson was planning to take on Tom Dewey's New York State machine.[101]

Simpson attributed Willkie's defeat not to his liberalism but to the "baggage"—cranks, crackpots, and conservative special interests—that weighed down the party. He included Dewey among these burdens. In Theodore Roosevelt's time, he wrote, the Republican Party had truly represented all citizens. He insisted that "we need, as never before, not unity, but a tolerant majority, a functioning minority, and the emphatic resolve of the Republican Party to become the agent not of special privilege, but of the entire people."[102] These were noble sentiments, not entirely wrong, and it is likely that Simpson sincerely believed them. But Simpson, no less than his idol Theodore Roosevelt, had built a reputation as not merely an idealist but also as a practical politician, and that entails putting enthusiasms and grudges aside. Somewhere in the tumult, the unexpected opportunities, and the heartbreaking setbacks of recent years, Simpson had forgotten that. He lost the sense of proportion and perspective essential for a politician who wants to keep his focus—and his following.

Although he had been elected to the United States Congress, Simpson was determined to retain his position as chairman of the New York County Republican Party. One reason was simple—his friends and allies occupied the county offices, and he wanted to protect them. Nor could he bring himself to withdraw for good from city politics. The county chairmanship was also the power base that he had held the longest and understood the best, and he believed that he could use it to take back the state party—specifically by putting his candidate in the governor's seat in 1942. But for all of that, Wendell Willkie had come and gone, and the New York County Republican chairman was just as isolated as he had been on June 12. Regardless, in early December, Simpson set out to regain lost influence, beginning in his own back yard.[103]

David Costuma was a long-time Republican Assembly District leader who, in 1935, with Simpson's backing, was named to the New York City Board of Elections. Reappointed in 1938, Costuma sized up the political situation and began moving from the Simpson wing of the party into the Dewey camp. By 1940, that transition was complete, giving Dewey a strong presence in the city and providing yet another irritant to Simpson.

Then, in time-honored New York tradition, a corruption investigation seemed to offer Simpson a way out of his predicament. In 1940, New York commissioner of investigation William B. Herlands issued a report on the administration of election law in the city. Herlands noted that Costuma "failed to take full advantage" of opportunities to eliminate waste. This was hardly a scathing indictment. Costuma had, in fact, been the only member of the board to cooperate fully with the investigation, but it was a straw and Simpson grasped

The Buffalo Courier-Express highlights Simpson's isolation from—and indignation over—the New York State Republican establishment in late 1940.

at it. He declared that he would oppose Costuma's reappointment to the board, calling it a move against "illegality, inefficiency, laxity and waste."[104] Simpson put forth his own candidate, Gabriel Kaplan, a close advisor and head of the law committee of the New York County Republican Committee.[105]

Trouble began immediately. Kaplan was far too close to Simpson, and he had provided legal help to the American Labor Party, which in recent years had veered much farther leftward even than it had been in 1937. Fifteenth Assembly District liberals Joseph Baldwin and Newbold Morris backed up Simpson, but their stock was also falling citywide. Dewey took up Costuma's cause, enlisting the help of notables such as Allen Dulles and Herbert Brownell. He also put two enterprising assistants to work on the matter full time.[106]

Simpson had a difficult task ahead of him. Out of solidarity, if not common sense, nearly all of the district leaders backed Costuma. Simpson, therefore, had to split the membership away from their leaders in a number of election districts. The New York County Republican Committee meeting held the evening of December 16 was understandably contentious. In a series of bitter contests, Simpson partisans challenged district leaders and called for delegation polls. In a remarkable indiscretion, Simpson even called upon Kaplan, acting in his capacity as chairman of the law committee, to make a ruling on one of the votes. In the end, Kaplan's nomination was badly defeated by a vote of 2445 to 1163; Simpson had obtained the solid backing of only five of the county's thirty-two districts. Worst of all, there had been no point to the exercise. The next day, the city council voted overwhelmingly to reelect all the election commissioners—most with records far more tarnished than Costuma's.[107]

Rather than confess his own colossal miscalculation, Simpson blamed Dewey and the forces of reaction. "I did my best, as was my plain duty, to get the party organization to go down the line for good government," he said. Even some who had backed Kaplan believed this to be an overstatement. Costuma called it "a shameful betrayal by a neurotic county chairman."[108] The New York Times was kinder, noting that even though it was not clear how much the controversy owed to Simpson's feud with Dewey, "in resisting official inefficiency and the politics of the trough he was everlastingly right."[109]

Simpson had put himself out on a very small limb, and Dewey started sawing. The district leaders planned to strip Simpson of nearly all of his powers and rest authority in a committee that would include Costuma. Simpson dutifully called a County Executive Committee meeting for the night of December 20 at the Mecca Temple. He had a year to go in office, but rather than submit, Simpson had decided to resign. He called the meeting to order and entertained a motion for a new chairman. Thomas J. Curran had voted for Dewey down to the last ballot in Philadelphia. He succeeded Simpson and cleared Dewey's way to a win in the 1942 governor's race.[110]

TWO WEEKS IN CONGRESS

Even as he approached the end of his career in city politics, Simpson was launching another in the nation's capital. By early December, when he attended a session of the House as a guest of Bruce Barton, Simpson had already begun to direct his broader concerns about international affairs into specific policy areas. During the campaign, Simpson had grown interested in the question of how best to mobilize the nation's industrial capacity for the national defense. He was hoping for a seat on the House Committee on Labor, where he could "make a study of the labor situation in this country with a view to facilitating the defense."[111] Simpson was understandably inspired when, on the night of Tuesday, December 29, Roosevelt gave his "Arsenal of Democracy" fireside chat, calling on the American people to assist Britain with every available measure while it was still possible. Wendell Willkie had already called on Republicans to act as "loyal opposition" during the crisis, and Simpson responded with a statement that put him squarely within those ranks. "The president's argument against appeasement and for all possible aid to Britain was unanswerable," claimed Simpson. "He has closed the door to compromise with a courageous challenge. There should be no room for obstruction, regardless of party affiliations."[112]

On January 3, 1941, Simpson took an early morning train to Washington, was sworn in at noon, and returned a congressman. He was emerging from the morass of New York politics, but he had hardly forgotten it. "There is no man from Buffalo to the Battery that can tell me, when I stand on the floor of the House of Representatives, to sit down in the interest of party harmony," he told one reporter.[113] Back in New York over the weekend, Simpson toured his district by car, calling especially on West Side constituents.[114]

On Monday morning, January 6, Simpson returned to Washington accompanied by regular house guest Alexander Kerensky. At lunch he introduced himself to Speaker of the House Sam Rayburn, who later whispered to Simpson, "I was talking to old man Franklin D. Roosevelt and he said he thought you were all right."[115] Simpson amply earned the praise that after-noon when Roosevelt delivered the annual message soon to be dubbed his "Four Freedoms" Speech. As the President defined the liberties that all people should enjoy and elaborated upon America's commitment to international-ism, Simpson was one of only two congressmen on the Republican side of the aisle who applauded. Roosevelt noticed. Afterward, in the corridor of the Capitol, Simpson encountered Franklin P. Adams, who asked why he had applauded. "Why not?" Simpson replied. "I thought it was swell."[116] A state-ment that he dictated for the Associated Press read: "I believe the American people will overwhelmingly subscribe to these principles, and that Congress should recognize them as a proper basis for our national policy."[117]

That night Simpson moved into the Willard hotel; he met Adams and two other friends at the hotel bar and spent the evening at the National Press Club. The next day came meetings with New York legislators—Republican, Democrat, and even the American Labor Party's only congressman, Vito Marcantonio. On Wednesday, Simpson took a call from a "constituent," Secretary of Labor Frances Perkins, who hoped Simpson would take a seat on the House Committee on Labor. He also sent copies of the *Congressional Record* to son Kelly to keep "as a recollection of your 13th birthday."[118]

Late in the week Simpson hired a secretary, Grace Sonfield—"the first one to show up who didn't seem grim and to know it all," he wrote Helen—just in time to handle the mounting piles of constituent mail for and against aid to embattled Britain.[119] Indeed, Simpson had come to Washington at one of the great turning points in American history, for Great Britain was broke. Still in question was whether the United States would open the door to a free Europe or close it on a continent lost to dictators.

On Friday evening, January 10, Simpson stepped off the train from Washington and went straight to the set of *Information Please*. That night, fellow contestant Judge James G. Wallace got off the best remarks. Simpson spoke overly long about the Constitution and struggled to recall the name of Charles Evans Hughes. He was clearly preoccupied, and with good reason. That afternoon, the administration had sent to Congress a bill numbered H.R. 1776 that would vastly expand the power of the federal government and could sink the United States more deeply into European affairs—possibly even into war. But it also offered the only hope for the survival of Great Britain and the restoration of freedom in Europe. That was a lot to think about.[120]

The bill, soon to be called "Lend Lease," had been authored by Simpson's best friend at Harvard Law School, John J. McCloy. After a highly successful stint as an international corporate lawyer, McCloy had joined Secretary of War Henry Stimson's staff. He soon demonstrated an ability to get things done despite political constraints, helping devise the "destroyers for bases" deal by which Roosevelt had offered earlier assistance to Great Britain. In December, McCloy became special assistant to the Secretary of War, and in early January he turned the ideas expressed in Roosevelt's "Arsenal of Democracy" speech into legislation.[121]

The response to H.R. 1776 signaled the beginning of a new wartime political alignment in the United States. Southern Democrats, who had fought Roosevelt on most New Deal measures, backed it. The usually solid Republican opposition split cleanly in half, with Eastern internationalists supporting the legislation and Midwestern isolationists against it. Tom Dewey, still on the isolationist side of the Republican fence, called it "an attempt to abolish free government in the United States."[122] Robert Taft attacked the clever rationale for the plan—that the United States would "lend" arms to Britain for the duration—as an absurdity, saying that military materiel was like chewing gum—"once it had been used, you didn't want it back."[123] On Sunday, January 12, Wendell Willkie announced that he favored the measure "with modifications," including a time limit on the President's extraordinary powers.[124]

Simpson spent the weekend thinking about the measure. To Willkie's modifications he added the idea that the President's ability to extend aid—and thus potentially ensnare the United States in foreign conflicts—should be tightly limited. Then, on the morning of Monday, January 13, Simpson encountered fellow commuter and former classmate McCloy in Washington's Pennsylvania Station. Over breakfast, they talked through Simpson's ideas, and in his office on Capitol Hill they framed the first amendment to Lend Lease. Simpson's measure called for a two-year time limit on the President's extraordinary powers and allowed him to extend aid only to the British Commonwealth and Ireland without congressional approval. When the draft was complete, Simpson reached Wendell Willkie by phone and read him the amendment.[125]

In Congress that morning, partisan punches had already been thrown over Lend Lease. A hostile Kentucky legislator tried unsuccessfully to get the bill shunted from the Foreign Affairs Committee to his own Military Affairs Committee. Isolationist Republican Hamilton Fish—a New Yorker and ranking member of the Foreign Affairs Committee—called the bill "a confession that representative government has failed in America."[126] Another Republican predicted the demise of freedom in America. A considerably cooler Simpson sat in the House chamber wondering how to introduce a bill. A colleague told him to push a button on his chair. He did and a page appeared, took the document, and disappeared. "I wasn't sure that my bill had been introduced until I read about it in the papers," Simpson confessed to Helen later.[127]

Lend Lease marked the point at which a nation divided over the Great Depression began to unite for war, and with that push of a button Simpson had played a part. Roosevelt had sprung his last big New Deal measure, the court packing plan, on an unwary Congress, made it a personal issue, and created a legislative debacle. Now the President was determined to work with Congress, framing a bill by consensus rather than command. That is why McCloy was happy to work with Simpson on an amendment—it was all in the plan. Indeed, Roosevelt's legislative point man, House Speaker Sam Rayburn, promptly suggested that he had no problem with Simpson's amendment.[128]

Isolationist Republicans on Capitol Hill understood what was going on. They were happy neither with Willkie's remarks on Sunday nor Simpson's amendment on Monday, and ranking members bristled at the freshman's impudence. But acting alone, entirely focused on the subject at hand and with no thought to political advantage, Kenneth Simpson had legislated, and it had been to the nation's benefit. He had also struck a nerve with the American people. By January 15, Simpson was receiving more mail than any other member of Congress. Simpson kept two secretaries—Esther Hogue, recently of the New York campaign, and Grace Sonfield—busy helping answer letters late into the night.[129]

On Thursday, Simpson made a modest maiden speech on the floor of Congress, asking unanimous consent to extend his remarks in the record and to include a statement by Wendell Willkie. "I am enjoying my work here tremendously," he wrote Hilles.[130] Simpson expressed some regret, now that Lend Lease had gone to the Committee on Foreign Affairs, that his involvement had been brief, but he seemed happy again to be taking up the problem of industrial mobilization. On Friday evening he dined with Adolph Berle, the former brain truster and La Guardia aide who, as Assistant Secretary of State, was now deeply immersed in that issue. He returned to New York on Saturday morning, put in some rare time at his law office, and then went into a self-described "panic."[131] Bantering with friends on *Information Please* was one thing, but now Simpson, speaking as an expert on Lend Lease, was scheduled to join left-wing playwright Lillian Hellman on the public affairs show *People's Platform*. Simpson turned in a creditable performance, but then something went very wrong.

CRASH

The appearance on *People's Platform* was Simpson's last public engagement. The enthusiasm of the previous two weeks evaporated—his fighting spirit, gone for good. Monday, January 20, was Franklin D. Roosevelt's third inauguration. Simpson had tickets for three on the platform, but he stayed home. Simpson's old co-counsel on the Coty case, Judge John Biggs Jr. of Delaware, escorted Helen and Kelly to Washington instead. "Hope you will be well soon," wired secretaries Sonfield and Hogue, "don't worry about office."[132]

But Simpson was not ill: he was drinking again—and to excess. Both Joseph Baldwin and Dewey later acknowledged that Simpson had returned to alcohol after the Costuma defeat, and Baldwin recalled that his doctor warned that it could kill him. Helen appears to have confided in the staff either on Monday or shortly after, so Simpson's secretaries were "noncommittal" to inquirers as to when he would return to Washington. But on Tuesday, January 22, Grace Sonfield told Helen that a problem had arisen: Thomas W. Lamont, financier, Morgan partner, and one of Simpson's most important political contacts, was anxious to talk with him—by telephone if not in person. "If it will be a few days before Mr. Simpson is available, perhaps it would be better for us to say that he is ill," she wrote.[133]

As Simpson dropped from view, the international crisis continued. Also on January 22, Congress passed the Vinson Bill, which strengthened the nation's aviation industry, and Wendell Willkie left for London in a move widely interpreted as a "mission" for Franklin Roosevelt that would essentially end his political career.[134]

At home on 91st Street, Simpson passed an agitated week, plagued by a host of demons, real and imagined. Since youth, Simpson had been a bundle of energy. In adulthood he was too often a bundle of nerves.

Political pressures written all over his face, Kenneth Simpson late in his life. This photograph was used in his congressional campaign booklet. *(Courtesy of Dr. Kelly Simpson)*

Smoking—particularly lighting and relighting his pipe—helped calm those nerves, but by late 1940, according to one account, Simpson was going through a box of cooking matches every two hours. The old problem with insomnia had also reappeared, and Simpson's efforts to overcome it led again to dependence on drugs: at one point, he was taking two kinds of sleeping pills at night, stimulants during the day, and paregoric for intestinal problems.[135] The late-night notes to Helen had turned desperate. One read: "3-4 AM or so and no sleep yet on account of Benzedrine etc. so please let me sleep until I wake up. Love—despite everything, K."[136] Politics had become a torment rather than a solace. Helen described him as "restless" and irritated, particularly when he read the newspapers. "He is not ready to go back yet," she wrote an unidentified confidante.[137]

As much as anything else, it seems, Simpson was unhappy about what he might be going back to. In Congress—the House in particular—the committee system provides the key to power and influence. In the 1930s and 1940s, the seniority system was at its strongest. Power came from tenure rather than from qualifications or achievement, and junior legislators were expected to wait their turn, not merely for leadership but even for membership on the more influential committees. Shortly after the election, Hilles warned Simpson that his chances would be "circumscribed by reason of the minority position of the party," but suggested that mutual friend and minority leader Joe Martin might come up with something.[138] It was quite likely Martin's influence that landed Simpson a spot on the highly important House Committee on Labor. For a time Simpson seemed content, although he also applied for the Committees on Interstate and Foreign Commerce and Immigration and Naturalization.[139]

But Simpson's part in the Lend Lease debate seems to have raised expectations—by mid-January he was hoping for a spot on the influential House Committee on Foreign Affairs, and he asked Wendell Willkie to weigh in. Simpson might have expected seats on both Labor and Foreign Affairs since predecessor Bruce Barton had served on them both—but Barton had waited for the seat on Foreign Affairs. There was little that could be done: the committee was already packed with New Yorkers, and far senior men were waiting.[140]

On Friday Simpson was to have attended a reunion of the Yale Class of 1917 with Prescott Bush. Instead, he stayed home. Outside, a winter storm blanketed the city with two inches of snow. That afternoon, Grace Sonfield wired Simpson his committee assignments. He had gotten the labor seat, but Simpson was otherwise sidelined in the backwater committees of Patents and the Election of President, Vice President, and Representatives in Congress. At 4:20 he wired back a curt reply: "Please inform whom it may concern that I will not accept membership on committees on patents or election of president and vice president. Simpson."[141]

On Saturday, January 25, the sky cleared, the sun shone, and city crews went to work shoveling the New York streets. In Washington, Britain's Foreign

Secretary conferred with Navy Secretary Frank Knox. With help from the United States, Lord Halifax said, the United Kingdom would hold out until spring. Help was coming. On Capitol Hill, the House Committee on Foreign Affairs wrapped up its hearings on Lend Lease with testimony from Yale man and former Ambassador to France William Bullitt. When the sun set, the temperature headed back below freezing.[142]

Sometime after eleven o'clock that night, Simpson sat alone in his walnut-paneled study when he suffered a heart attack. Helen heard his cries for help. She called Dr. Shearer, who rushed over from East 85th Street. Simpson was still breathing when the doctor arrived, but he never revived. Kenneth Simpson died at 11:30 that night: he was only forty-five years old. A medical examiner later attributed Simpson's death to "chronic hypertension, acute myocardial insufficiency, and acute alcoholism."[143]

The news was in the last editions of the morning papers and spread during the day. Among those who called on Helen and the children were Joseph Baldwin, Gabriel Kaplan, Gertrude Hess, and opera singer Lily Pons, wife of Simpson's friend Andre Kostelanetz. Notes of condolence—cards, letters, and telegrams numbering in the thousands—arrived at the house. One of the first was from Eleanor Roosevelt. Wendell Willkie cabled from Europe that "he was one of my dearest friends and I admired him very much."[144] Those who did not know Simpson well were shocked when they heard of the heart attack. Those who did—those familiar with the breakneck schedules, the enthusiasms and disappointments, and the all-too-human frailties—understood better. Bruce Barton was among the first callers on Sunday. He told reporters that in service to the public, Simpson had "cheerfully sacrificed every personal consideration—time and money, his law practice, and finally his own life."[145]

On Monday in New York City, snow was falling again. In Washington, flags flapped at half staff in a drizzling gray sky. In a brief service on Capitol Hill, Congressman Francis Culkin, who had taken his side in the fight with Dewey, praised Simpson's "promotion and advocacy of decency in municipal politics."[146] Congress adjourned until Wednesday. From Buffalo, Ed Jaeckle sent a telegram of condolence to Helen Simpson.[147]

The funeral was held on the afternoon of Tuesday, January 28, at St. James's Episcopal Church, where Kenneth Simpson had been baptized, confirmed, and married. More than six hundred eminent New Yorkers crowded in for a simple service. Mrs. Wendell Willkie attended on behalf of her husband;

Tom Dewey was there, as was Fiorello La Guardia. Colonel William Hayward, who had hired Simpson as assistant United States Attorney, attended, as did boyhood friend Alfred Bellinger. Two hundred honorary pallbearers preceded a flag-draped mahogany coffin down an aisle banked with roses, lilies of the valley, and chrysanthemums. Helen must have believed that enough had been said already: there was no eulogy. A bugler sounded taps in the chancel, echoed by another in the choir loft, and mourners filed out into the white, winter afternoon. The next day, in Hudson, New York, Simpson's family said goodbye alone. He was buried beside his father, mother, and infant brother on the side of the highest hill in the Hudson City Cemetery.[148]

THE FINAL HAND

The sudden death of Kenneth Simpson left a tremendous void in a still-young family. Kelly, the oldest of the four children, had only just turned thirteen. Helen never remarried. She raised the children alone and remained in the house at 109 East 91st Street until her death forty years later. Simpson's death also left an empty seat in Congress that New York Republicans were eager to fill. Wendell Willkie was an obvious candidate, but he refused to run, believing that he would be more influential as a private citizen. Bruce Barton could likely have retaken the seat, but he was tired of politics. Russell Davenport, who had done so much to make Willkie a candidate, began a "boom" of sorts for Helen Simpson to succeed her husband in Congress, arguing that she had been his "constant advisor in mapping out the liberal and constructive course he followed."[149] Helen was wise enough to decline. She had neither the temperament for politics nor had she been her husband's political advisor. Instead, Joseph Clark Baldwin made the run and kept the seat for city Republicans.[150]

Elections came and went, and the wounds of the 1930s healed, even though Republican politics long bore the scars. Although the party remained in the electoral wilderness for another eleven years, it emerged from World War II better attuned to the social, economic, and cultural conditions of twentieth-century America. This was all that Simpson had hoped. He had learned the themes from Theodore Roosevelt but had elaborated upon them out of the experience of a new generation. The Republican Party, he argued again and again, had to accept regulation and restraint upon the unbridled power of business. It had to make a place for working-class as well as white-collar

Americans, give a wide scope to cultural difference, and allow the nation to take its natural place on the international stage. Republicans of the 1920s and 1930s were pessimists, unconvinced that the government could ameliorate social ills yet also safeguard basic freedoms. Simpson was an optimist: he believed that popular institutions were as capable as the people who had shaped his life—Theodore Roosevelt, his father, his friends at Yale, colleagues on Wall Street, and cohorts in countless smoke-filled political clubs up and down the island of Manhattan.[151]

Simpson had correctly anticipated the party's near-term future. As World War II gave way to the postwar *Pax Americana*, the influence of the old, insular progressivism died with its champions. A small government, "main street" Republican movement remained, led until the early 1950s by Robert Taft, but in the immediate postwar years it was liberal Republicanism—a coalition built upon white-collar workers, businessmen, and urban educated elites comfortable with big institutions and, within reason, big government—that held sway. Its standard bearer was a New York politician who, early in the war, saw the train of history, climbed aboard, and rode it through two unsuccessful presidential runs, the last lost in 1948 to Harry Truman by an agonizingly thin margin. It is unfortunate that the leading liberal Republican of the mid-twentieth century never realized that, irritating as he was, Kenneth Simpson had in fact helped make the Republican Party safe for Thomas E. Dewey.

It is tragic that Simpson did not live to build up the national liberal Republicanism that he helped to create out of the maelstrom of New York politics. Chase Mellen Jr. expressed a common sentiment when he wrote to Helen that "it is terribly cruel that he should have died just as he had crossed the threshold to a useful and important national career and when he had at last got free of local and petty politics."[152] As the *Washington Post* put it, "his 20 days showed what 20 years might have meant in a position where leadership is at a premium."[153]

But if Simpson did not live to see the triumph of liberal Republicanism during the Eisenhower years, neither did he live to see its collapse. During the 1960s, latter-day liberals like Nelson Rockefeller and John Lindsay failed in their attempts to bring together wide coalitions under the Republican banner. Instead, Barry Goldwater and Ronald Reagan, neither of whom had much faith in the potential of government, built up a new insular party based on laissez-faire economics and cultural intolerance that offered little hope to the impoverished in America.

What could Simpson have accomplished had he lived? It is unlikely that he could have reversed his party's ultimate turn away from liberalism, but given what his colleagues at the 15th Assembly District called "his impatience with the false, the fraud, the fake," he would certainly have raised a voice against it.[154] He may have remained in Congress, but he may just as likely have impatiently returned to the urban arena that he truly loved. It is doubtful that he would have risen to the level of presidential politics where positions must be malleable and sharp edges are soon worn smooth. Kenneth Simpson was all sharp edges. Shortly after his death, the *Herald Tribune*, a newspaper that had stood with him in nearly all of his fights, wrote that "if there were ten ways of doing a thing, nine of which would irritate no one and the tenth of which would irritate everybody, Mr. Simpson always preferred the tenth course."[155]

There can be no denying that some of Simpson's abrasiveness stemmed from the ambition so evident since his days at the Hill School. "I've been trying to make something out of my life," he wrote Helen in one of his late-night notes from the 1930s, "to leave the children a good name and reputation if no money."[156] There was also a heedlessness that stemmed from the joy with which Simpson entered the fray—a joy that was infectious. Franklin Roosevelt once despaired of "the stupid action of throwing out Simpson in New York City." "On the whole," Roosevelt wrote William Chadbourne, "while he was leader there was a 'lift' to the general scheme of office holding by all parties."[157] Bruce Barton recalled that "I never would have been in politics except for Ken Simpson. After he died I realized that his enthusiasm had been my mainspring and that most of the fun and the color had gone out of the game for me when he went."[158]

Kenneth Simpson's greatest political assets, and also his chief liabilities, were his sense of justice and deeply held convictions. "He was a hard fighter but a fair one," wrote Rolland Marvin.[159] The drummer boy in the Knickerbocker Greys was probably always better at setting the beat for others than at marching himself. He loved the race, but he cared too much about the destination to run it with the detachment that other candidates were capable of. Tom Dewey could never forgive Simpson for going back on their "deal," but he could not understand that for at least one man in politics, the cost of keeping one's word could outweigh the consequences of breaking it. Simpson had a gambler's instinct and a fighting spirit, but he took losing much too personally.

One evening in the fall of 1940, before he won his congressional seat and lost the county chairmanship, Simpson joined the usual suspects around the green baize table of the Hoyle Club. In a game of stud poker, Simpson had a pair of kings showing: another player had a pair of treys turned up. "Drop out. You can't win," Simpson muttered over and over with a characteristic lack of subtlety. Into his final hand, Simpson pulled a queen for two pair, but the opponent picked up a third trey to win. Afterward, as they walked back uptown together, Simpson turned to a fellow player. "You want to know something? What happened to me in poker tonight is symbolic—of almost everything in my life. Just when I get to the point of really winning—I always get kicked in the face."[160] Pipe smoke mixed with the scent of decaying leaves and hung in the autumn air as the two men walked on toward the close of an era and the end of a life, then disappeared into the New York night.

FOR CONGRESS

KENNETH F.
SIMPSON

ENDNOTES

CHAPTER 1

1. *New York Times*, March 11, 2007; "Knickerbocker Greys," *New Yorker*, May 1, 1926, 11-12.

2. Thomas Lee Jones, "Marching Along—The Knickerbocker Greys," *Social Register Observer*, Summer 2006, 24-28; *New York Times*, May 3, 1908; Stephen Birmingham, *The Right People: A Portrait of the American Social Establishment* (Boston, 1958), 46; "Twenty-Fifth Annual Reception and Drill of the Knickerbocker Greys," April 27, 1906. All Knickerbocker Greys Program material is courtesy of Dave Menegon, Commander, The Knickerbocker Greys.

3. "Twenty-Third Annual Reception and Drill of the Knickerbocker Greys," April 15, 1904.

4. The Kenneth Farrand Simpson Papers, Yale University Manuscripts and Archives (hereafter KFS Papers), Box 10, contain highly detailed preliminary drafts of an article, which, greatly shortened, appeared in the October 28, 1939, *New Yorker* (hereafter, Large Draft, *New Yorker*). See Noel F. Busch, "Boss Without Cigar," *New Yorker*, October 28, 1939.

5. *New York Times*, October 21, 1994.

6. Seventh Census of the United States, 1850; Stephen B. Miller, *Historical Sketches of Hudson* (Hudson, N.Y., 1862), 118; *New York Times*, January 20, 1860.

7. *New York Times*, January 20, 1860; *New York Times*, January 24, 1860; *New York Times*, February 8, 1860; Edward Hungerford, *Men and Iron: The History of the New York Central* (New York, 1938), 162; Eighth Census of the United States, 1860.

8. *New York Times*, April 15, 1897; Ninth Census of the United States, 1870.

9. "Resolutions on the Death of Dr. William Kelly Simpson," n.d. (circa 1914), Kelly Simpson Papers; Kenneth F. Simpson (hereafter KFS) to Evelyn Adams, September 19, 1936, KFS Papers, Box 1; Large Draft, *New Yorker*; *Medical Record*, February 14, 1914.

10. New York Naturalization Petition, Joseph Steevens Farrand, August 3, 1850; U.S. Passport Application, Joseph Steevens, April 23, 1851; "The Farrand Connection," n.d., Kelly Simpson Papers; Ninth Census of the United States, 1870.

11. Information from George Nicholas Simpson entry, *www.findagrave.com*, January 31, 2003, by Barbara Doxey; the author is indebted to Mrs. Doxey for providing additional information on the Simpson and Farrand families. "Resolutions on the Death of Dr. William Kelly Simpson," n.d. (circa 1914), Kelly Simpson Papers; *Medical Record*, February 14, 1914.

12. *New York Times*, February 15, 1898; *New York Times*, February 7, 1914; see, for example, *New York Tribune*, April 18, 1904.

13. City of New York Department of Records, Birth Certificate, Kenneth Farrand Simpson, May 4, 1895.

14. In choosing the Indian word "Taminend," club founders sought to cultivate a truly American identity. On "honest graft," see William L. Riordan, *Plunkitt of Tammany Hall: A Series of Very Plain Talks on Very Practical Politics* (New York, 1995).

15. Edwin G. Burrows and Mike Wallace, *Gotham: A History of New York City to 1898* (New York, 1999), 1200.

16. Ibid., 1077; Twelfth Census of the United States, 1900.

17. *New York Times*, April 15, 1897; Twelfth Census of the United States, 1900; W. K. Simpson to Arthur Farrand, June 4, 1900, Kelly Simpson Papers.

18. Large Draft, *New Yorker*.

19. *New York Times*, December 9, 1912; Large Draft, *New Yorker*; Thirteenth Census of the United States, 1910; Large Draft, *New Yorker*; see for example, debtor judgment in *New York Times*, April 3, 1906.

20. William Henry Harbaugh, *Power and Responsibility: The Life and Times of Theodore Roosevelt* (New York, 1961), 108; Large Draft, *New Yorker*.

21. *New York Times*, August 13, 1899; Robert Howard Syms, "Life and Needs of the City School Boy," *Town and Country*, August 19, 1905.

22. *New York Times*, May 4, 1909.

23. Large Draft, *New Yorker*.

24. KFS to Anna Farrand Simpson, June 16, 1919, Kelly Simpson Papers; KFS to Mrs. Walter Mack, December 6, 1937, KFS Papers, Box 2.

25. Elmer Rice, "A New York Childhood—1," *New Yorker*, September 8, 1928, 19-21.

26. Cass Gilbert Jr. to KFS, May 30, 1912, Kelly Simpson Papers.

27. *Town and Country*, May 6, 1905.

28. "Twenty-Ninth Annual Reception and Drill of the Kickerbocker Greys," April 22, 1910.

29. See Twenty-Third through Twenty-Seventh Annual Reception and Drill Programs; "Twenty-Eighth Annual Reception and Drill of the Kickerbocker Greys," April 23, 1909; "Twenty-Ninth Annual Reception and Drill of the Kickerbocker Greys," April 22, 1910.

30. Large Draft, *New Yorker*; John A. Garraty, *Right-Hand Man: The Life of George W. Perkins* (New York, 1957), 158.

31. *New York Times*, November 8, 1911; Edmund Wilson, "Mr. Rolfe," *The Atlantic*, March 1943, 97-107, see p. 100.

32. *Hill School News*, March 5, 1913; *Hill School News*, October 1, 1912; *The Hill School Dial*, 1911; Edmund Wilson, "A Prelude: Landscapes, Characters, and Conversations from the Earlier Years of My Life," *New Yorker*, April 29, 1967, 50-131, see p. 113.

33. The tough times included time in the Hill School dispensary for a severe ear infection that sent Kenneth home for a time. George Perkins Jr., who had a cold at the same time, wrote, "Kenneth Simpson is in the san which all helps to make things nice and cheerful around here." See George Perkins Jr. to George Perkins Sr., January 18, 1912, Columbia University Archives and Manuscripts, George W. Perkins Papers, Box 12.

34. Paul Chancellor, *The History of the Hill School, 1851-1976* (Pottstown, PA, 1976), 48, 37; Wilson, "Mr. Rolfe," 100.

35. *The Hill School Dial*, 1913; KFS to Anna Farrand Simpson, October 16, 1918, Kelly Simpson Papers; *The Hill School Dial*, 1912; *The Hill School Dial*, 1913; Large Draft, *New Yorker*, discusses Simpson's early acting aspirations.

36. "Kenneth F. Simpson," biographical sketch, n.d. (circa 1936), KFS Papers, Box 33; *Hill School News*, December 3, 1912; *Hill School News*, April 9, 1913; see George W. Perkins Jr. to Mrs. George W. Perkins, April 7, 1913, and George W. Perkins Jr. to George W. Perkins Sr., April 9, 1913, Columbia University Archives and Manuscripts, George W. Perkins Papers, Box 13.

37. Chancellor, *The History of the Hill School*, 35; *The Hill School Dial*, 1912.

38. *The Hill School Dial*, 1913; *Hill School News*, May 20, 1913; Large Draft, *New Yorker*; Chancellor, *The History of the Hill School*, 62.

39. George Brown Tindall, *America: A Narrative History, Volume II* (New York, 1988), 941.

40. George E. Mowry, *Theodore Roosevelt and The Progressive Movement* (New York, 1946), 18.

41. *New York Times*, December 30, 1911.

42. The Kenneth Farrand Simpson Papers, Box 10, contain miscellaneous draft pages, out of order, for the same article discussed in note 4 (hereafter "*New Yorker* Drafts").

43. *Hill School News*, October 8, 1912; *The Hill School Dial*, 1913; *The Hill School Dial*, 1912.

44. *Hill School News*, October 1, 1912; *Hill School News*, January 14, 1913.

45. Large Draft, *New Yorker*; see George W. Perkins Jr. to Mrs. George W. Perkins, April 7, 1913, Columbia University Archives and Manuscripts, George W. Perkins Papers, Box 13; *The Hill School Dial*, 1913.

46. *The Hill School Dial*, 1913.

47. *Hill School News*, October 8, 1912; *The Hill School Dial*, 1913.

48. *Hill School News*, October 22, 1912; Large Draft, *New Yorker*.

49. *The Hill School Dial*, 1913; *Hill School News*, May 20, 1913; Large Draft, *New Yorker*.

50. *The Hill School Dial*, 1912.

51. *The Hill School Dial*, 1913.

52. See *The Snooze*, Thanksgiving 1911, included in the John W. Overton Scrapbook, The Hill School Library.

53. George W. Perkins Sr. to George W. Perkins Jr., April 21, 1913, Columbia University Archives and Manuscripts, George W. Perkins Papers, Box 13.

54. *New York Times*, June 10, 1913; *Hill School News*, June 10, 1913.

55. *The Outlook*, August 2, 1913.

56. *New York Times*, June 10, 1913.

57. *The Hill School Dial*, 1913.

58. *The Hill School Record*, June 1913, 270; William Kelly Simpson to KFS, October 4, 1913, KFS Papers, Box 1.

59. William Kelly Simpson to KFS, October 4, 1913, KFS Papers, Box 1.

60. Chancellor, *The History of the Hill School*, 47; *Hill School News*, January 14, 1913.

61. *The Hill School Dial*, 1913.

62. See John W. Overton Scrapbook, The Hill School Library.

63. William Kelly Simpson to KFS, October 4, 1913, KFS Papers, Box 1; Willam Kelly Simpson to KFS, November 23, 1913, KFS Papers, Box 1; description from Draft Registration Card, May 29, 1917.

64. Twenty-two entering freshmen were from The Hill School. See *History of the Class of Nineteen Hundred and Seventeen, Yale College* (New Haven, 1917), 1, 294; *Hill School News*, April 15, 1913; William Kelly Simpson to KFS, October 4, 1913, KFS Papers, Box 1.

65. William Kelly Simpson to KFS, October 4, 1913, KFS Papers, Box 1; see William A. James to KFS, January 12, 1936, KFS Papers, Box 1.

66. William Kelly Simpson to KFS, November 23, 1913, KFS Papers, Box 1.

67. *New York Times*, February 7, 1914; William Kelly Simpson Estate Settlement, June 9, 1916, KFS Papers, Box 33; Anna Farrand Simpson to Mrs. Cunningham, n.d. (circa October 1918), Kelly Simpson Papers; *History of the Class of Nineteen Hundred and Seventeen*, 294.

68. *New Yorker* Drafts.

69. See journal entry for May 28, 1931, in Kelly Simpson Papers; *History of the Class of Nineteen Hundred and Seventeen,* 294; KFS to Helen Simpson, March 11, 1927, Kelly Simpson Papers.

70. *History of the Class of Nineteen Hundred and Seventeen,* 294; quoted in Walter Isaacson and Evan Thomas, *The Wise Men: Six friends and the World They Made* (New York, 1986), 80.

71. Henry F. Pringle, "Young Men on the Make," *Harpers,* January, 1929, 149-57.

72. Kenneth does not show up in the newspaper social listings until the 1920s.

73. *History of the Class of Nineteen Hundred and Seventeen,* 4; Lewis Sheldon Welch and Walter Camp, *Yale: Her Campus, Class-Rooms, and Athletics* (Boston, 1899), 80; John Kobler, *Luce: His Time, Life, and Fortune* (Garden City, NY, 1968), 37.

74. *History of the Class of Nineteen Hundred and Seventeen,* 294.

75. The buildings of the Berkeley Oval were replaced in the 1930s by Berkeley College.

76. KFS to Anna Farrand Simpson, April 21, 1914, Kelly Simpson Papers.

77. *Yale Daily News,* February 11, 1916; Kenneth knew of his selection long in advance. He was designated chairman in May 1915.

78. Garraty, *Right-Hand Man,* 298; *New York Times,* August 22, 1914; Garraty, *Right-Hand Man,* 312.

79. *New York Times,* September 25, 1915.

80. *New York Times,* September 26, 1915. Simpson frankly discussed his enjoyment of "flirting and related sports" in a private journal kept later in life. See May 28, 1931, entry in KFS loose-leaf journal, Kelly Simpson Papers.

81. Garraty, *Right-Hand Man,* 33.

82. His "letter of authority" as assistant sergeant-at-arms is in the George W. Perkins Papers, Box 8, Columbia University Archives and Manuscripts. The George W. Perkins Papers contain transcripts of some of these private wire conversations, but Kenneth's participation is indicated in none of them. Although the Papers provide no evidence that he was there, it is still likely that he was, given that Simpson told this story a number of times and in such highly visible venues as the *New Yorker* without refutation. Also, nearly all of Simpson's other stories can be corroborated—there is no evidence that he ever embellished his past. For the account mentioned, see Noel F. Busch, "Boss Without Cigar," *New Yorker,* October 28, 1939.

83. Large Draft, *New Yorker*; Busch, "Boss Without Cigar."

84. Garraty, *Right-Hand Man,* 334.

85. Harbaugh, *Power and Responsibility,* 489; Garraty, *Right-Hand Man,* 351.

86. Welch and Camp, *Yale,* 107.

87. See Pringle, "Young Men on the Make."

88. *Yale Daily News*, May 18, 1916; *History of the Class of Nineteen Hundred and Seventeen*, 415.

89. *Yale Daily News*, May 19, 1916.

90. KFS to Anna Farrand Simpson, October 16, 1918, Kelly Simpson Papers; *History of the Class of Nineteen Hundred and Seventeen*, 49, 294.

91. *History of the Class of Nineteen Hundred and Seventeen*, 29; Isaacson and Thomas, *The Wise Men*, 90; KFS to Anna Farrand Simpson, October 16, 1918, Kelly Simpson Papers.

92. Large Draft, *New Yorker*; *Hartford Courant*, October 10, 1915; *History of the Class of Nineteen Hundred and Seventeen*, 49; *New York Times*, September 1, 1916.

93. *History of the Class of Nineteen Hundred and Seventeen*, 55, 49; *New York Times*, June 21, 1916.

94. *History of the Class of Nineteen Hundred and Seventeen*, 401.

95. *New York Times*, September 1, 1916.

96. *History of the Class of Nineteen Hundred and Seventeen*, 55, 408.

97. *History of the Class of Nineteen Hundred and Seventeen*, 294; "Kenneth F. Simpson," biographical sketch, n.d. (circa 1936), KFS Papers, Box 33; Welch and Camp, *Yale*, 77.

98. Pringle, "Young Men on the Make," 154.

99. *Yale Daily News*, October 14, 1916.

100. *Yale Daily News*, September 30, 1916.

101. *Yale Daily News*, November 9, 1916.

102. *Yale Daily News*, October 6, 1916.

103. *History of the Class of Nineteen Hundred and Seventeen*, 430; *Yale Daily News*, October 10, 1916.

104. *Yale Daily News*, October 10, 1916.

105. Large Draft, *New Yorker*.

106. Ibid.; *Hartford Courant*, October 29, 1916.

107. *Yale Daily News*, October 25, 1916; *History of the Class of Nineteen Hundred and Seventeen*, 59.

108. "Kenneth F. Simpson," biographical sketch, n.d. (circa 1936), KFS Papers, Box 33.

109. Large Draft, *New Yorker*; *Yale Daily News*, November 7, 1916.

110. Large Draft, *New Yorker*; *Yale Daily News*, November 8, 1916.

111. Large Draft, *New Yorker*; *Yale Daily News*, November 11, 1916.

112. *History of the Class of Nineteen Hundred and Seventeen,* 65; *Yale Daily News,* January 24, 1917.

113. *History of the Class of Nineteen Hundred and Seventeen,* 66.

114. *Yale Alumni Weekly,* n.d. (circa March 1917), Kelly Simpson Papers.

115. *History of the Class of Nineteen Hundred and Seventeen,* 430-32.

116. On Phelps, see Isaacson and Thomas, *The Wise Men,* 86; Wilson, "A Prelude," 52-149, see p. 131.

117. Kenneth Farrand Simpson, "The Students in the War," in George Henry Nettleton, *Yale in the World War, Part One* (New Haven, 1925), 411-14, see p. 411.

118. *Yale Daily News,* February 3 and 5, 1917; Draft Registration Card, May 29, 1917; *Hartford Courant,* April 1, 1917.

119. *Yale Daily News,* April 12, 1917; Simpson, "The Students in the War," 411.

120. *Yale Daily News,* April 24, 1917.

121. F. Scott Fitzgerald, *This Side of Paradise* (New York, 1920), 282.

CHAPTER 2

1.   KFS to Livingston W. Cleveland, November 4, 1917, Kelly Simpson Papers.

2.   302nd Field Artillery Association, *The 302nd Field Artillery, United States Army* (New York, 1919), 45, 35.

3.   *The 302nd Field Artillery,* 31-42. The Kenneth Farrand Simpson Papers, Yale University Manuscripts and Archives (hereafter KFS Papers), Box 10, contain miscellaneous draft pages, out of order, of highly detailed preliminary drafts of an article which, greatly shortened, appeared in the October 28, 1939, *New Yorker* (hereafter "*New Yorker* Drafts").

4.   Regimental History, 302nd Field Artillery, April 1918, National Archives and Records Administration, College Park, Maryland (NARA), RG 120 (Records of the American Expeditionary Forces), Entry 1241, Box 2; *New Yorker* Drafts; *The 302nd Field Artillery,* 45.

5.   Regimental History, 302nd Field Artillery, August 1918, NARA, RG 120, Entry 1241, Box 2.

6.   Kenneth Farrand Simpson, "The Students in the War," in George Henry Nettleton, *Yale in the World War, Part One* (New Haven, 1925), 411-14, see p. 413; *The 302nd Field Artillery,* 61, 69; KFS to Anna Farrand Simpson, October 16, 1918, Kelly Simpson Papers.

7. *The 302nd Field Artillery*, 61, 69, 72; Regimental Return, 302nd Field Artillery, November 1918, NARA, RG 407 (Records of the Adjutant General's Office), Entry UD 111, Box 210; *The 302nd Field Artillery*, 90.

8. See collected field messages in NARA, RG 120, Entry 1241, Box 2; see "Headquarters, 302nd Field Artillery, American Expeditionary Forces, France, Log of Operations," NARA, RG 120, Entry 1241, Box 2; *The 302nd Field Artillery*, 102.

9. KFS to T. Louis A. Britt, Esq., September 12, 1938, KFS Papers, Box 3; Alfred E. Cornebise, *Soldier-Scholars: Higher Education in the AEF, 1917-1919* (Philadelphia, 1997), xiii, 8.

10. KFS to Anna Farrand Simpson, June 22, 1919, Kelly Simpson Papers; Regimental History, 302nd Field Artillery, January 1919, NARA, RG 120, Entry 1241, Box 2; Cornebise, *Soldier-Scholars*, 141; KFS to Veterans Administration Board of Appeals, May 25, 1936, KFS Papers, Box 1; Lieutenant Colonel Gordon R. Catts to Assistant Chief of Staff, C-5, May 5, 1919, NARA, RG 120, Entry 420, Box 1965.

11. Lieutenant Colonel Gordon R. Catts to Assistant Chief of Staff, C-5, May 5, 1919, NARA, RG 120, Entry 420, Box 1965.

12. Noel F. Busch, "Boss Without Cigar," *New Yorker*, October 28, 1939, 22; Cornebise, *Soldier-Scholars*, 155-57.

13. *New Yorker* Drafts; KFS to Anna Farrand Simpson, June 22, 1919, Kelly Simpson Papers.

14. Kai Bird, *The Chairman: John J. McCloy, The Making of the American Establishment* (New York, 1992), 48; Ivan Chen, "Alger Hiss, 1926-1929" (2008), available at http://works.bepress.com/ivan_chen/1, 15-16.

15. Harvard Law School, Registrar's Office, KFS transcripts; Chen, "Alger Hiss, 1926-1929," 25; *Boston Daily Globe*, October 4, 1919; Simpson's roommate was Edward Stevenson Pinney II; Bird, *The Chairman*, 49-50.

16. *Hartford Courant*, February 10, 1920, and December 12, 1920.

17. Membership card (n.d.) can be found in KFS Papers, Box 34; Arthur E. Sutherland, *The Law at Harvard: A History of Ideas and Men, 1817-1967* (Cambridge, 1967), 248; KFS to J. Watson Webb, December 29, 1937, KFS Papers, Box 3.

18. Joel Seligman, *The High Citadel: The Influence of Harvard Law School* (New York, 1978), 58; Bird, *The Chairman*, 53-54.

19. *New York Times*, June 23, 1922; see May 19, 1922, Kenneth Farrand Simpson Passport Application, U.S. Department of State; KFS Papers, Box 10, contain highly detailed preliminary drafts of an article, which, greatly shortened, appeared in the October 28, 1939, *New Yorker* (hereafter, Large Draft, *New Yorker*).

20. *Harvard Crimson*, December 10, 1921.

21. Bird, *The Chairman*, 58.

22. Deborah S. Gardner, *Cadwalader, Wickersham & Taft: A Bicentennial History, 1792-1992* (New York, 1994), 16; Bird, *The Chairman*, 58.

23. *New York Times*, December 5, 1924; KFS to Richard C. Buck, Esq., June 16, 1923, KFS Papers, Box 16; KFS to Daniel F. Daily, Esq., March 20, 1924, KFS Papers, Box 20.

24. John Kobler, *Luce: His Time, His Life, His Fortune* (Garden City, NY, 1968), 46; *New Yorker* Drafts.

25. Large Draft, *New Yorker*.

26. Ibid.

27. Roy V. Peel, *The Political Clubs of New York City* (New York, 1935), 56.

28. Frederic C. Bellinger, "The Story of Ken Simpson and How He Put Thomas E. Dewey on the Political Map" (unpublished manuscript), KFS Papers, Box 33, 4; Reminiscences of Stanley Isaacs, Columbia University Oral History Research Office (hereafter CUOHRO), 14; Peel, *The Political Clubs of New York City*, 160.

29. Peel, *The Political Clubs of New York City*, 221.

30. Reminiscences of Walter Mack Jr., CUOHRO, 9-10.

31. "Nize Sam, Ett Opp all the G.O.P.," *New Yorker*, March 6, 1926, 15-16.

32. Reminiscences of Samuel S. Koenig, CUOHRO, 47.

33. *New York Times*, May 3, 1964.

34. *New York Times*, January 21, 1924.

35. *New York Times*, March 15, 1924; Reminiscences of Walter Mack Jr., CUOHRO, 9; "Alderwoman," *Time*, November 16, 1925; *New York Times*, March 30, 1924.

36. *New Yorker* Drafts; Bird, *The Chairman*, 63-64.

37. Busch, "Boss Without Cigar," 23; *New York Times*, April 2, 1924.

38. Ibid.; Reminiscences of Joseph Clark Baldwin, CUOHRO, 11.

39. *New Yorker* Drafts.

40. *News Record*, September 23, 1925; *New York Times*, April 28, 1925.

41. Reminiscences of Samuel S. Koenig, CUOHRO, 40; Burton W. Peretti, *Nightclub City: Politics and Amusement in Manhattan* (Philadelphia, 2007), 79; "Mr. Buckner Explains," *New Yorker*, November 14, 1925.

42. *Daily News Record*, May 12, 1925.

43. Martin Mayer, *Emory Buckner* (New York, 1968), 177; KFS to Helen Porter, April 29, 1925, Kelly Simpson Papers.

44. Peretti, *Nightclub City*, 80; Mayer, *Emory Buckner*, 184; KFS to Helen Porter, April 28, 1925, Kelly Simpson Papers.

45. See for example, *New York Times*, January 20 and February 4, 1923; Joseph
     Fulford Folsom, ed., *The Municipalities of Essex County, New Jersey, 1666-1924*
     (New York, 1925), 352; Henry Whittmore, *History of Montclair Township, State
     of New Jersey: Including the History of the Families Who Have Been Identified
     With Its Growth and Prosperity* (New York, 1894), 233.

46. The two could have met in France, but it is unlikely. They were stationed at
     opposite ends of the front, and no correspondence between the two exists until
     early 1925.

47. Helen Porter to KFS, February 5, 1925, Kelly Simpson Papers.

48. KFS to Helen Porter, May 15, 1925, Kelly Simpson Papers.

49. Helen Porter to KFS, May 1, 1925, KFS Papers, Box 1; KFS to Helen Porter,
     April 30, 1925, Kelly Simpson Papers; KFS to Helen Porter, May 13, 1925, Kelly
     Simpson Papers.

50. Caroline Porter to KFS, April 26, 1925, KFS Papers, Box 1; *New York Times*, June
     19, 1925; *New York Times*, June 26, 1925; KFS to Helen Simpson, June 25, 1938,
     Kelly Simpson Papers; *New York Times*, June 26, 1925.

51. See June 3, 1921, Helen L. K. Porter Passport Application, U.S. Department of
     State; Kenneth Simpson Passport, June 29, 1927, Kelly Simpson Papers.

52. William E. Leuchtenberg, *The Perils of Prosperity, 1914-32* (Chicago, 1958), 150.

53. Unidentified Correspondent to KFS, September 1919; KFS to M. Maurice Le
     Clerc, February 28, 1939, KFS Papers, Box 3.

54. Large Draft, *New Yorker*; *Christian Science Monitor*, March 2, 1927; Ernest
     Hemingway, *A Moveable Feast* (New York, 1964), 20.

55. See June 17, 1924, passport in KFS Papers, Box 34.

56. William H. Whyte, ed., *The WPA Guide to New York City, The Federal Writers
     Project Guide to 1930s New York* (New York, 1982), 233-34; *Hartford Courant*,
     June 19, 1932.

57. See "Inventory of Paintings etc.," May 1, 1931, in KFS Papers, Box 33; KFS to
     Helen Simpson, May 19, 1926, Kelly Simpson Papers; KFS to Helen Simpson,
     May 15, 1929, Kelly Simpson Papers; KFS to Helen Simpson, March 11, 1927,
     Kelly Simpson Papers.

58. *Pittsburgh Courier*, April 2, 1927; *New York Times*, May 27, 1930; *New York
     Times*, May 10, 1928; *New Yorker* Drafts.

59. When Simpson sought to obtain a passport in 1922, his mother was too ill to
     vouch for him. Sarah Simpson to KFS, November 23, 1926, Kelly Simpson
     Papers; KFS to Helen Simpson, May 17, 1929, Kelly Simpson Papers.

60. *New York Herald* (Paris Edition), February 27, 1926; "Kenneth F. Simpson,"
     biographical sketch, n.d. (circa 1936), KFS Papers, Box 33; Maritza Colau
     (Littleton) to KFS, December 15, 1938, KFS Papers, Box 3; see February 17,
     1926, passport in KFS Papers, Box 34.

61. *New York Sun*, September 3, 1926; *Christian Science Monitor*, May 7, 1926.

62. Mayer, *Emory Buckner*, 211; *New York Telegram*, January 22, 1926; *New York Times*, February 2, 1926.

63. Mayer, *Emory Buckner*, 215.

64. See notes for *New Yorker* article in KFS Papers, Box 33.

65. *New York Times*, May 8, 1926.

66. *Evening Post*, October 4, 1926; KFS to Helen Simpson, April 7, 1926, Kelly Simpson Papers; *Christian Science Monitor*, May 7, 1926.

67. Mayer, *Emory Buckner*, 217.

68. *New York American*, April 6, 1927.

69. *Evening Post*, October 4, 1926.

70. *Evening World*, September 15, 1926; see notes for *New Yorker* article in KFS Papers, Box 33; *New York Times*, October 12, 1926.

71. *New York Times*, December 9, 1926; *Los Angeles Times*, February 11, 1927; James N. Giglio, *H.M. Daugherty and the Politics of Expediency* (Kent, OH, 1978), 181-92.

72. *New York Times*, July 21, 1927; *Evening World*, July 19, 1927; *New York Times*, July 19, 1927.

73. *New York Times*, July 21, 1927.

74. *New York World*, September 20, 1927; *New York World*, August 17, 1927; "The Nigger of the 'Kingsway,'" *New Yorker*, August 20, 1927.

75. *New York World*, August 9, 1927; *New York Times*, August 17, 1927.

76. KFS to Helen Porter, May 5, 1925, Kelly Simpson Papers; see Bank Book entries for January 1926 in KFS Papers, Box 33; KFS to Helen Porter, April 28, 1925, Kelly Simpson Papers; KFS to Charles H. Tuttle, September 12, 1927, and Charles H. Tuttle to KFS, September 15, 1927, KFS Papers, Box 1; *New York Times*, September 13, 1927.

77. *New York Times*, September 13, 1927; *New York Times*, December 24, 1927; KFS to Albert F. Horton, October 22, 1927, KFS Papers, Box 30; George Gordon Battle to KFS, January 30, 1928, KFS Papers, Box 16; KFS to Merrill N. Gates, Esq., November 22, 1927, KFS Papers, Box 28.

78. J. Callendar Heminway, ed., *History of the Class of 1917, Yale College* (New Haven, 1928), 187.

79. *New York Times*, March 8, 1928.

80. Herbert Mitgang, *The Man Who Rode the Tiger: The Life and Times of Judge Samuel Seabury* (New York, 1963), 192; *The People of the State of New York v. Carol Bodmer*, January 6, 1928, KFS Papers, Box 16.

81. Elizabeth Frank, *Louise Bogan: A Portrait* (New York, 1985), 1985.

82. Recounted in KFS to Dorothy Harvey, May 4, 1935, KFS Papers, Box 8.

83. Dorothy Harvey to KFS, n.d. (circa August to October 1930), KFS Papers, Box 8; Dorothy Harvey to KFS, November 21, 1930, KFS Papers, Box 8; see for example, Dorothy Dudley to KFS, May 4, 1934, KFS Papers, Box 8.

84. *New York Times*, March 23, 1928; *New York Times*, March 16, 1929; KFS to Frederick R. Coudert, March 15, 1929, Frederic R. Coudert Jr. Papers, Columbia University Archives and Manuscripts, Box 8 (hereafter Coudert Papers).

85. KFS to Frederic R. Coudert Jr., August 16, 1929, Coudert Papers, Box 7; *Herald Tribune*, March 16, 1929.

86. *Brooklyn Daily Eagle*, November 12, 1929.

87. *Evening World*, September 26, 1929; *Brooklyn Times*, May 15, 1930.

88. KFS to Helen Simpson, May 17, 1930, Kelly Simpson Papers. The verdict was set aside on a technicality. The case went to trial again but was dropped.

89. *New York Times*, June 19, 1929; *New York Times*, December 18, 1929; see Howard Carter Dickinson to KFS, April 30, 1929, KFS Papers, Box 29.

90. "Dinosaur Hunt," *New Yorker*, December 19, 1931; *New York City Telegram*, February 27, 1931.

91. "Kenneth F. Simpson," biographical sketch, n.d. (circa 1936), KFS Papers, Box 33.

92. Marvin G. Weinbaum, "A Minority's Survival: The Republican Party of New York County, 1897-1960" (Ph.D. diss., Columbia University, 1965), 13.

93. Frederic C. Bellinger, "The Copeland Primary Fight in New York and La Guardia in 1940" (unpublished manuscript), KFS Papers, Box 10, p. 22; *New York Times*, August 29, 1949; "Kenneth F. Simpson," biographical sketch, n.d. (circa 1936), KFS Papers, Box 33.

94. Judith Stein, "The Birth of Liberal Republicanism in New York State, 1932-1938" (Ph.D. diss., Yale University, 1968), 12.

95. Lewis L. Gould, *Grand Old Party, A History of the Republicans* (New York, 2003), 247, 249.

96. Stein, "The Birth of Liberal Republicanism in New York State," 30; KFS to Helen Simpson, June 19, 1928, Kelly Simpson Papers.

97. Reminiscences of Walter Mack Jr., CUOHRO, 15.

98. KFS to Helen Simpson, June 19, 1928, Kelly Simpson Papers.

99. Ibid.

100. *New York Times*, June 16, 1929.

101. *New York Times*, October 10, 1929; KFS to Helen Simpson, May 17, 1929, Kelly Simpson Papers; *New York Times*, November 15, 1930.

102. Reminiscences of Walter Mack Jr., CUOHRO, 15.

103. Leuchtenberg, *The Perils of Prosperity*, 243.

104. KFS to Donald Ogden Stewart, April 26, 1930, KFS Papers, Box 30.

105. KFS to Helen Simpson, June 3, 1930, Kelly Simpson Papers; KFS to Helen Simpson, June 10, 1930, Kelly Simpson Papers.

106. *New York Times*, May 27, 1930; Dorothy Kenyon to KFS, n.d. (circa May 1930), Kelly Simpson Papers.

107. KFS to Dorothy Harvey, March 13, 1933, KFS Papers, Box 8; KFS to Helen Simpson, May 31, 1929, Kelly Simpson Papers; KFS to Helen Simpson, June 10, 1930, Kelly Simpson Papers.

108. KFS Memo, "Maximum Lump Sum Offer," n.d. (circa April 1932), KFS Papers, Box 34; for various club resignations, see Kenneth Simpson correspondence, KFS Papers, Box 1; KFS to Snell Smith, December 2, 1932, KFS Papers, Box 1.

109. KFS to Snell Smith, December 2, 1932, on the Union League Club. One of the few clubs he did not resign was the Yale Club. KFS to John A. Maher, Esq., February 7, 1933, KFS Papers, Box 1.

110. KFS to Helen Porter, April 28, 1925, and May 8, 1925, Kelly Simpson Papers.

111. *New Yorker* Drafts; see May 19, 1922, passport photo in KFS Papers, Box 34; *New Yorker* Drafts; Dorothy Harvey to KFS, July 29, 1930, KFS Papers, Box 8; Dorothy Harvey to KFS, August 18, 1930, KFS Papers, Box 8.

112. Dorothy Harvey to KFS, August 15, 1932, KFS Papers, Box 8.

113. May 26, 1931, entry in KFS loose-leaf journal, Kelly Simpson Papers; Henry B. Harvey to KFS, December 17, 1931, KFS Papers, Box 8.

114. Dorothy Harvey to KFS, October 6, 1931, KFS Papers, Box 8; see "Poor Dreiser," in *The Bookman: A Review of Books and Life*, November 1932, 75.

115. Dorothy Harvey to KFS, December 18, 1932, KFS Papers, Box 8; "Waggoner's Gesture," *Time*, September 16, 1929; handwritten "brief review of legal work," n.d. (circa January 1935), KFS Papers, Box 34.

116. Kenneth Walser to KFS, April 4, 1933, KFS Papers, Box 25; KFS to Dorothy Harvey, March 13, 1933, KFS Papers, Box 8.

117. KFS to Dorothy Harvey, May 4, 1933, KFS Papers, Box 8.

118. Large Draft, *New Yorker*.

119. Handwritten self-evaluation, n.d. (circa May 1931), Kelly Simpson Papers.

120. Ibid. He wrote in his journal: "How are the mighty fallen feeling—Yale—Army etc. and now."

121. KFS to Helen Simpson, September 9, 1932, Kelly Simpson Papers.

122. Dorothy Harvey to KFS, August 15, 1932, KFS Papers, Box 8.

123. Charles Hilles to Richard Scandrett, February 4, 1932, Charles Hilles Papers, Yale University Manuscripts and Archives, Box 119.

124. Leuchtenberg, *The Perils of Prosperity*, 265.

125. KFS to Dorothy Harvey, October 10, 1932, KFS Papers, Box 8.

126. Keyes Winter to KFS, November 25, 1932, KFS Papers, Box 1.

127. Warren Moscow, *Politics in the Empire State* (New York, 1948), 71; Stein, "The Birth of Liberal Republicanism in New York State," 38; Weinbaum, "A Minority's Survival," 56; "The Sick Man of Politics," *New Yorker*, August 5, 1933.

128. Reminiscences of Walter Mack Jr., CUOHRO, 26.

129. "More Bounce to the Ounce II" *New Yorker*, July 8, 1950, 34.

130. Ibid.; Reminiscences of Walter Mack Jr., CUOHRO, 26, 27.

131. Reminiscences of Walter Mack Jr., CUOHRO, 39.

132. "Nize Sam, Ett Opp all the G.O.P.," *New Yorker*, March 6, 1926; Weinbaum, "A Minority's Survival," 60; *New York Times*, January 1, 1933.

133. *New York Times*, May 17, 1933; *New York Times*, May 18, 1933; KFS to Dorothy Harvey, May 17, 1933, KFS Papers, Box 8.

134. *New York Times*, June 6, 1933.

CHAPTER 3

1. The cards, ace of clubs signed by the players, are in the Kenneth Farrand Simpson Papers, Yale University Manuscripts and Archives (hereafter KFS Papers), Box 33; undated, unattributed newspaper clipping in Kenneth Simpson Scrapbooks, Yale University Microfilm Collection.

2. *New York Times*, March 14, 1937.

3. KFS to "Dear Voter," November 4, 1933, Kelly Simpson Papers.

4. Judith Stein, "The Birth of Liberal Republicanism in New York State, 1932-1938" (Ph.D. diss., Yale University, 1968), 52-53.

5. Newbold Morris, *Let the Chips Fall: My Battles Against Corruption* (New York, 1955), 87; Frederic C. Bellinger, "The Story of Ken Simpson and How He Put Thomas E. Dewey on the Political Map" (unpublished manuscript), KFS Papers, Box 33, 9.

6. KFS to J. C. Heminway, October 11, 1934, KFS Papers, Box 1. Most politicians, noted colleague Stanley Isaacs, were "not interested in the mechanics of it. He was intensely interested in it." Reminiscences of Stanley Isaacs, Columbia University Oral History Research Office (hereafter CUOHRO), 81; Simpson to Charles Hilles, October 9, 1934, KFS Papers, Box 1.

7. KFS to Charles Hilles, September 8, 1935, Charles Hilles Papers, Yale University Manuscripts and Archives (hereafter Hilles Papers), Box 123.

8. *New York Times*, September 16, 1934; Morris, *Let The Chips Fall*, 97; *New York Times*, October 8, 1934; Simpson to J. C. Heminway, October 11, 1934, KFS Papers, Box 1.

9.   Stein, "The Birth of Liberal Republicanism in New York State," 73-78.

10. Ibid., 77; *Time*, December 24, 1934.

11. KFS to G. Herbert Semler, December 5, 1934, KFS Papers, Box 1.

12. KFS to J. C. Heminway, October 11, 1934, KFS Papers, Box 1.

13. Attachment to "Report of the Hack Bureau, Police Department, City of New York," Citizens Budget Commission, April 23, 1934, KFS Papers, Box 9.

14. KFS to Kenneth E. Walser, April 6, 1935, KFS Papers, Box 34.

15. KFS to J. C. Heminway, October 11, 1934, KFS Papers, Box 1; KFS to Dorothy Dudley Harvey, April 26, 1934, and August 31, 1934, KFS Papers, Box 8.

16. KFS to Dorothy Dudley Harvey, August 31, 1934, KFS Papers, Box 8.

17. Dorothy Dudley Harvey to KFS, November 21, 1934, KFS Papers, Box 8.

18. Biographical sketch, n.d., KFS Papers, Box 3; *New York Times*, May 23, 1935.

19. *New York Times*, May 1, 1934, and April 27, 1934; *New York Times*, February 9, 1935; *New York Times*, May 8, 1934; *New York Times*, June 27, 1934; *New York Times*, April 8, 1935; unidentified to "Maitre Moulin," August 16, 1935, KFS Papers, Box 18; KFS to David Brady, June 18, 1935, KFS Papers, Box 18; KFS to Michel Brault, May 2, 1935, KFS Papers, Box 18.

20. The KFS Papers, Box 10, contain miscellaneous draft pages, out of order, of highly detailed preliminary drafts of an article which, greatly shortened, appeared in the October 28, 1939, *New Yorker* (hereafter "*New Yorker* Drafts").

21. See notes in KFS Papers, Box 33. In 1937, Simpson was contributing three times his salary to the firm's income. KFS to Dorothy Dudley Harvey, August 31, 1934, KFS Papers, Box 8. The house was owned by renowned illustrator of the 1920s John Held, Jr.

22. *New Yorker* Drafts; *New York Times*, December 13, 1936. The KFS Papers, Box 10, contain highly detailed preliminary drafts of an article, which, greatly shortened, appeared in the October 28, 1939, *New Yorker* (hereafter, Large Draft, *New Yorker*).

23. KFS to Helen Simpson, n.d. (circa August 15, 1935), Kelly Simpson Papers.

24. KFS to Raymond Harper, June 2, 1937, KFS Papers, Box 32.

25. Warren Moscow, *Politics in the Empire State* (New York, 1948), 70; Charles Hilles to James R. Sheffield, September 23, 1934, Hilles Papers, Box 123.

26. *New York Times*, September 29, 1935.

27. *New Yorker* Drafts; Bellinger, "The Story of Ken Simpson," 8.

28. *New York Times*, September 19, 1935; *New York Times*, September 20, 1935.

29. New Yorker Drafts; G. Herbert Semler to KFS, December 8, 1934, KFS Papers, Box 1.

30. *New York Times*, September 21, 1935; *New York Times*, September 22, 1935.

31. *New York Times*, September 22, 1935.

32. *New York Times*, September 26, 1935; Large Draft, *New Yorker*, KFS Papers, Box 10.

33. Large Draft, *New Yorker*; *New York Times*, September 26, 1935.

34. *New Yorker* Drafts; Mellen to KFS, September 25, 1935, KFS Papers, Box 1.

35. KFS to Charles C. Burlingham, August 17, 1937, KFS Papers, Box 1.

36. *New York Times*, September 27, 1935.

37. *New York Times*, October 1 and 2, 1935.

38. George Brown Tindall, *America: A Narrative History, Volume Two* (New York, 1988), 1127.

39. Charles Hilles to Mrs. Preston Davie, February 12, 1936, Hilles Papers, Box 124.

40. Charles Hilles to KFS, February 13, 1936, KFS Papers, Box 1.

41. Stein, "The Birth of Liberal Republicanism in New York State," 139; *New York Times*, February 15, 1936.

42. Minutes of the New York Republican State Committee, February 18, 1936, Records of the New York Republican State Committee, M.E. Grenander Department of Special Collections & Archives, State University of New York, Albany (hereafter SUNY Albany Archives), Box 1.

43. Gertrude Hess to Alexander L. Steinert, March 3, 1936, KFS Papers, Box 29; *New York Times*, February 28, 1936, and April 2, 1936.

44. The law committee included Gabriel Kaplan and Mark McClay, both of whom would become Simpson confidants. See *New York Times*, October 30, 1935; *New York Times*, February 3, 1936.

45. Stein, "The Birth of Liberal Republicanism in New York State," 87-89, 94, 97-98.

46. Ibid., 102.

47. Minutes of the New York Republican State Committee, August 19, 1936, Records of the New York Republican State Committee, SUNY Albany Archives, Box 1; KFS to Edwin F. Jaeckle, December 15, 1936, University of Rochester Rare Books and Special Collections, Edwin F. Jaeckle Papers, Box 2.

48. *New York Times*, May 26, 1936.

49. *New York Times*, June 2, 1936; Hamilton Fish Jr. to KFS, May 15, 1936, KFS Papers, Box 1.

50. KFS to Charles Hilles, February 19, 1936, Hilles Papers, Box 124.

51. Minutes of the New York Republican State Committee, April 16, 1936, Records of the New York Republican State Committee, SUNY Albany Archives, Box 1.

52. *New York Times*, June 14, 1936. The souvenir menu for the "Simpson-Griffiths Special" is in the KFS Papers, Box 36. *New York Times*, May 26, 1936; *New York Times*, June 8, 1936.

53. KFS to Helen Simpson, June 9, 1936, Kelly Simpson Papers.

54. *New York Times*, June 9, 1936; KFS to Helen Simpson, June 9, 1936, Kelly Simpson Papers.

55. *New York Times*, June 9, 1936; *New York Times*, June 11, 1936; Stein, "The Birth of Liberal Republicanism in New York State," 147-49.

56. KFS to Helen Simpson, June 13, 1936, Kelly Simpson Papers.

57. Ibid.; *New York Times*, June 14, 1936.

58. KFS to Helen Simpson, June 14-17, 1936, Kelly Simpson Papers.

59. Stein, "The Birth of Liberal Republicanism in New York State," 127-28.

60. *New York Times*, June 18, 1936.

61. Telegram to multiple recipients, n.d., (circa June 1936), KFS Papers, Box 1; *New York Times*, June 22, 1936; *New Yorker*, September 5, 1936.

62. Richard Norton Smith, *Thomas E. Dewey and His Times* (New York, 1982), 219.

63. Stein, "The Birth of Liberal Republicanism in New York State," 91; Terry Jane Ruderman, *Stanley M. Isaacs: The Conscience of New York* (New York, 1982), 93; Bellinger, "The Story of Ken Simpson," 9.

64. KFS to Thomas S. Lamont, October 5, 1937, KFS Papers, Box 2.

65. KFS always went to opening or closing night—not in between. Norman Bel Geddes to KFS, November 6, 1936, KFS Papers, Box 1.

66. Stein, "The Birth of Liberal Republicanism in New York State," 130-32.

67. James W. Wadsworth to Charles Hilles, June 26, 1936, Hilles Papers, Box 125.

68. KFS to Dorothy Dudley Harvey, January 8, 1937, KFS Papers, Box 8.

69. Smith, *Thomas E. Dewey and His Times*, 224.

70. George J. Lankevich, *American Metropolis: A History of New York City* (New York: 1998), 165.

71. The Norris-La Guardia Act prohibited the use of injunctions in labor disputes.

72. This is a paraphrase of Henry Clay's "I'd rather be right than president" quip; Morris, *Let the Chips Fall*, 79-80; *New York Times*, January 21, 1934.

73. Reminiscences of Walter Mack Jr., CUOHRO, 54.

74. KFS to Dorothy Dudley Harvey, August 31, 1934, KFS Papers, Box 8.

75. *New York Times*, January 1, 1936; *New York Times*, July 10, 1936.

76. *New York Times*, July 15, 1936.

77. *New York Times*, July 20 and August 6, 1936.

78. These letters are in the Kenneth Simpson Papers, Box 1. See Hylda M. Goldsmith to KFS, February 15, 1937, KFS Papers, Box 1.

79. William Hard to KFS, February 6, 1937, KFS Papers, Box 1.

80. KFS to Stanley Isaacs, March 12, 1937, Columbia University Archives and Manuscripts, Stanley Isaacs Papers, Box 1.

81. Dorothy Dudley Harvey to KFS, March 23, 1937, KFS Papers, Box 8.

82. Stein, "The Birth of Liberal Republicanism in New York State," 157; Bellinger, "The Story of Ken Simpson," 10.

83. Frederic C. Bellinger, "The Copeland Primary Fight in New York and La Guardia in 1940" (unpublished manuscript), KFS Papers, Box 10, 3-5.

84. Lewis Gregory Cole, M.D., and William Gregory Cole, M.D., to KFS, April 30, 1937. The x-ray did find serious dental problems. KFS to Raymond Harper, June 2, 1937, KFS Papers, Box 32.

85. Bellinger, "The Copeland Primary Fight," 7.

86. *New York Times*, May 27, 1937.

87. Ibid.; Bellinger, "The Copeland Primary Fight," 9.

88. *New York Times*, May 27, 1937.

89. Ibid.

90. Transcript of statement by Charles E. Hughes Jr., George Z. Medalie, Thomas D. Thatcher, and Charles H. Tuttle, May 27, 1937, KFS Papers, Box 9.

91. Stein, "The Birth of Liberal Republicanism in New York State," 158; handwritten comments on reverse side of transcript of statement by Charles E. Hughes Jr., George Z. Medalie, Thomas D. Thatcher, and Charles H. Tuttle, May 27, 1937, KFS Papers, Box 9.

92. Gertrude Hess to Hon. Jehil M. Roeder, June 7, 1937, KFS Papers, Box 1; KFS to Stanley Howe, June 17, 1937, New York City Municipal Archives, Office of the Mayor Mayoralty Campaign Series, Box 4105; KFS to Charles Hilles, July 20, 1937, KFS Papers, Box 1; draft press releases, July 19 and 20, 1937, KFS Papers, Box 9; Ruderman, *Stanley M. Isaacs*, 87; Joseph Clark Baldwin, *Flowers for the Judge* (New York, 1950), 186.

93. Bellinger, "The Story of Ken Simpson," 13; KFS to Mrs. James Russell Parsons, July 28, 1937, KFS Papers, Box 1.

94. Morris, *Let the Chips Fall*, 103; Bellinger, "The Copeland Primary Fight," 90; Ruderman, *Stanley M. Isaacs*, 87.

95. The date of this meeting is difficult to set. KFS thought it was the 24th, but that put it too late. In Simpson's papers is the telegram from the Hoyle Club indicating that Simpson would be with La Guardia that evening. See Bamberger to KFS, July 22, 1937, KFS Papers, Box 1; *New York Times*, July 22, 1937.

96. Large Draft, *New Yorker*; *New Yorker* Drafts.

97. Large Draft, *New Yorker*.

98. Noel F. Busch, "Boss Without Cigar," *New Yorker*, October 28, 1939, 26.

99. Large Draft, *New Yorker*.

100. *New Yorker* Drafts.

101. *New York Daily News*, July 25, 1937.

102. Beatrice Bishop Berle and Travis Beal Jacobs, ed., *Navigating the Rapids, 1918-1971: From the Papers of Adolph A. Berle* (New York, 1973), 129.

103. Bellinger, "The Copeland Primary Fight," 19.

104. See transcript of "September 25th Conversation with R.H.," KFS Papers, Box 1.

105. Bellinger, "The Copeland Primary Fight," 21.

106. Bellinger, "The Story of Ken Simpson," 7.

107. *New Yorker* Drafts; KFS to Alex Rose, September 11, 1937, KFS Papers, Box 1.

108. *New York Times*, July 30, 1937.

109. *New Yorker* Drafts; Stein, "The Birth of Liberal Republicanism in New York State," 37.

110. Berle and Jacobs, *Navigating the Rapids*, 128; Reminiscences of Stanley Isaacs, CUOHRO, 82.

111. *New Yorker* Drafts; Large Draft, *New Yorker*.

112. Reminiscences of Stanley Isaacs, CUOHRO, 82.

113. Ruderman, *Stanley M. Isaacs*, 86-95.

114. Another fall 1936 race involved a young Texan named Lyndon Johnson. Richard M. Fried, *The Man Everybody Knew: Bruce Barton and the Making of Modern America* (Chicago, 2005), 157, 116-38.

115. Large Draft, *New Yorker*.

116. Ibid.; Bruce Barton to Ray Howard, October 21, 1937, Bruce Barton Papers, Wisconsin State Historical Society, Box 30 (hereafter Barton Papers).

117. Smith, *Thomas E. Dewey and His Times*, 86.

118. Ibid., passim.

119. Bellinger, "The Story of Ken Simpson," 18; Smith, *Thomas E. Dewey and His Times*, 229.

120. Smith, *Thomas E. Dewey and His Times*, 230; Berle and Jacobs, *Navigating the Rapids*, 130-31.

121. *New York World Telegram*, August 14, 1937; Bellinger, "The Story of Ken Simpson," 19-20.

122. KFS to Charles Burlingham, August 17, 1937, KFS Papers, Box 1.

123. Unidentified to KFS, August 18, 1937, KFS Papers, Box 1; Bellinger, "The Story of Ken Simpson," 13.

124. *New York Times*, August 30, 1937.

125. Stein, "The Birth of Liberal Republicanism in New York State," 163-64; Bellinger, "The Copeland Primary Fight," 41-42.

126. KFS to Helen Simpson, October 14, 1937, Kelly Simpson Papers.

127. KFS to Alf M. Landon, October 13, 1937, KFS Papers, Box 2; Charles Gold to KFS, September 30, 1937, KFS Papers, Box 1.

128. *New York Times*, September 10, 1937.

129. *Washington Post*, September 13, 1937.

130. Bellinger, "The Copeland Primary Fight," 42; press release, September 18, 1937, KFS Papers, Box 9.

131. KFS, "Memorandum on the So-Called City Fusion Party and Their Recent Activities," September 29, 1937, New York City Municipal Archives, Office of the Mayor, Mayoralty Campaign Series, Box 4120; KFS to Helen Simpson, October 14, 1937, Kelly Simpson Papers.

132. Ruderman, *Stanley M. Isaacs*, 96-98.

133. Fried, *The Man Everybody Knew*, 161-64; Bruce Barton to Roy Howard, November 20, 1937, Barton Papers, Box 30.

134. KFS to Helen Simpson, October 14, 1937, Kelly Simpson Papers.

135. Smith, *Thomas E. Dewey and His Times*, 232-38; KFS to Helen Simpson, October 14, 1937, Kelly Simpson Papers; Busch, "Boss Without Cigar," 23; Reminiscences of Thomas E. Dewey, CUOHRO, 384.

136. The amount of money that Simpson "demanded" would grow with the retelling—in a 1939 account, it was $20,000; more than twenty years later, it was $50,000. See John Hamilton memorandum, June 9, 1939, in the John D. M. Hamilton Papers, Library of Congress, Box 2, and Reminiscences of Thomas E. Dewey, CUOHRO, 411-12.

137. John Mantle Clapp to KFS, November 16, 1937, KFS Papers, Box 2.

138. *New York Times*, October 31, 1937.

139. *Time*, November 15, 1937.

140. Stein, "The Birth of Liberal Republicanism in New York State," 166; Charles Hilles to KFS, November 3, 1937, KFS Papers, Box 2.

141. Thomas Kessner, *Fiorello La Guardia and the Making of Modern New York* (New York, 1989), 142.

142. Smith, *Thomas E. Dewey and His Times*, 239.

143. *New York Times*, November 3, 1937.

144. Smith, *Thomas E. Dewey and His Times*, 239.

145. *Time*, November 15, 1937. The Board of Estimate included the mayor, comptroller, president of the Board of Aldermen, and five borough presidents. Extra votes for the officials and some borough representatives accounted for the fifteen vote count. *New Yorker* Drafts; KFS to Henry Huntington, November 22, 1937, KFS Papers, Box 2; Smith, *Thomas E. Dewey and His Times*, 239; Stein, "The Birth of Liberal Republicanism in New York State," 167.

146. *New York Times*, December 12, 1937.

147. Large Draft, *New Yorker*; Stein, "The Birth of Liberal Republicanism in New York State," 172.

148. Charles D. Hilles to William S. Murray, September 20, 1937, Records of the New York Republican State Committee, SUNY Albany Archives, Box 1; Charles Hilles to KFS, September 20, 1937, Hilles Papers, Box 127.

149. KFS to Stanley M. Isaacs, November 9, 1937, KFS Papers, Box 2.

150. *New York Daily Mirror*, December 9, 1937.

151. Simpson tendered his resignation in advance of the expiration of his first two-year term (fully expecting reelection). His explanation to Roy Howard was that he did not intend to go through with it but was determined to go within the next year and wanted it on notice. See transcript of "September 25th Conversation with R.H.," KFS Papers, Box 1. Simpson wrote to Helen that despite the accolades for his accomplishments, "some day I think I'll really go into politics." See KFS to Helen Simpson, October 8, 1937, Kelly Simpson Papers.

152. Minutes of the New York Republican State Committee, December 16, 1937, Records of the New York Republican State Committee, SUNY Albany Archives, Box 1.

153. Ibid.

154. Emory Buckner to KFS, December 17, 1937, KFS Papers, Box 2.

CHAPTER 4

1. *New York Post*, November 28, 1939; *Young Republican*, March 1939.

2. A Leo Hirschfield cartoon from the *New York Times*, March 21, 1938, showed this detail, to Simpson's delight. See KFS to Leo Hirschfield, March 21, 1938, Kenneth Farrand Simpson Papers, Yale University Manuscripts and Archives (hereafter KFS Papers), Box 3.

3. Bel Geddes to Players Club, August 16, 1938, KFS Papers, Box 3.

4. Undated document in Kelly Simpson Papers.

5. KFS to John R. Davies, December 30, 1937, KFS Papers, Box 3; *Jewish Morning Journal*, November 5, 1939.

6. KFS to Helen Simpson, June 7, 1938, Kelly Simpson Papers.

7. *Washington Post*, March 13, 1938.

8. *Washington Post*, March 14, 1938.

9. Undated document in Kelly Simpson Papers.

10. KFS to Norman Bel Geddes, May 18, 1938, KFS Papers, Box 3.

11. Norman Bel Geddes to KFS, October 14, 1938, KFS Papers, Box 3; Players Club to KFS, October 28, 1938, KFS Papers, Box 3.

12. In attendance at the convention were 92 Republicans, 75 Democrats, and one Democrat elected on the Republican ALP ticket.

13. Undated press release featuring contents of telegram sent to all Republican delegates, KFS Papers, Box 9; Minutes of the New York Republican State Committee, June 15, 1938, Records of the New York Republican State Committee, M.E. Grenander Department of Special Collections & Archives, State University of New York, Albany (hereafter SUNY Albany Archives), Box 1.

14. Richard Norton Smith, *Thomas E. Dewey and His Times* (New York, 1982), 253; KFS to Helen Simpson, June 14, 1938, Kelly Simpson Papers. Late in the year, Simpson believed that his "usefulness to the party" would be in inverse proportion to his public appearances. See KFS to Alfred L. Simon, December 29, 1937, KFS Papers, Box 3.

15. KFS to Arthur L. Marvin, December 9, 1937, KFS Papers, Box 2.

16. KFS to William M. Chadbourne, October 7, 1937, KFS Papers, Box 2; KFS to Bruce Barton, February 1, 1938, KFS Papers, Box 3; *Washington Post*, March 19, 1938.

17. KFS to Bruce Barton, February 1, 1938, KFS Papers, Box 3; Reminiscences of Stanley Isaacs, Columbia University Oral History Research Office (hereafter CUOHRO), 91; Reminiscences of Thomas E. Dewey, CUOHRO, 416.

18. "Statement from: Kenneth F. Simpson, Republican National Committee Member from New York," November 29, 1939, KFS Papers, Box 14.

19. "Remarks of Kenneth F. Simpson, Member of Republican National Committee from New York State," October 13, 1939, KFS Papers, Box 14.

20. See "Excerpts from Speech of Kenneth F. Simpson to Young Republican Leaders," May 27, 1939, KFS Papers, Box 14, for conservative achievement in England.

21. Grand Street Boys Club *Wuxtra*, January 1940. Simpson was far ahead of the curve here, but later politicians like Richard Nixon and Ronald Reagan proved him right. Judith Stein, "The Birth of Liberal Republicanism in New York State, 1932-1938" (Ph.D. diss., Yale University, 1968), 44; Remarks: "Legislative Correspondents Dinner," March 10, 1938, KFS Papers, Box 14.

22. *Christian Science Monitor,* July 27, 1938.

23. KFS to William Hard, May 2, 1938, KFS Papers, Box 3.

24. KFS to Fred A. Young, November 23, 1938, KFS Papers, Box 3; Stein, "The Birth of Liberal Republicanism in New York State," 45; Capitol Hill Club Speech attached to KFS to Thomas E. Dewey, December 18, 1938, University of Rochester Rare Books and Special Collections, Thomas E. Dewey Papers, Box 43 (hereafter Dewey Papers).

25. Hilles laid out the strategy as he got it from Simpson. See Hilles to Albert L. Warner, August 29, 1938, Charles Hilles Papers, Yale University Manuscripts and Archives (hereafter Hilles Papers), Box 129.

26. The other top purge targets were from Georgia, South Carolina, and Maryland. Hilles to Albert L. Warner, August 29, 1938, Hilles Papers, Box 129.

27. KFS to Robert McMarsh, August 23, 1938, KFS Papers, Box 3.

28. *New York Times*, November 15, 1938; John Burke to KFS, July 21, 1938, KFS Papers, Box 3.

29. *Washington Post*, August 9, 1938.

30. For letters, see for example, R. F. Migdalski to KFS, July 28, 1938, KFS Papers, Box 3; KFS to Robert McMarsh, August 23, 1938, KFS Papers, Box 3; Stein, "The Birth of Liberal Republicanism in New York State," 47; Charles Hilles to James R. Sheffield, August 23, 1938, Hilles Papers, Box 129.

31. *Daily Mirror*, August 12, 1938.

32. *New York Post*, November 28, 1938; *New York Times*, September 15, 1938.

33. William E. Leuchtenberg, *Franklin D. Roosevelt and the New Deal, 1932-1940* (New York, 1963), 268.

34. Richard Scandrett to Charles Hilles, June 12, 1939, Hilles Papers, Box 129.

35. KFS to Alf Landon, August 10, 1938, KFS Papers, Box 3.

36. Stein, "The Birth of Liberal Republicanism in New York State," 45; KFS to Norman Bel Geddes, October 17, 1938, KFS Papers, Box 3.

37. Bronson Cutting died in a plane crash in 1935. Frederic C. Bellinger, "The Story of Ken Simpson and How He Put Thomas E. Dewey on the Political Map" (unpublished manuscript), KFS Papers, Box 33, 24.

38. Bronson Trevor to KFS, September 8, 1938, KFS Papers, Box 3; Bellinger, "The Story of Ken Simpson," 25.

39. *New York Post*, November 28, 1938.

40. *New York Post*, November 28, 1938.

41. Barton to "Fellow Republicans," September 17, 1938, KFS Papers, Box 3; KFS to Bruce Barton, December 8, 1938, KFS Papers, Box 3; *Young Republican*, September 5, 1939, KFS Papers, Box 10; New York Young Republican Club, "Report of Campaign Committee re: Activities in Republican Primaries of 1939," October 12, 1939, 6, KFS Papers, Box 3.

42. KFS to Lester Hoffman, September 27, 1938, KFS Papers, Box 3; KFS to Flo Renyx, December 8, 1938, KFS Papers, Box 3.

43. KFS to James H. Hatch, October 5, 1938, KFS Papers, Box 3.

44. Bellinger, "The Story of Ken Simpson," 27. Simpson consulted only with Gabriel Kaplan, a lawyer specialized in electoral procedure who had become one of his most valued assistants.

45. Plaque text, undated document in KFS Papers, Box 3.

46. *New York Times*, March 5, 1939; Thomas Dewey to KFS, March 4, 1939, Kelly Simpson Papers.

47. Marvin G. Weinbaum, "A Minority's Survival: The Republican Party of New York County, 1897-1960" (Ph.D. diss., Columbia University, 1965), 80.

48. Richard Norton Smith, *Thomas E. Dewey and His Times* (New York, 1982), 250; undated document in Kelly Simpson Papers.

49. Richard Scandrett to KFS, January 11, 1938, KFS Papers, Box 3.

50. Charles Hilles to Charles Francis Adams, January 12, 1938, Hilles Papers, Box 128.

51. Smith, *Thomas E. Dewey and His Times*, 251; KFS to Helen Simpson, June 18, 1938, Kelly Simpson Papers; *Christian Science Monitor*, July 27, 1938.

52. Smith, *Thomas E. Dewey and His Times*, 260; KFS Papers, Box 10, contain miscellaneous draft pages, out of order, of highly detailed preliminary drafts of an article which, greatly shortened, appeared in the October 28, 1939, *New Yorker* (hereafter "*New Yorker* Drafts"); *New York Times*, September 23, 1938.

53. Bellinger, "The Story of Ken Simpson," 25, on KFS talking Medalie into serving as campaign manager.

54. Veteran U.S. Senator James W. Wadsworth who, along with county leader Thomas R. Broderick from Rochester, hoped to put his son James W. Wadsworth Jr. on the ticket. See Bellinger, "The Story of Ken Simpson," 28-30.

55. Bellinger, "The Story of Ken Simpson," 30; "For Release on Delivery Expected about 12 Noon," September 29, 1938, KFS Papers, Box 14; see the Minutes of the Convention in Records of the New York Republican State Committee, SUNY Albany Archives, Box 1; Smith, *Thomas E. Dewey and His Times*, 264.

56. Reminiscences of Thomas E. Dewey, CUOHRO, 474.

57. See for example, *Atlanta Constitution*, October 21, 1938.

58. Smith, *Thomas E. Dewey and His Times*, 276; Reminiscences of Warren Moscow, CUOHRO, 19; KFS to Thomas E. Dewey, November 5, 1938, KFS Papers, Box 3.

59. Reminiscences of Warren Moscow, CUOHRO, 18.

60. KFS to James D. Williams, November 16, 1938, KFS Papers, Box 3; KFS to Fred A. Young, November 23, 1938, KFS Papers, Box 3.

61. "KFS in Buffalo," December 7, 1938, KFS Papers, Box 14.

62. Weinbaum, "A Minority's Survival," 81.

63. Smith, *Thomas E. Dewey and His Times*, 269.

64. *Washington Post*, June 28, 1938; *Hartford Courant*, November 27, 1938; KFS to John D. M. Hamilton, October 11, 1938, KFS Papers, Box 3.

65. *New York Times,* November 15, 1938.

66. *New York Post*, November 28, 1938.

67. Reminiscences of Thomas E. Dewey, CUOHRO, 415.

68. Smith, *Thomas E. Dewey and His Times*, 274, 253.

69. Undated memo, "Kenneth Simpson" in Library of Congress Manuscripts, John D. M. Hamilton Papers, Box 2. As of the 22nd, Simpson still had not heard about the meeting. KFS to Edwin Jaeckle, November 22, 1938, University of Rochester Rare Books and Special Collections, Edwin F. Jaeckle Papers, Box 43 (hereafter Jaeckle Papers); *Washington Post,* November 29, 1938; undated memo, "Kenneth Simpson" in Library of Congress Manuscripts, John D. M. Hamilton Papers, Box 2.

70. Minutes of the New York Republican State Committee, November 28, 1938, Records of the New York Republican State Committee, SUNY Albany Archives, Box 1.

71. KFS to Alan Fox, December 30, 1938, KFS Papers, Box 3.

72. Herbert Hoover to Charles Hilles, September 21, 1937, Hilles Papers, Box 127; KFS to Alan Fox, December 30, 1938, KFS Papers, Box 3.

73. *New Republic,* June 1939.

74. *New York Sun,* November 30, 1938.

75. *New York Sun,* November 30, 1938; KFS to Phelps Adams, December 8, 1938, KFS Papers, Box 3; *New York Sun,* November 30, 1938.

76. *New York Sun,* November 30, 1938. Simpson claimed that a number of Republican National Committee members told him later that they would have stood up for him if a vote was taken—"but they were glad it was not." See KFS to J. Russel Sprague, December 8, 1938, KFS Papers, Box 3; *Washington Post,* November 30, 1938.

77. *Washington Post,* December 2, 1938.

78. *New York Times,* November 30, 1938.

79. KFS to Richard Scandrett, December 8, 1938, KFS Papers, Box 3.

80. Information on Hoover's grievance from memo, "Meeting L.A.R. – F.S.C. Feb. 7, 1939" attached to Franck S. Cushner to KFS, February 9, 1939, KFS Papers, Box 3; Noel F. Busch, "Boss Without Cigar," *New Yorker,* October 28, 1939.

81. KFS to Thomas E. Dewey, November 4, 1937, Dewey Papers, Box 43.

82. See for example, Thomas E. Dewey to KFS, May 3, 1938, KFS Papers, Box 3.

83. Reminiscences of Thomas E. Dewey, CUOHRO, 519.

84. Ibid., 522. Smith, *Thomas E. Dewey and His Times,* repeats this story.

85. *Washington Post,* November 30, 1938.

86. Reminiscences of Stanley Isaacs, CUOHRO, 184; *New York Times,* March 5, 1939.

87. *New Yorker* Drafts; unattributed newspaper article, January 1939, Kenneth Simpson Scrapbooks, Yale University Microfilm Collection.

88. KFS to Thomas E. Dewey, February 3, 1939, KFS Papers, Box 3.

89. *New York Times*, February 14, 1939; KFS to Franck S. Cushner, February 17, 1939, KFS Papers, Box 3; Smith, *Thomas E. Dewey and His Times*, 292.

90. See the program in KFS Papers, Box 35; *New York Times*, March 24, 1939.

91. Clarence E. Wunderlin, ed., *The Papers of Robert A. Taft, Volume 2, 1939-1944* (Kent, OH, 2001), 50.

92. The drafts are in the Dewey Papers, Box 4.

93. "Thomas E. Dewey Speech—Legislative Correspondents' Dinner," March 23, 1939, Dewey Papers, Box 4.

94. Warren Moscow, *Politics in the Empire State* (New York, 1948), 77.

95. KFS to Helen Simpson, March 24, 1939, Kelly Simpson Papers.

96. Moscow, *Politics in the Empire State*, 77; *New York Times*, March 28, 1939.

97. *New York Times*, April 7, 1939; Stanley M. Isaacs to Charles D. Hilles, October 13, 1939, Columbia University Archives and Manuscripts, Stanley Isaacs Papers, Box 1; *Christian Science Monitor*, April 26, 1939.

98. *New York Times*, April 27, 1939.

99. *Christian Science Monitor*, May 27, 1939.

100. Cornelius M. Shannon to Edwin F. Jaeckle, December 12, 1938, Jaeckle Papers, Box 3.

101. *New York Times*, June 6, 1939; *New York Times*, June 19, 1939.

102. Moscow, *Politics in the Empire State*, 77; *New York Times*, April 17, 1939.

103. *Wall Street Journal*, May 24, 1939; *Remarks of Hon. Francis D. Culkin of New York in the House of Representatives* (Washington, D.C., 1939); reprint from *Congressional Record* in KFS Papers, Box 10.

104. *New York Times*, June 26, 1939; Moscow, *Politics in the Empire State*, 78.

105. Memo, June 9, 1939, Library of Congress Manuscripts, John D. M. Hamilton Papers, Box 2; Smith, *Thomas E. Dewey and His Times*, 293; anonymous memo, July 7, 1939, attached to Thomas E. Dewey to John R. Davies, September 6, 1939, Dewey Papers, Box 19.

106. Hamilton memo on conversation with Charles Hilles, July 7, 1939, Library of Congress Manuscripts, John D. M. Hamilton Papers, Box 2; anonymous memo, July 7, 1939, attached to Thomas E. Dewey to John R. Davies, September 6, 1939, Dewey Papers, Box 19.

107. Reminiscences of Thomas E. Dewey, CUOHRO, 520.

108. KFS to Alf Landon, July 20, 1939, KFS Papers, Box 3.

109. KFS to Alan Fox, December 30, 1938, KFS Papers, Box 3; New York City *North Side News*, August 11, 1939.

110. *Washington Post*, September 20, 1939; Weinbaum, "A Minority's Survival," 83; John R. Davies to KFS, attached to John R. Davies to Thomas E. Dewey, October 4, 1939, Dewey Papers, Box 36; *New York Times*, November 5, 1939.

111. KFS to Dorothy Harvey, January 8, 1937, Kelly Simpson Papers.

112. Undated document in Kelly Simpson Papers.

113. Undated handwritten document in KFS Papers, Box 10.

114. Dorothy Harvey to KFS, January 10, 1939, March 24, 1939, October 18, 1939, and February 16, 1940, in Kelly Simpson Papers.

115. Bellinger, "The Story of Ken Simpson," 22; telegrams, Dewey to KFS and KFS to Dewey, February 19, 1938, Dewey Papers, Box 43; see the many letters from the summer of 1938 in KFS Papers, Box 3.

116. *New York Times*, December 24, 1939; *New Yorker* Drafts.

117. Trevor listed ten fees totaling more than $24,000 collected by Simpson in the late 1930s. See Bronson Trevor to Kenneth Simpson, September 12, 1939, KFS Papers, Box 4; *New York Times*, March 17, 1939; *New York Times,* May 1, 1939.

118. *New York Post*, April 18, 1939.

119. Joseph Mitchell, "All You Can Hold for Five Bucks," *New Yorker*, April 15, 1939.

120. Bellinger, "The Story of Ken Simpson," 26.

121. Undated document circa November 1939 in Kelly Simpson Papers. Simpson was "laid up" immediately after the 1939 primary fight, for example. See Stanley M. Isaacs to KFS, October 6, 1939, KFS Papers, Box 4; Large Draft, *New Yorker*.

122. *New Yorker* Drafts.

123. This quotation had made many appearances, but the original source is unclear. It appears to be featured first in *Time*, February 26, 1940, and then in *New Yorker*, May 25, 1940.

124. See May 7, June 9, and July 7, 1939, memos in Library of Congress Manuscripts, John D. M. Hamilton Papers, Box 2; Lewis L. Gould, *Grand Old Party: A History of the Republicans* (New York, 2003), 281.

125. Rolland Marvin to Russel Sprague, June 2, 1939, Dewey Papers, Box 41.

126. *Washington Post*, November 27, 1939; *New York Times*, November 23, 1939.

127. *Christian Science Monitor,* December 18, 1939; unidentified newspaper, December 29, 1939, Kenneth Simpson Scrapbooks, Yale University Microfilm Collection.

128. *Christian Science Monitor,* December 18, 1939.

129. *New York Times*, January 31, 1940.

130. *New York Times*, January 6, 1940; *New York Times*, February 2, 1940; *New York Times*, February 3, 1940.

131. Lincoln Day Dinner remarks are reprinted in *Congressional Record*, February 10, 1940, copy in KFS Papers, Box 14; *New York Times,* February 21, 1940.

132. See the program in KFS Papers, Box 35.

133. "Remarks of Kenneth F. Simpson, Member of National Republican Committee, New York State," March 2, 1940, KFS Papers, Box 14.

134. Unidentified newspaper article excerpt in Kenneth Simpson Scrapbooks, April 8, 1940.

135. Troy, New York, *Times*, April 13, 1940.

136. George Brown Tindall, *America: A Narrative History, Volume Two* (New York, 1988), 1169.

137. Conrad Joyner, *The Republican Dilemma: Conservatism or Progressivism* (Tucson, AZ, 1963), 22, 24.

138. *New York Times,* September 7, 1939.

139. Dewey knew that all of this was going on. For one thing, his lieutenants and friends forwarded correspondence to him—his papers are full of other people's letters. For another, as the campaign began, his people generated daily news reports separating articles into favorable and unfavorable. Too many of the latter featured Simpson.

140. This analysis is from a memo prepared by Simpson in 1939 or early 1940 (undated document in Kelly Simpson Papers).

141. Richard Scandrett to Charles Hilles, June 12, 1939, Hilles Papers, Box 129.

142. This is from a memo prepared by Simpson (undated document in Kelly Simpson Papers).

143. Joyner, *The Republican Dilemma,*18.

144. See drafts in Jaeckle Papers, Box 1.

145. *New York Times*, April 13, 1940.

146. The source for this and subsequent paragraphs is Minutes of the New York Republican State Committee, April 12, 1940, Records of the New York Republican State Committee, SUNY Albany Archives, Box 1, pp. 9-45.

147. Reminiscences of Thomas E. Dewey, CUOHRO, 539.

148. KFS to George M. Murray, April 29, 1940, KFS Papers, Box 4.

CHAPTER 5

1.   *New York Times*, April 14, 1940.

2.   *New York Times*, April 15, 1940.

3.   *Chicago Tribune*, April 15, 1940; *New York Times*, April 17, 1940.

4. *Washington Post*, July 21, 1948.

5. A copy of the pamphlet, somewhat vindictively entitled, "Don't Say We Didn't Warn You," is in the Kenneth Farrand Simpson Papers, Yale University Manuscripts and Archives (hereafter KFS Papers); *New York Times*, April 22, 1940.

6. Steve Neal, *Dark Horse: A Biography of Wendell Willkie* (New York, 1984), 104; Conrad Joyner, *The Republican Dilemma: Conservatism or Progressivism* (Tucson, 1963), 29; *Washington Post*, May 15, 1940.

7. *Washington Post*, April 17, 1940.

8. *New York Times*, April 24, 1940.

9. *Christian Science Monitor*, May 15, 1940.

10. *New York Times*, April 17, 1940. For a time, Jaeckle even considered running Syracuse mayor Rolland Marvin rather than Long Island leader Russel Sprague for Simpson's seat on the Republican National Committee. See *New York Times*, April 19, 1940.

11. *New York Times*, April 20 and 26, 1940.

12. *New York Times*, April 21, 1940; Joyner, *The Republican Dilemma*, 18.

13. *New York Times*, May 23 and 24, 1940.

14. Reminiscences of Paul Windels, Columbia University Oral History Research Office (hereafter CUOHRO), 171.

15. *New York Times*, June 10 and 13, 1940.

16. Minutes of the New York Republican State Committee, June 12, 1940, Records of the New York Republican State Committee, M.E. Grenander Department of Special Collections & Archives, State University of New York, Albany (hereafter SUNY Albany Archives), 26.

17. *New York Times*, June 13, 1940.

18. George W. Perkins to KFS, June 13, 1940, KFS Papers, Box 4.

19. John Foster Dulles to Edwin Jaeckle, June 13, 1940, University of Rochester Rare Books and Special Collections, Edwin F. Jaeckle Papers (hereafter Jaeckle Papers), Box 3.

20. *New York Times*, February 16, 1940.

21. Richard Norton Smith, *Thomas E. Dewey and His Times* (New York, 1982), 303.

22. Joyner, *The Republican Dilemma*, 21; Lewis L. Gould, *Grand Old Party: A History of the Republicans* (New York, 2003), 281; Smith, *Thomas E. Dewey and His Times*, 303.

23. Richard M. Fried, *The Man Everybody Knew: Bruce Barton and the Making of Modern America* (Chicago, 2005), 186.

24. Joyner, *The Republican Dilemma*, 23.

25. *Chicago Tribune*, May 28, 1952.

26. Bruce Barton to Thomas E. Dewey, June 13, 1940, KFS Papers, Box 4.

27. Charles Peters, *Five Days in Philadelphia* (New York, 2005), 124.

28. Reminiscences of Mary Lasker, CUOHRO, 719, 62; KFS to Lyttleton B. P. Gould, January 11, 1941, KFS Papers, Box 7.

29. Kai Bird, *The Chairman: John J. McCloy, The Making of the American Establishment* (New York, 1992), 110.

30. Joyner, *The Republican Dilemma*, 34.

31. Ibid., 35; Peters, *Five Days in Philadelphia*, 35; Gould, *Grand Old Party*, 282; Smith, *Thomas E. Dewey and His Times*, 295.

32. Willkie had even attended both the 1924 and 1932 conventions. See Peters, *Five Days in Philadelphia*, 65, 36; Neal, *Dark Horse*, 49, 52.

33. Smith, *Thomas E. Dewey and His Times*, 294.

34. Neal, *Dark Horse*, 53; Joyner, *The Republican Dilemma*, 35.

35. Peters, *Five Days in Philadelphia*, 38; Neal, *Dark Horse*, 67-69.

36. *Christian Science Monitor*, April 17, 1940, and *New York Times*, April 17, 1940. Clearly, this was just a way to get Wendell Willkie's name in play. Charles Hilles, secretary of the committee on arrangements, turned down the idea on grounds that Willkie himself might be a candidate. Simpson and Hilles were too close not to have discussed this in advance.

37. Joyner, *The Republican Dilemma*, 43; *New York Times*, May 19, 1940.

38. For an extended statement of this thesis, see Peters, *Five Days in Philadelphia*.

39. *New York Times*, June 26, 1940.

40. *New York Times*, June 18, 1940.

41. *New York Times*, June 20, 1940.

42. Peters, *Five Days in Philadelphia*, 64; Neal, *Dark Horse*, 87.

43. John D. M. Hamilton, "Notes on the Willkie Campaign," July 1, 1940, Library of Congress Manuscripts, John D. M. Hamilton Papers, Box 4; *New York Times*, June 24, 1940; Smith, *Thomas E. Dewey and His Times*, 308.

44. July 1, 1940, Morris Mogelever column in unidentified newspaper in KFS Scrapbooks; *Chicago Tribune*, June 28, 1940; Hamilton, "Notes on the Willkie Campaign," Library of Congress Manuscripts, John D. M. Hamilton Papers, Box 4.

45. KFS to Col. R. B. Creager, December 3, 1940, KFS Papers, Box 6.

46. John D. M. Hamilton interview by Dr. Karl Lamb on "Willkie's Nomination and Campaign," n.d., Library of Congress Manuscripts, John D. M. Hamilton Papers, Box 15.

47. Peters, *Five Days in Philadelphia*, 76.

48. *New York Times*, June 26, 1940; Neal, *Dark Horse*, 101; *Time*, July 8, 1940.

49. Peters, *Five Days in Philadelphia*, 82.

50. Ibid., 84; *Honolulu Star Bulletin*, July 4, 1940; KFS to William Clark, August 12, 1940, KFS Papers, Box 4; July 1, 1940, Morris Mogelever column in unidentified newspaper, Kenneth Simpson Scrapbooks, Yale University Microfilm Collection.

51. June 27, 1940, unidentified newspaper article in Kenneth Simpson Scrapbooks, Yale University Microfilm Collection.

52. Smith, *Thomas E. Dewey and His Times*, 311.

53. Joe Martin, *My First Fifty Years in Politics* (New York, 1960), 153; Peters, *Five Days in Philadelphia*, 95; Kenneth Simpson Scrapbooks, Yale University Microfilm Collection.

54. Peters, *Five Days in Philadelphia*, 51; Murray Friedman, Notes from Interview with John Hamilton, October 27, 1945, Library of Congress Manuscripts, John D. M. Hamilton Papers, Box 4; Martin, *My First Fifty Years in Politics*, 154-55.

55. Neal, *Dark Horse*, 108; Peters, *Five Days in Philadelphia*, 58; *Chicago Tribune*, June 28, 1940; *Time*, July 8, 1940.

56. Neal, *Dark Horse*, 110; *Honolulu Star Bulletin*, July 4, 1940; *New York World-Telegram*, June 29, 1940; *Chicago Tribune*, June 28, 1940.

57. Reminiscences of Walter Mack, CUOHRO, 57; *Chicago Tribune*, June 28, 1940; Peters, *Five Days in Philadelphia*, 102.

58. Bruce R. Tuttle to KFS, July 2, 1940, KFS Papers, Box 4; James E. Bennett Jr. to KFS, July 15, 1940, KFS Papers, Box 4; Smith, *Thomas E. Dewey and His Times*, 312; *Chicago Tribune*, June 28, 1940. "On a crucial vote at the convention he led the group in a poll of the delegation to break the solidarity of the New York delegation," Dewey told an interviewer in 1973 (Reminiscences of Thomas E. Dewey, CUOHRO, 520).

59. *Chicago Tribune*, June 28, 1940; *New York World-Telegram*, June 29, 1940.

60. *Time*, July 8, 1940.

61. *New York World-Telegram*, June 29, 1940; *Chicago Tribune*, June 28, 1940; Neal, *Dark Horse*, 114.

62. People wrote and said they saw him. See "Jenkintown Republican" to KFS, June 28, 1940, KFS Papers, Box 4; *New York Daily Mirror*, n.d., Kenneth Simpson Scrapbooks, Yale University Microfilm Collection.

63. Smith, *Thomas E. Dewey and His Times*, 313.

64. *Honolulu Star Bulletin*, July 4, 1940; *Chicago Tribune*, June 28, 1940; Neal, *Dark Horse*, 117-19.

65. *Time*, July 8, 1940.

66. *New York World-Telegram*, June 29, 1940.

67. *Christian Science Monitor,* July 9, 1940; *Paterson New Jersey Call,* July 17, 1940.

68. John D. M. Hamilton interview by Dr. Karl Lamb on "Willkie's Nomination and Campaign," n.d., Library of Congress Manuscripts, John D. M. Hamilton Papers, Box 15; KFS to Mrs. MacDonald DeWitt, August 8, 1940, and KFS to Warren Leslie Jr., August 16, 1940, both in KFS Papers, Box 4.

69. Gertrude Hess to KFS, July 1, 1940, KFS Papers, Box 4; James E. Bennett Jr. to KFS, July 15, 1940, KFS Papers, Box 4; KFS to Mrs. MacDonald DeWitt, August 8, 1940, KFS Papers, Box 4; *New York World-Telegram,* August 10, 1940; KFS to Warren Leslie Jr., August 16, 1940, KFS Papers, Box 4; Victor Kaufmann to KFS, August 23, 1940, KFS Papers, Box 4; Martin, *My First Fifty Years in Politics,* 112-13; *New York Times,* August 20, 1940.

70. Reminiscences of Stanley Isaacs, CUOHRO, 185.

71. KFS to Wendell Willkie, n.d., KFS Papers, Box 12. The phrase "conspiracy of state bastards" is provided in a penciled note on the back of the document.

72. *Chicago Tribune,* September 13, 1940.

73. *Washington Post,* July 1, 1940.

74. *New York Times,* September 11, 1940.

75. Murray Friedman, Notes from Interview with John Hamilton, October 27, 1945, Library of Congress Manuscripts, John D. M. Hamilton Papers, Box 4; Fried, *The Man Everybody Knew,* 188.

76. Smith, *Thomas E. Dewey and His Times,* 327; *New York Times,* September 28, 1940; *Time,* October 7, 1940.

77. Smith, *Thomas E. Dewey and His Times,* 327; *New York Times,* September 30, 1940; Murray Friedman, Notes from Interview with John Hamilton, October 27, 1945, Library of Congress Manuscripts, John D. M. Hamilton Papers, Box 4.

78. Gerald Nachman, *Raised on Radio* (Berkeley, 1998), 332.

79. *New York Times,* May 14, 1940.

80. Undated Albany newspaper articles in Kenneth Simpson Scrapbooks, Yale University Microfilm Collection.

81. Both Baldwin and Dewey erroneously stated that Simpson elbowed Barton out. See their reminiscences in the Columbia Oral History Project.

82. *New York Times,* October 8, 1940.

83. KFS to Mrs. Keyes Winter, October 10, 1940, KFS Papers, Box 5; KFS to William M. Wener, October 23, 1940, KFS Papers, Box 6; see Asae Konokawa, "The Invisible Legacies (Mrs. Simpson and I)," n.d., Kelly Simpson Papers.

84. See Knight Wolley to KFS and Clare Luce to KFS, October 10, 1940, Kelly Simpson Papers; Charles Hilles to KFS, October 25, 1940, KFS Papers, Box 6; KFS to Morris Mogelever, October 24, 1940, KFS Papers, Box 6.

85. *New York Times,* October 9, 1940; *New York World-Telegram,* October 19, 1940.

86. *New York World-Telegram*, October 19, 1940; M. Fischer to KFS, October 9, 1940, KFS Papers, Box 5.

87. Joan Pratt to KFS, October 9, 1940, KFS Papers, Box 5.

88. Howard S. Burton to KFS, October 29, 1940, KFS Papers, Box 6.

89. *New York World-Telegram*, October 31, 1940.

90. *New York Times*, November 1, 1940.

91. Gould, *Grand Old Party*, 285; Neal, *Dark Horse*, 121.

92. Bruce Barton to Donald Bruce Johnson, May 10, 1960, Wisconsin State Historical Society, Bruce Barton Papers, Box 72.

93. Martin, *My First Fifty Years in Politics*, 109.

94. Gould, *Grand Old Party*, 286.

95. "Madison Square Garden Rally," November 2, 1940, KFS Papers, Box 14; see *New York Times*, October 29, 1940; "Keynote Speech of Kenneth F. Simpson," November 3, 1940, KFS Papers, Box 14.

96. Gould, *Grand Old Party*, 287; KFS to Charles Hilles, December 2, 1940, KFS Papers, Box 6. KFS got 54,628 votes, the Democrat got 47,318, and the ALP candidate got 5,945. Simpson would have won even without the ALP having split the Democratic vote, but it would have been close. See *New York Times*, November 7, 1940.

97. KFS to South Trimble, November 10, 1940, KFS Papers, Box 6; KFS to David W. Kempner, November 29, 1940, and W. Carl Moore to KFS, November 20, 1940, KFS Papers, Box 6.

98. KFS to Arthur Ballantine, November 14, 1940, KFS Papers, Box 6; *PM*, November 10, 1940.

99. Arthur Ballantine to KFS, November 12, 1940, KFS Papers, Box 6.

100. KFS to Arthur Ballantine, November 14, 1940, KFS Papers, Box 6.

101. Noel Busch to KFS, November 19, 1940, KFS Papers, Box 6; *New York World-Telegram*, November 16, 1940.

102. *Life*, November 18, 1940.

103. Vincent Fanelli to KFS, December 28, 1940, KFS Papers, Box 7. In the optimism just after the election, some had suggested that Simpson himself might fit the bill; he himself named more seasoned possibilities like Syracuse mayor Rolland Marvin or city planner extraordinaire Robert Moses.

104. *Christian Science Monitor*, December 12, 1940. Isaacs confirmed that Simpson was determined to root out Dewey influence in the city and was starting with Costuma. See Reminiscences of Stanley Isaacs, CUOHRO, 199.

105. *New York Times*, December 12, 1940.

106. *New York Post*, December 17, 1940; *New York Times*, December 13, 1940; Reminiscences of Thomas E. Dewey, CUOHRO, 521.

107. *New York Times*, December 16, 1940; Marvin G. Weinbaum, "A Minority's Survival: The Republican Party of New York County, 1897-1960" (Ph.D. diss., Columbia University, 1965), 86; *New York Times*, December 18, 1940.

108. *New York Times*, December 17, 1940.

109. *New York Times*, December 18, 1940.

110. Ibid.; *New York Times*, December 20 and 21, 1940; *New York Times*, December 30, 1940; Weinbaum, "A Minority's Survival," 87; *New York Times*, December 27, 1940.

111. *New York Enquirer*, December 2, 1940; *New York Times*, December 25, 1940; KFS to William M. Calder, December 5, 1940, KFS Papers, Box 6.

112. *New York Times*, December 30, 1940.

113. KFS to Robert H. Schaffer, January 3, 1941, KFS Papers, Box 7; *New York Daily News*, n.d., in Kenneth Simpson Scrapbooks, Yale University Microfilm Collection.

114. KFS to Thomas Stephens, January 8, 1941, KFS Papers, Box 7.

115. KFS to Helen Simpson, January 7, 1941, KFS Papers, Box 7.

116. The other was James Wadsworth, from upstate, a sponsor of the selective service bill and a former backer of Kenneth Simpson in state politics. Franklin Delano Roosevelt to William M. Chadbourne, January 9, 1941, KFS Papers, Box 7; *New York Post*, January 28, 1941.

117. Press Statement, n.d., KFS Papers, Box 7.

118. KFS to Helen Simpson, January 7, 1941, KFS Papers, Box 7; KFS to Helen Simpson, January 8, 1941, KFS Papers, Box 7; KFS to William Kelly Simpson, January 8, 1941, KFS Papers, Box 7.

119. KFS to Helen Simpson, January 8, 1941, KFS Papers, Box 7.

120. KFS to Helen Simpson, January 10, 1941. Recordings of the January 11, 1941, episode of "Information Please" are available on the Internet.

121. Bird, *The Chairman*, 119-22.

122. *Christian Science Monitor*, January 14, 1941; *Chicago Tribune*, May 28, 1952.

123. Bird, *The Chairman*, 123.

124. *New York Times*, January 13, 1941.

125. KFS to Helen Simpson, January 14, 1941, KFS Papers, Box 7; *Christian Science Monitor*, January 14, 1941.

126. *New York Times*, January 14, 1941.

127. KFS to Helen Simpson, January 14, 1941, KFS Papers, Box 7.

128. *New York Times*, January 14, 1941.

129. *Christian Science Monitor*, January 27, 1941; KFS to Mark Maclay, January 15, 1941, KFS Papers, Box 7; Esther Hogue to Helen Simpson, January 15, 1941, KFS Papers, Box 7.

130. KFS to Charles Hilles, January 16, 1941, KFS Papers, Box 7.

131. KFS to Helen Simpson, January 17, 1941, KFS Papers, Box 7; on going into a "panic," see KFS to Richard C. Patterson, January 18, 1941, KFS Papers, Box 7.

132. See the ticket in KFS Papers, Box 35; "Sonfield and Hogue" to KFS, January 20, 1941, KFS Papers, Box 7.

133. Reminiscences of Joseph Clark Baldwin, CUOHRO, 69; Reminiscences of Thomas E. Dewey, CUOHRO, 522. Dewey knew a great deal about his political enemy. A copy of Simpson's death certificate can be found in the Dewey papers. Hogue or Sonfield to Helen Simpson, January 21, 1941, KFS Papers, Box 7.

134. *New York Times*, January 22, 1941; Peters, *Five Days in Philadelphia*, 185.

135. *PM*, November 10, 1940. A note indicates that in one evening he took 3 sodium amytal, 2 teaspoons of paregoric, and a seconal (Kelly Simpson Papers).

136. Undated document but clearly very late, judging from the subject matter, papers, and writing. See Kelly Simpson Papers.

137. Undated memo by Helen Simpson, Kelly Simpson Papers.

138. Charles Hilles to KFS, November 8, 1940, KFS Papers, Box 7.

139. KFS to Lyttleton B. P. Gould, January 11, 1941, KFS Papers, Box 7.

140. Charles Hilles to KFS, January 13, 1941, KFS Papers, Box 7; Wendell Willkie to Joe Martin, January 13, 1941, The Lily Library, Indiana University-Bloomington, Manuscripts Department, Wendell Willkie Manuscripts, Box 51; Rose Hornstein to KFS, December 21, 1940, Kelly Simpson Papers; Fried, *The Man Everybody Knew*, 184; Joe Martin to Wendell Willkie, January 14, 1941, The Lily Library, Indiana University-Bloomington, Manuscripts Department, Wendell Willkie Manuscripts, Box 51.

141. Gertrude Hess to KFS, n.d., KFS Papers, Box 7; *New York Times*, January 25, 1941; see the series of correspondence, January 24, 1941, in KFS Papers, Box 7.

142. *New York Times*, January 26, 1941.

143. Helen, of course, was almost totally deaf and not likely wearing a hearing aid. Although accounts credit Helen, it is possible that someone else first heard the call (*New York Times*, January 26, 1941); Death Certificate No. 2369, January 28, 1941, Kenneth Farrand Simpson, New York City Municipal Archives.

144. Eleanor Roosevelt to Helen Simpson, January 26, 1941, Kelly Simpson Papers; *Washington Post*, January 27, 1941.

145. *New York Daily Mirror*, n.d. (circa January 1941); *Washington Post*, January 27, 1941.

146. *Hartford Courant*, January 28, 1941; *New York Times*, January 28, 1941.

147. Edwin F. Jaeckle to Helen Simpson, January 27, 1941, Jaeckle Papers, Box 3.

148. Typescript, funeral program, January 28, 1941, Kelly Simpson Papers; *New York Times*, January 29, 1941.

149. *New York Times*, February 5, 1941.

150. *New York Times*, January 29, 1941; *Washington Post*, February 3, 1941.

151. In his November 1940 article in *Life*, Simpson quoted Theodore Roosevelt: "To remain a democracy must not have horizontal division between parties. It must continue to have a vertical cleavage with all interests represented by both parties."

152. Chase Mellen Jr. to Helen Simpson, January 27, 1941, Kelly Simpson Papers.

153. *Washington Post*, January 28, 1941.

154. "15th Activities Digest," January 1942, in Records of the New York Republican State Committee, SUNY Albany Archives, Box 8.

155. Cited in the *Hartford Courant*, January 28, 1941.

156. Undated note from KFS to Helen Simpson, Kelly Simpson Papers.

157. Franklin D. Roosevelt to William M. Chadnourne, January 9, 1941, KFS Papers, Box 7.

158. Bruce Barton to Helen Simpson, November 26, 1946, Kelly Simpson Papers.

159. Rolland Marvin to Helen Simpson, March 11, 1941, Kelly Simpson Papers.

160. This account is from the Louis Sobel "New York Cavalcade" column in the *San Francisco Examiner*, February 11, 1941; Sobel himself often played poker with Simpson, and the confidante may well have been Sobel himself.

BIBLIOGRAPHY

BOOKS

302nd Field Artillery Association. *The 302nd Field Artillery, United States Army.* New York, 1919.

Berle, Beatrice Bishop, and Travis Beal Jacobs, eds. *Navigating the Rapids, 1918-1971: From the Papers of Adolph A. Berle.* New York, 1973.

Bird, Kai. *The Chairman: John J. McCloy, The Making of the American Establishment.* New York, 1992.

Birmingham, Stephen. *The Right People: A Portrait of the American Social Establishment.* Boston, 1958.

Burrows, Edwin G., and Mike Wallace. *Gotham: A History of New York City to 1898.* New York, 1999.

Chancellor, Paul. *The History of the Hill School, 1851-1976.* Pottstown, PA, 1976.

Cornebise, Alfred E. *Soldier-Scholars: Higher Education in the AEF, 1917-1919.* Philadelphia, 1997.

Fitzgerald, F. Scott. *This Side of Paradise.* New York, 1920.

Folsom, Joseph Fulford, ed. *The Municipalities of Essex County, New Jersey, 1666-1924.* New York, 1925.

Frank, Elizabeth. *Louise Bogan: A Portrait.* New York, 1985.

Fried, Richard M. *The Man Everybody Knew: Bruce Barton and the Making of Modern America.* Chicago, 2005.

Gardner, Deborah S. *Cadwalader, Wickersham & Taft: A Bicentennial History, 1792-1992.* New York, 1994.

Garraty, John A. *Right-Hand Man: The Life of George W. Perkins.* New York, 1957.

Giglio, James N. *H.M. Daugherty and the Politics of Expediency.* Kent, OH, 1978.

Gould, Lewis L. *Grand Old Party, A History of the Republicans.* New York, 2003.

Harbaugh, William Henry. *Power and Responsibility: The Life and Times of Theodore Roosevelt.* New York, 1961.

Hemingway, Ernest. *A Moveable Feast.* New York, 1964.

Heminway, J. Callendar, ed. *History of the Class of 1917, Yale College.* New Haven, 1928.

Hungerford, Edward. *Men and Iron: The History of the New York Central.* New York, 1938.

Isaacson, Walter, and Evan Thomas. *The Wise Men: Six Friends and the World They Made.* New York, 1986.

Joyner, Conrad. *The Republican Dilemma: Conservatism or Progressivism.* Tucson, AZ, 1963.

Kessner, Thomas. *Fiorello La Guardia and the Making of Modern New York.* New York, 1989.

Kobler, John. *Luce: His Time, Life, and Fortune.* Garden City, NY, 1968.

Lankevich, George J. *American Metropolis: A History of New York City.* New York, 1998.

Leuchtenberg, William E. *The Perils of Prosperity, 1914-32.* Chicago, 1958.

Martin, Joe. *My First Fifty Years in Politics.* New York, 1960.

Mayer, Martin. *Emory Buckner.* New York, 1968.

Miller, Stephen B. *Historical Sketches of Hudson.* Hudson, NY, 1862.

Mitgang, Herbert. *The Man Who Rode the Tiger: The Life and Times of Judge Samuel Seabury.* New York, 1963.

Morris, Newbold. *Let the Chips Fall: My Battles Against Corruption.* New York, 1955.

Moscow, Warren. *Politics in the Empire State.* New York, 1948.

Mowry, George E. *Theodore Roosevelt and The Progressive Movement.* New York, 1946.

Murray, George Mosher, and James Callender Heminway, eds. *History of the Class of Nineteen Hundred and Seventeen, Yale College.* New Haven, 1917.

Nachman, Gerald. *Raised on Radio.* Berkeley, 1998.

Neal, Steve. *Dark Horse: A Biography of Wendell Willkie.* New York, 1984.

Nettleton, George Henry. *Yale in the World War, Part One.* New Haven, 1925.

Peel, Roy V. *The Political Clubs of New York City.* New York, 1935.

Peretti, Burton W. *Nightclub City: Politics and Amusement in Manhattan.* Philadelphia, 2007.

Peters, Charles. *Five Days in Philadelphia.* New York, 2005.

Riordan, William L. *Plunkitt of Tammany Hall: A Series of Very Plain Talks on Very Practical Politics.* New York, 1995.

Ruderman, Terry Jane. *Stanley M. Isaacs: The Conscience of New York.* New York, 1982.

Seligman, Joel. *The High Citadel: The Influence of Harvard Law School.* New York, 1978.

Smith, Richard Norton. *Thomas E. Dewey and His Times.* New York, 1982.

Sutherland, Arthur E. *The Law at Harvard: A History of Ideas and Men, 1817-1967.* Cambridge, 1967.

Tindall, George Brown. *America: A Narrative History, Volume II.* New York, 1988.

Welch, Lewis Sheldon, and Walter Camp. *Yale: Her Campus, Class-Rooms, and Athletics.* Boston, 1899.

Whittmore, Henry. *History of Montclair Township, State of New Jersey: Including the History of the Families Who Have Been Identified With Its Growth and Prosperity.* New York, 1894.

Whyte, William H., ed. *The WPA Guide to New York City, The Federal Writers Project Guide to 1930s New York.* New York, 1982.

Wunderlin, Clarence E., ed. *The Papers of Robert A. Taft, Volume 2, 1939-1944.* Kent, OH, 2001.

ARTICLES

Chen, Ivan. "Alger Hiss, 1926-1929". Unpublished, 2008. Available at http://works.bepress.com/ivan_chen/1.

NEWSPAPERS

Boston Daily Globe, October 4, 1919.

Brooklyn Daily Eagle, November 12, 1929.

Brooklyn Times, May 15, 1930.

Chicago Tribune, 1940-1952.

Christian Science Monitor, 1926-1940.

Daily Mirror, August 12, 1938.

Daily News Record, May 12, 1925.

Evening Post, October 4, 1926.

Evening World, 1926-1929.

Hartford Courant, 1917-1941.

Harvard Crimson, December 10, 1921.

Hill School News, 1912-1913.

Honolulu Star Bulletin, July 4, 1940.

Jewish Morning Journal, November 5, 1939.

Los Angeles Times, February 11, 1927.

Medical Record, February 14, 1914.

News Record, September 23, 1925.

New York American, April 6, 1927.

New York City Telegram, February 27, 1931.

New York Daily Mirror, 1937-1941.

New York Enquirer, December 2, 1940.

New York Herald (Paris Edition), February 27, 1926.

New York Post, 1938-1940.

New York Sun, 1926-1938.

New York Telegram, January 22, 1926.

New York Times, 1860-2007.

New York World, August-September 1927.

New York World-Telegram, 1937-1940

Paterson New Jersey Call, July 17, 1940.

Pittsburgh Courier, April 2, 1927.

PM, November 10, 1940.

San Francisco Examiner, February 11, 1941.

Wall Street Journal, May 24, 1939.

Washington Post, 1937-1948.

Yale Daily News, 1916-1917.

DISSERTATIONS

Stein, Judith. "The Birth of Liberal Republicanism in New York State, 1932-1938." Ph.D. diss., Yale University, 1968.

Weinbaum, Marvin G. "A Minority's Survival: The Republican Party of New York County, 1897-1960." Ph.D. diss., Columbia University, 1965.

MAGAZINES

Harpers, January 1929.

Life, November 18, 1940.

New Republic, June 1939.

New Yorker, 1925-1967.

Social Register Observer, Summer 2006.

The Atlantic, March 1943.

The Bookman: A Review of Books and Life, November 1932.

The Hill School Dial, 1911-1913.

The Hill School Record, June 1913.

The Outlook, August 2, 1913.

Time, 1925-1940.

Town and Country, May-August 1905.

Young Republican, March 1939 and September 5, 1939.

ORAL HISTORIES

(All in Columbia University Oral History Research Office Collection)

Baldwin, Joseph Clark, 1949-1950.

Dewey, Thomas E., interviewed by Harlan B. Phillips, 1973.

Isaacs, Stanley, 1949-1950.

Koenig, Samuel S., interviewed by Dean Albertson, 1950.

Lasker, Mary, interviewed by John T. Mason Jr., 1962-1982.

Mack, Walter Jr., interviewed by Owen Bombard, 1950.

Windels, Paul, interviewed by Owen Bombard, 1949-1950.

GOVERNMENT DOCUMENTS

New York Naturalization Petition, Joseph Steevens Farrand, August 3, 1850.

U.S. Bureau of the Census. Seventh Census of the United States, 1850.

_____. Eighth Census of the United States, 1860.

_____. Ninth Census of the United States, 1870.

_____. Twelfth Census of the United States, 1900.

_____. Thirteenth Census of the United States, 1910.

U.S. Department of State, Washington, DC. Kenneth Farrand Simpson U.S. Passport Application.

_____. Helen L. K. Porter U.S. Passport Application.

_____. Joseph Steevens U.S. Passport Application, April 23, 1851.

ARCHIVES

Columbia University Archives and Manuscripts, New York, NY. Frederic R. Coudert Jr. Papers.

_____. Stanley Isaacs Papers.

_____. George W. Perkins Papers.

Library of Congress, Washington, D.C. John D. M. Hamilton Papers.

_____. Congressional Record, February 10, 1940.

National Archives and Records Administration, College Park, MD. RG 120 (Records of the American Expeditionary Forces), Entry 1241, Box 2.

_____. RG 407 (Records of the Adjutant General's Office), Entry UD 111, Box 210.

New York City Municipal Archives, New York, NY. Office of the Mayor Mayoralty Campaign Series.

State University of New York (SUNY), Albany, NY. M.E. Grenander Department of Special Collections & Archives, Records of the New York Republican State Committee.

The Hill School Library Archives and Manuscripts, Pottstown, PA. Student Scrapbook Collection.

The Knickerbocker Greys Archives, New York, NY.

The Lilly Library, Indiana University-Bloomington. Wendell Willkie Manuscripts.

University of Rochester Rare Books and Special Collections, Rochester, NY. Thomas E. Dewey Papers.

_____. Edwin F. Jaeckle Papers.

Wisconsin State Historical Society, Madison, WI. Bruce Barton Papers.

Yale University Manuscripts and Archives, New Haven, CT. Kenneth Farrand Simpson Papers.

_____. Charles Hilles Papers.

INDEX

Boldface page numbers indicate illustrations.

DATE DUE

GAYLORD			PRINTED IN U.S.A.

F 124 .D87 2009

Durr, Kenneth D.

Life of the party